THE REVISED

CHARTER AND ORDINANCES

OF THE

CITY OF DETROIT,

PUBLISHED BY ORDER OF

COMMON COUNCIL.

DETROIT:
WILBUR F. STOREY, PRINTER TO THE CITY.

1855.

NOTE.

The present arrangement of the Charter and Ordinances of the City of Detroit has been prepared in conformity with the following resolution, adopted by the Common Council of said city, on the 13th day of February, 1855:

RESOLVED, That the Recorder, City Attorney, and City Auditor be a special committee, whose duty it shall be to proceed and collate the Charter of the city of Detroit, and all the present existing amendments thereto, all the Ordinances of said city now in force or existing, omitting all amendments or Ordinances repealed or not now in force, together with the standing rules of this Council, and have the same published at the expense of the city, and furnished to each member and officer of the Common Council, with all convenient speed.

The faithful discharge of the duty enjoined by this resolution has been no easy task. The acts of the Legislature, constituting the Charter of the City, and the Ordinances of the Council, passed in pursuance of such Charter, have undergone so many changes and modifications since the last collation of the Charter and Ordinances, in 1848, that much time and labor, and very careful discrimination, were required to ascertain what remain in force, both of legislative and municipal enactments, and to bring all together in proper form and appropriate connection. A constant effort seems to have been maintained, as well in the Legislature as in the Council, for a succession of years, to "ring changes" upon the laws of the city, and to keep its Charter and Ordinances in an unsettled state. The wisdom and expediency of *permanent laws*, though often imperfect, seems to have been entirely unheeded by the law makers, and the old maxim upon this subject entirely forgotten. A state of confusion and uncertainty, in regard to the powers of the corporation and the laws of the city, greatly to be lamented, has been the result; and a new collation of the Charter and Ordinances had become an absolute necessity. To bring order out of the confusion which has thus existed has been the aim of the Committee, and they indulge the hope that their efforts in this regard have not failed of success.

The Committee have aimed at both accuracy and convenience in their arrangement of the Charter and Ordinances, and trust that the results of their labors will commend itself, in both these respects, to the Common Council and officers of the city, as also to the citizens of Detroit, and the Courts of the State.

The legislative enactments, constituting the Charter of the city, have been brought together in distinct parts—all provisions relating to a particular subject, so far as practicable, being placed under an appropriate sub-division, without regard to the time when the same were passed into laws. This arrangement, it is believed, will prove of much convenience. The citations at the ends of sections refer to the acts of the Legislature in which such sections are contained. Where no such citations are found at the ends of sections, it will be understood that such sections are contained in the acts referred to in the next citation.

Acts of the Legislature, which are not purely amendments to the Charter, but which, nevertheless, either grant powers to the city or its officers, or relate in some way to its government, are added to the Charter, under the head of "Acts relative to the City of Detroit."

In collating the Ordinances, the Committee have collected and arranged all such as relate to the same class of subjects under separate titles, and have inserted amendments in their appropriate place. The Ordinances passed during the past few years not having been copied into the book of Ordinances, the collection and arrangement of them has been attended with difficulty.

In the haste of proof reading a few errors, chiefly typographical, have been overlooked, which are noticed in the appended "Errata," to which reference is made.

DETROIT, August, 1855.

Erratum.—The following note should have been placed at the foot of page 10 referring to section 22 of Act of 1841, cited on that page:

† The official term of the Mayor of the City is one year from the time of his election. See section 3, of Revised Charter, approved April 4, 1827, which having been entirely repealed, except as regards the limitation therein contained of the Mayor's term of office, is not inserted.

TABLE OF CONTENTS OF ORDINANCES.

TITLE I.

Of City Officers.

TITLE II.

Of Taxes and Assessments.

TITLE III.

Of Streets and Alleys.

TITLE IV.

Of Drains and Sewers.

TITLE V.

Of Markets and Sales.

TITLE VI.

Of the Prevention of Fires.

TITLE VII.

Of the Public Health.

TITLE VIII.

Of the Public Peace.

TITLE IX.

Of Stray Animals.

TITLE X.

Of Ferries, Hacks and Drays.

TITLE XI.

Of Places of Recreation and Refreshment.

TITLE XII.

Of Porters, Runners, and the Arrival and Departure of Boats and Cars.

TITLE XIII.

Of the City Poor.

TITLE XIV.

Miscellaneous.

REVISED CHARTER

OF THE

CITY OF DETROIT,

AS ALTERED AND AMENDED BY

SUCCESSIVE LEGISLATURES,

DOWN TO AND INCLUDING THE SESSION OF 1855.

PART I.

RELATIVE TO INCORPORATION—BOUNDARIES—WARDS, ETC.

SECTION 1. *Be it enacted by the Legislative Council of the Territory of Michigan*, That the district of country contained within the following limits, to wit: beginning at a point on the national boundary line in the river Detroit, directly opposite, and in a line with the south-west or lower line of the farm now owned by DeGarmo Jones; thence, in the course of said line, three miles from the margin of the said river Detroit; thence north-eastwardly, on a line parallel to the course of Jefferson Avenue, in said city, until the said parallel line shall intersect a line continued from, and on a course with, the division line between the two farms commonly known by the names of the Beaubien farm and the Brush farm; thence along the said division line, so continued, and in the course thereof, to the margin of the river Detroit, and until the said line, on the said course, shall intersect the said national boundary line in said river; thence along the said national boundary line, down stream, to the place of beginning, shall continue to be a city, by the name of the "City of Detroit;" and all the freemen of said city, from time to time, being inhabitants thereof, shall be, and continue to be, a body corporate and politic, by the name

Original boundaries of the city.

Freemen of city a body corporate, &c

of "The Mayor, Recorder, Aldermen and Freemen of the City of Detroit," and by that name, they and their successors shall be known in law, and shall be, and are hereby made, capable of suing and being sued, of pleading and being impleaded, of answering and being answered unto, and of defending and being defended, in all Courts of Record, and any other place whatsoever; and may have a common seal, and may change and alter the same at pleasure; and by the same name shall be, and are hereby made capable of purchasing, holding, conveying, and disposing of any real and personal estate, for the use of the said corporation.—*Revised Charter, approved April* 4, 1827.

Style of corporation.

May have a seal.

And hold real estate.

Additional boundaries.

SEC. 1. *Be it enacted, &c.*, That the district of country contained within the following limits, to wit: beginning at a point in the national boundary line, in the river Detroit, directly opposite and in a line with the easterly or upper line of the Brush farm, now being the easterly or upper boundary of the city of Detroit; thence easterly, in the course, and on the said line, until it intersects the rear or northerly boundary line of said city; thence easterly, in the course of said rear or northern boundary line of said city, to a point opposite to, and in the line of the westerly or lower line of the Guoin farm, in the township of Hamtramck, or if said farm extends so far northerly, then to a point in said westerly or lower line of said farm; thence southerly, in the course, and on said line, to a point in the said national boundary line in Detroit river; thence on the said boundary line to the place of beginning, be and the same is hereby annexed to, and made a part of the city and township of Detroit; and that the said district hereby annexed and the inhabitants thereof be, and they are hereby made subject to the provisions, and shall be entitled to all the rights, privileges, and franchises of an act entitled "An Act relative to the City of Detroit," approved April 4, 1827; and the by-laws and ordinances made and now in force, or that may hereafter be made, in pursuance and under the authority of said act, shall have full force and effect within the said district, and from and after the day on which this act is to take effect and be in force, the said district shall not be subject to the regulations or government of said township of Hamtramck.—*Act approved May* 28, 1832.*

* This act took effect March 31, 1833.

SEC. 1. *Be it enacted, &c.*, That the district of country contained within the following limits, to wit: beginning at a point in the national boundary line in the river Detroit; thence easterly, in the course of said river or northerly boundary line of said city, to a point opposite to, and in the line of the easterly or upper line of the Witherell farm, so called, in the township of Hamtramck, or if said farm extend so far northerly, thence to a point in said easterly or upper line of said farm; thence southerly in the course and on said line to a point in said national boundary line in the Detroit river; thence on the said boundary line to the place of beginning, be and the same is hereby annexed and made a part of the township and city of Detroit, and that the said district hereby annexed and the inhabitants thereof be, and they are hereby made subject to the provisions and shall be entitled to all the rights and privileges and franchises of an act entitled "An Act relative to the City of Detroit," approved the fourth of April, one thousand eight hundred and twenty-seven, and the by-laws and ordinances made and now in force, or that may hereafter be made, in pursuance and under the authority of said act, shall have full force and effect within the said district, and from and after the day on which this act is to take effect and be in force the said district shall not be subject to the regulations or government of the said township of Hamtramck.—*Act approved March* 26, 1836.* Additional boundaries.

SEC. 1. *Be it enacted, &c.*, That the eastern boundary line of the City of Detroit shall hereafter be as follows, to wit: beginning on the national boundary line in the river Detroit, directly opposite and in a line with the south-west, or lower line of the farm formerly owned and occupied by the late James Witherell, deceased, and thence north-eastwardly on the line between the said farm and the farm commonly called the Dequinde farm, three miles to the northern line of said city.—*Act approved February* 15, 1842. Witherell Farm detached from the city.

SEC. 1. *Be it enacted, &c.*, That the district of country contained within the following limits, to wit: beginning at a point on the national boundary line in the Detroit river, directly opposite and in a line with the westerly or lower line of the Jones farm, [so called,] Additional boundaries.

---

* This act took effect on the first Monday in April, 1836. The section cited is somewhat ambiguous in its terms, though the intention is obvious. By Section 1, of the Act of 1842, next cited, it will be seen that so much of the act of 1836 as annexes the "Witherell farm" to the city, is virtually repealed.

on private claim number two hundred and forty-seven, and now being ing the lower boundary of said city of Detroit; thence in a straight line northerly in the course of the said lower line of the Jones farm, until it intersects the rear or northerly boundary line of said city; thence westerly on the line and in the course of the rear or northerly boundary line of private claims number twenty-three [Forsyth farm], number two hundred and forty-six, [La Brosse farm], and number twenty four [or Baker farm], to a point on the easterly or upper line of private claim number twenty-four, and known as the Woodbridge farm, in the Township of Springwells; thence southerly, and in the course of and on said upper line of said Woodbridge farm to a point on the said national boundary line in the Detroit river; thence on said boundary line to the place of beginning, be, and the same is hereby annexed to and made part of the township and city of Detroit; and that the said district hereby annexed, and the inhabitants thereof, be and they are hereby made subject to the provisions, and shall be entitled to all the rights, privileges and franchises created or conferred by the several acts of the Legislative Council of the late Territory of Michigan, or of the Legislature of the State of Michigan, relative to the city of Detroit, now in force or hereafter to be created, and the by-laws and ordinances lawfully made and now in force, or that may hereafter be made under the authority of said several acts, shall have full force and effect within the said district from and after the day on which this act is to take effect and be in force: and from and after that day, the said district shall not be subject to the regulations or government of the township of Springwells.

Eighth Ward

SEC. 2. The district by this act annexed to the city of Detroit, shall be and is hereby established as the eighth ward of said city, and said ward is hereby attached to and made a part of the first assessment district of the city of Detroit.—*Act approved February* 20, 1849.

City divided into Wards.

SEC. 14. The several wards in said city shall be, and they are hereby set of as follows:

First Ward.

The First Ward to embrace that part of the said city situate west of the centre line of Shelby, and south of the centre of Michigan Avenue.

Second Ward

The Second Ward, all south of the centres of Monroe and Michigan Avenues, and between the centres of Shelby and Randolph streets.

The Third Ward, all south of the centre of Croghan street, and between the centre lines of Randolph and St. Antoine streets. Third Ward.

[The Fourth Ward, all south of the Gratiot Road, between the centre of St. Antoine and Rivard streets.*] Fourth Ward

The Fifth Ward, all north of the centre of Michigan Avenue, and west of the centres of Woodward Avenue and the Saginaw turnpike. Fifth Ward.

The Sixth Ward, all east of the centre of Woodward Avenue, north of the centres of Monroe Avenue, Croghan street, and the Gratiot road, and west of the centre line of St. Antoine street. Sixth Ward.

[The Seventh Ward, all south of the Gratiot road, east of the centre of Rivard street.*]—*Act approved March* 27, 1839, *as amended by act approved January* 25, 1848. Seventh Ward.

[The Eighth Ward, comprises the Forsyth, Labrosse and Baker Farms.—See Sec. 2. of act approved February 20, 1849, *ante*, p. 4.] Eighth Ward

PART II.

RELATIVE TO OFFICERS.

Officers of city.

SEC. 2. There shall be the following officers in and for the said city, to wit: one Mayor, one Recorder, five (*now sixteen*†) Aldermen, one Clerk, one Marshal, one Treasurer, one Supervisor,‡ one Assessor,§ one Collector, (*in each ward*,‖) and three (*now eight*¶) Constables, of whom the Mayor, Recorder and Aldermen shall be freeholders.—*Revised Charter, approved April* 4, 1827.

Mayor, Recorder and Aldermen to be freeholders.

Certain corporate officers elective.

SEC. 1. *Be it enacted, &c.*, That the corporation officers of the city of Detroit, who are hereinafter named, may hereafter, at the an-

---

* See Sec. 4 of act approved January 25, 1848.

† See act approved June 28, 1851.

‡ Sec. 146 of act No. 87, approved February 14, 1853, provides that the *Assessors* in Detroit, shall exercice the powers and duties of *Supervisors.*

§ Act approved January 30, 1850, provides for dividing the city into three assessment districts, and for the election of *one* Assessor for *each* district. See pp. 9 and 10, Laws of 1850. But the bill passed at the session of 1855, to amend the charter of the City, repeals the provisions of the act of 1850, in regard to Assessors and assessment districts, and provides for the election of one Assessor in each ward in the city.—See Sec. 10 of said bill, cited post p. 6.

‖ See Sec. 2, of act approved February 21, 1849.

¶ See Sec. 3, of act approved March 27, 1839, and Section 3, of act approved February 20, 1849.

nual charter election, be annually elected by the qualified electors of said city, and by a plurality of votes, viz: One Recorder, one Attorney, one Clerk, one Treasurer, one Marshal, one Superintendent of the Water Works,* one Physician, one Director of the Poor, one Sexton, one Clerk for each public market, one Surveyor, three Inspectors of Firewood, and as many other such Inspectors as shall from time to time be directed by the Common Council; two Weigh Masters, and as many other such Weigh Masters as shall from time to time be directed by the Common Council.

One collector and supervisor to be elected in each Ward.

SEC. 2. There shall be elected annually, at the time aforesaid, one Supervisor in and for each road district of said city, and one Collector in and for each ward of said city.

Provisions of charter to apply to election of above officers.

SEC. 7. The provisions of the Charter of said city, respecting the qualifications of electors and officers, the notice, conduct and determination of election and vacancy in, and removal from office, shall apply to elections held under this act.—*Act approved Feb.* 21, 1849.

One constable to be elected in each Ward.

SEC. 3. There shall also be elected in each of the said wards, annually, one Constable, and the seven† Constables thus chosen shall be the Constables for said city in lieu of those now provided by law.—*Act approved March* 27, 1839.

One assessor to be elected in each Ward

SEC. 9. The official term of the Assessor to be elected in said city at the charter election for the present year, 1855, shall expire on the first Monday of March next thereafter; and at the annual charter election held in said city in the year 1856, and every year thereafter, there shall be elected by the qualified voters of each ward in said city one Assessor for each ward, who shall hold his office until the first Monday in March next succeeding his election, or until his successor shall have been duly qualified; and each person elected to the office of Assessor shall take and subscribe the usual oath of office, and enter into a bond in such sum, and with such sureties, as shall be directed or approved by the Common Council: *Provided, however*, That the person elected to the office of Assessor in said city at the charter election for the year 1854, shall be the Assessor of the ward in which he shall reside until the expiration of his pre-

Their oath and bond.

Proviso.

* The Water Commissioners now appoint their own Superintendent.

† The Section, as originally adopted, is thus amended by Section 3 of act approved January 25, 1848. By the addition of the Eighth Ward the number of Constables is increased to *eight*.

sent term of office; and no Assessor shall be elected in such ward until the charter election for the year 1857, and the Assessor elected at that election in such ward shall enter upon his duties on the expiration of the term of the Assessor elected in 1854.*—*Act approved February* 12, 1855.

Sec. 3. The Common Council may appoint a suitable person as City Auditor, who shall hold his office for and during the term of three years, to be removed only by a vote of two-thirds of all the members of said Council, whose duty it shall be to audit all accounts and claims presented against the city, and examine and adjust, at least once in every three months, the accounts of all officers of said city, in such manner as the Common Council shall direct, and shall receive for his services such compensation as the Common Council may from time to time allow.

Common Council may appoint a city auditor.

His duties.

His compensation.

Sec. 4. The said City Auditor, previous to entering upon the duties of his office, shall take and subscribe an oath for the faithful discharge of the same, and also enter into a bond in such a sum, and with such sureties as the Common Council shall approve of —*Act approved March* 11, 1844.

His oath.

His bond.

Sec. 40. That hereafter the office of "City Auditor" shall be called "City Comptroller;" and such officer shall perform such duties as the Common Council shall prescribe by ordinance, in addition to those now required to be performed by law. It shall be competent for the City Comptroller, in the discharge of his duties, whenever he shall deem it necessary or advisable, to administer oaths, and to examine all parties, claimants and witnesses, in reference to all claims and demands preferred against the Corporation of Detroit, or said Common Council; and any person who shall wilfully swear falsely in regard to any such matter or claim shall be deemed guilty of perjury, and shall be punished as in other cases of perjury, by the laws of this State. His term of office (on the expiration of the appointment of the present incumbent) shall be reduced to two years; and he shall be subject to removal from office by a majority of all the members elected of said Common Council.—*Act approved February*, 12, 1855.

Title of "Auditor" changed to "Comptroller."

His duties enlarged

May administer oaths.

Persons swearing false before Comptroller are guilty of perjury.

Comptrollers term reduced to two years.

May be removed by Council.

* As the provisions of the act approved January 30, 1850, relative to assessors and assessments are to be of no force after the year 1855, it has not been deemed necessary to insert them here. They may be seen on pages 9 and 10, Laws of 1850.

Assistant Marshal may be appointed

SEC. 9. Whenever to the Common Council it shall appear necessary, they may direct the Marshal of said city to nominate an Assistant Marshal, and when the person so nominated shall have been approved by the Council, and shall have filed such security as the Council shall direct and approve, he shall have full power and authority to do and perform all things that may now be done and performed by said Marshal. The Common Council shall have power to prescribe the compensation of said Assistant Marshal, and may remove him from office whenever in their judgment it shall be proper so to do, by a vote of a majority of the members present at any meeting of the Council.—*Act approved January* 30, 1850.

His bond. His powers. His compensation. May be removed by majority of Council.

Council may appoint a collector.

SEC. 3. The Common Council of the city of Detroit is hereby fully empowered and authorized to appoint an officer to be called a City Collector, who shall hold his office for the term of one year, whose powers, duties and compensation shall be prescribed by said Common Council. Such Collector, before entering upon the duties of his office, shall take and subscribe the usual oath of office, and may enter into a bond in such sum as the Council may direct, and with such securities as they may approve.—*Act approved Feb.* 12, 1855.

School Inspectors to be elected.

SEC. 2. In lieu of the School Inspectors now required to be elected in said city, there shall be twelve* School Inspectors, to be elected in the manner following: At the next annual charter election, there shall be elected in each ward of said city, two School Inspectors, one of whom shall hold his office for two years, and the other for one year; and at every annual (*charter*) election thereafter, there shall be elected in each ward, one School Inspector, who shall hold his office for two years. No School Inspector shall be entitled to receive any compensation for his services.

Their services to be gratuitous.

Vacancy in office, how filled.

SEC. 3. In case of a vacancy in the office of School Inspector, the Common Council of the city of Detroit may fill the same, until the next annual election, when, if such vacancy happen in the first year of the term of said office, the electors of the proper ward may choose a suitable person to fill the remainder of such term: *Provided*, The City Clerk shall give notice of such vacancy prior to such election, as may be required in other cases.

---

* The addition of two wards to the city since the passage of the act in which this section is contained, has increased the number of Inspectors to sixteen.

SEC. 4. Every person elected to the office of School Inspector, who, without sufficient cause, shall neglect or refuse to serve, shall forfeit to the board of education for the use of the library, the sum of ten dollars, to be recovered in an action of debt in some competent court: *Provided*, no person shall be compelled to serve two terms successively; and the said board shall make all necessary rules and regulations relative to its proceedings, and punish by fine, not exceeding five dollars for each offence of any member of the board, who may, without sufficient cause, absent himself from any meeting thereof, to be collected as they may direct.—*Act relative to Free Schools, approved February* 17, 1842.

Persons elected and refusing to serve may be fined.

Proviso.

Board may make rules and punish absent members.

SEC. 1. *Be it enacted, &c.*, That there shall be a Police Justice in the city of Detroit; the first election for said Justice shall be held on the first Monday of May next, in the city of Detroit, to be conducted in the same manner as Justices of the Peace are elected at the charter election of said city; and the first incumbent of said office shall hold his office from the time he is elected till the 4th day of July in the year 1854; and at the charter election of said city, and at the interval of every four years, the said Justice shall be elected in the manner provided for the election of Justices of the Peace in said city, to hold his office for four years, the term of which shall commence on the fourth day of July of the year in which he is elected; and in case of a vacancy occurring in the said office of Police Justice, the Common Council shall order a special election, giving twenty days' notice thereof. And said Police Justice shall, before entering upon the duties of his office, take and subscribe the oath prescribed by the Constitution of this State, before some officer authorized by law to administer oaths, and deposit the same with the Clerk of the county of Wayne, who shall file and preserve the same in his office.—*Act approved April* 2, 1850.

Police Justice to be elected.

Term of office

How often to be elected.

Council to order special election for, when office vacant.

Oath of Police Justice.

SEC. 5. [*Last part.*] The Council may from time to time, as they may deem requisite, designate the Mayor, Recorder, or any one of the Aldermen, a Police Magistrate, and he shall possess all the jurisdiction and exercise all the powers and authority in criminal cases, of a Justice of the Peace, or Police Justice, of said city, in addition to the powers heretofore or hereafter given by this or any other act.—*Act approved February* 12, 1855.

Council may designate a Police Magistrate.

His powers.

2

Justices of the Peace.

SEC. 1. *Be it enacted, &c.*, That in the township of Monroe and the city of Detroit, two additional Justices of the Peace shall be chosen, in the manner directed in the revised statutes of this State, and such additional Justices shall be classified as near as may be, in the manner prescribed in said Revised Statutes, and shall take the same oath and file the said bond, and have the same powers, and be subject to the same liabilities, as provided in Section 6, Chapter first, Title fourth and Part first of the Revised Statutes. — *Act approved Feb.* 29, 1840.

Idem.

SEC. 104. (*Last part.*) Two additional Justices of the Peace shall continue to be chosen in the township of Monroe and two in the city of Detroit, in the same manner, and with the like powers, and subject to the same duties and liabilities as provided in this chapter, in relation to election, powers, duties and liabilities of Justices of the the Peace.—*Rev. Stat.* 1846, *ch.* 16.

Recorder to act as Mayor in certain cases.

SEC. 8. That in case of the absence, sickness or death of the Mayor of said city, the Recorder of said city shall be, and hereby is authorized to do and perform all the duties and trusts appertaining to the said Mayor.—*Revised Charter, approved April* 4 1827.

His privileges.

SEC. 15. The Recorder shall be chosen as heretofore by the Mayor and Aldermen,* and shall be entitled to a seat within the Common Council, for the purposes of deliberation, and of acting on committees, but shall have no vote therein, except when the Mayor shall be absent or his office vacant, in which case he shall be the acting Mayor as heretofore.—*Act approved March* 27, 1839.

May exercise powers of Circuit Court Commissioner.

SEC. 1. *Be it enacted, &c.*, That the Recorder of the city of Detroit shall have and exercise the same powers as are now exercised by the Circuit Court Commissioner of the County of Wayne.

Recorder's fees when acting as Commissioner.

SEC. 2. The Recorder is authorized to demand and receive the same fees for the services so rendered as are now by law permitted to be demanded and received by the Circuit Court Commissioner.—*Act approved April* 2, 1849.

Officers to continue in office till successors are qualified.

SEC. 22. The Mayor, Recorder, Aldermen, Assessors and Constables, and all other officers of said city, elected from time to time, shall continue in office until their successors, respectively, are elected and qualified.—*Act approved April* 13, 1841.

---

* The Recorder is now elected by the freemen. See Sec. 1 of act approved February 21, 1849. Cited *ante*, p. 6.

Term of offices.

SEC. 8. The term of said offices shall be one year, to commence and be computed from the time assigned for holding the annual charter election, and they shall continue in office until their successors shall be elected and qualified: *Provided*, That the term of the Attorney and Clerk shall commence and be computed from the first Monday in April after such election.*—*Act approved Feb.* 21, 1849.

Proviso.

When term of certain elective officers to expire

SEC. 2. The official terms of the Mayor and Recorder elected at the charter election for the present year, 1855, and also of the Aldermen elected at the charter election for the year 1854, shall expire on the second Tuesday of February, in the year 1856; and the official term of the Aldermen elected at the charter election of the year 1855 shall expire on the second Tuesday in February, 1857; and the official terms of all other officers elected at the charter election for the year 1855, shall expire as soon as their successors, elected or appointed in the year 1856, shall have been qualified for the discharge of their duties.—*Act approved February* 12, 1855.

All ministerial officers removable by the Council

SEC. 4. That all ministerial officers of the city of Detroit shall be hereafter appointed by the Common Council † of said city, and all such officers as may be hereafter appointed, shall be removable at the pleasure of the said Common Council.—*Act approved April* 12, 1827.

Idem.

SEC. 11. The Common Council, by a vote of two-thirds‡ of all the members elected, may remove any ministerial officer of said city, for sufficient cause, and the proceedings in that behalf, shall be entered on their journal: *Provided*, That the Common Council shall previously cause a copy of the charges preferred against the officer sought to be removed, and notice of the time and place assigned for hearing the same, to be served on him, ten days at least, previous to the time so assigned.—*Act approved February* 21, 1849.

Proviso.

Majority of Council may remove city officers.

SEC. 45. That all city officers shall be subject to be removed from office by a vote of the majority of all the members elected of the said Common Council, for such cause as they may deem sufficient. All vacancies shall be filled by said Common Council for the

Vacancies to be filled for balance of term.

---

* This proviso is in effect repealed by section 2, of act approved February 12, 1855, next cited, so far as relates to officers elected in 1855.

† Most of the ministerial officers of the city are now elected by the freemen. See *ante*, pp. 5 and 6.

‡ By the section next cited from the act of 1855, it will be seen that all city officers are liable to be removed on the vote of a *majority* of the Council.

residue of the unexpired term of office.—*Act approved February* 12, 1855.

Certain persons ineligible to office.

SEC. 6. No person shall be eligible to any office in said city, except the offices of scavenger and chimney sweeper, unless he is able to read and write the English language; and if any such person unable, to read and write shall hereafter be appointed or elected to any office, it shall be the duty of the Common Council to declare said office vacant, and to appoint some competent citizen to fill and perform the duties of said office.—*Act approved February* 12, 1855.

Com. Council may dispense with services of any officer appointed by them.

SEC. 2. The Common Council of the city of Detroit are hereby authorized to dispense with the service of any particular officer of said city appointed by said Council, and require the duties of his office to be performed by such other officer as they, by resolution, or ordinance may designate.—*Act approved March* 11, 1844.

An officer removing from his ward vacates his office.

SEC. 3. If any officer has removed, or shall remove, from the ward for which he may have been elected or chosen, such removal shall be deemed a vacancy in such office, and whenever satisfactory evidence of such removal shall be presented to the Common Council, they shall hear the same and decide thereon according to the rights of the case.—*Act approved March* 4, 1843.

Com. Council to fill vacancies in offices

SEC. 9. The Mayor, Recorder and Aldermen of the said city, in Common Council convened, shall have power to fill all vacancies that may happen in any of the offices established by this act, so often as the same shall accrue, by death or removal from the city or otherwise; and all officers so appointed to fill vacancies as aforesaid, shall be notified, qualified and take upon themselves the said office to which they may be severally appointed, in the same manner, and under the same liabilities as is herein before provided, in cases of regular annual elections: *Provided*, That no person so appointed to fill such vacant office, shall hold the same longer than until the next annual election of charter officers.—*Revised Charter, approved April* 4, 1827.

Proviso.

Power to fill vacancies continued.

SEC. 12. The Common Council shall continue to have the same power they now have, to fill all vacancies that may happen in any ministerial office; and the person appointed to fill such vacancy, may continue in office for the period which his predecessor had to serve: and in case of temporary inability, by reason of sickness or otherwise, of any officer, to perform the duties of his office, the Common Coun-

Council may make temporary appointments in certain cases.

cil may appoint some suitable person in his place, who shall discharge the duities of such office during the inability of such officer.—*Act approved February* 21, 1849.

SEC. 10. That the Treasurer, Collector(s,) Marshal and Constables shall, respectively, before they enter upon the exercise of the duties of their respective offices, give such security, for the faithful discharge of the trust reposed in them, as the Mayor, Recorder and Aldermen, in Common Council convened, shall direct and require.—*Revised Charter, approved April* 4, 1827. Treasurer, Collectors, &c., to give bonds.

SEC. 15. The Common Council shall have power at all times, whenever they may deem it for the interest of the public, to require the officers under them, or over whom they may have control, or whose bonds they have approval of, to give such further sureties, in such further sums as may be requisite, in their opinion, for the public good.—*Approved April* 13, 1841. Additional securities may be required of officers.

SEC. 9. Said officers shall take and file the oath of office, and give bonds for the performance of their duties agreeably to the law, or the by-laws, ordinances or resolutions of the Common Council, as the case may be; and the compensation of said officers shall not be diminished after their election and during the term for which they were elected.—*Act approved Febiuary* 21, 1849. Officers oath bonds and compensation.

SEC. 44. It shall be competent for said Common Council, from time to time, as they may deem it expedient or necessary, to exact new and additional bonds from any city or corporation officer, whether elected or appointed under said city charter, or this act, and in such sum or sums as said Council shall prescribe; and in the event of any such officer failing to give such security, his office may be declared vacant, and said Common Council may proceed to fill such vacancy for the residue of his term.—*Act Approved February* 12, 1855. Council may require new bonds of officers.

SEC. 10. Said officers respectively shall perform such duties and be subject to such liabilities, as are, or may be, from time to time, prescribed by law, or by the by-laws, ordinances, or resolutions, duly passed by the Common Council, as the case may be. Powers and duties of officers to be prescribed by Council.

SEC. 14. The Common Council shall have power to prescribe the powers, duties and compensation of all ministerial officers of said city, in cases where the same are not prescribed by law.—*Act approved February* 21, 1849. Idem.

Member of Council may also be school inspector.

SEC. 7. Any law now in force, which prohibits the same person from holding the offices in said city, of member of the Common Council and of the Board of Education, is hereby repealed, in respect to said offices, and any Alderman or School Inspector, who shall remove from the ward in which he was elected, shall thereby vacate his office. *Act approved March* 16, 1847.

PART III.

RELATIVE TO ELECTIONS.

Election of members of Council.

SEC. 1. *Be it enacted, &c.*, The city shall be divided into six* wards, in the manner hereinafter mentioned, each of which shall elect as members of the Common Council two Aldermen; and from and after the first Monday of March, eighteen hundred and forty, each ward shall elect annually one Alderman, who shall serve for two years. They shall also elect the other city and township officers, which by law are now elective, in the manner hereinafter provided.

Term of office of Aldermen.

Vacancy in office of Aldermen.

In case of a vacancy in the office of Alderman, it shall be the duty of the Common Council to give notice of a special election, to be held by the freemen of the proper ward, to fill such vacancy, which notice shall designate the time and place in said ward of holding said election, as hereinafter mentioned.

When charter elections to be held.

Notice of election to be published.

The charter election shall be held on the first Monday of March† in each year, at such places in the respective wards as shall be designated by an order of the Common Council, at least eight days previous thereto, notice of which shall immediately or within three days from the date of such order be given by the city clerk by publication in the newspaper published by the city printer.—*Act approved March* 27, 1839.

Time of holding charter elections changed to 1st Tuesday in February.

SEC. 1. *The people of the State of Michigan enact:* That so much of an act of the Legislature of this State, entitled "An act relative to ward elections in the city of Detroit, and for other purposes," approved on the twenty-seventh day of March, 1839, as re-

---

* There are now eight wards. See Act approved February 20, 1849, cited *ante* p. 4. Also act approved January 25, 1848.

† Hereafter charter elections are to be held on the first Tuesday in February. See Section 1 of Act approved February 1855, cited next.

quires the charter election in said city to be held on the first Monday in March in each year, be, and the same is hereby repealed: *Provided*, That such repeal shall not apply to the charter election for the present year, 1855; and from and after the present year, the charter election in said city shall be held on the first Tuesday in February in each year, and shall be conducted in all respects in conformity with the laws now in force relative to charter elections in said city. The ward Inspectors of Elections in said city, or a majority thereof, shall, on the Saturday next succeeding each charter election, after the present year, at three o'clock, P. M., meet at the Common Council room in said city, and then and there proceed to open and canvass the returns, and declare the result of such election, in the manner heretofore required and prescribed by the laws relative thereto now in force.—*Act approved February* 12, 1855.

Official canvass to be made on Saturday after election.

SEC. 2. At all city elections, every freeman shall vote in the ward where he shall have resided for ten (*thirty**) days next preceding the day of election, otherwise he may vote in the ward from which he removed.

Freemen to vote in ward where they have resided 30 days.

The residence of an elector under this act, shall be the ward in which he boards, or takes his regular meals.

Residence of electors.

SEC. 11. The votes for the offices of Mayor, Justices of the Peace and other city and township officers, shall be given by the freemen in the wards in the manner provided for in the second section.—*Act approved March* 27, 1839.

Votes for Mayor, Justices, &c.

SEC. 5. At every ward election after the annual charter election for the year eighteen hundred and fifty, the ward Inspectors shall consist of the two Aldermen of their respective wards, and a third person, to be chosen, *viva voce*, by the electors present, from their number at the time of opening the polls, who shall be duly sworn to a faithful performance of their duties; and if, from any cause, either or both of said Aldermen shall fail to attend any such election, his or their places may be supplied for the time being, by the electors present, who shall elect any of their number, *viva voce.*—*Act approved January* 30, 1850.

Who to be inspectors of election.

SEC. 13. At all charter elections, if a vote shall be challenged,

Voters challenged to be sworn.

* See Section 21, Act approved April 13, 1841.

the Inspectors of election shall be authorized to swear or affirm the person whose vote is challenged, to answer such questions as may be put to him touching his qualifications, and the said Inspectors shall decide from the examination, as to the legality of such vote. All false swearing under this or any other act relating to the qualification of electors in said city, is hereby declared to be perjury, and punishable as such. And if any elector shall vote in more than one ward, or more than once in the same ward, at any election in said city, he shall be subject to indictment, and on conviction, punished by fine not exceeding five hundred dollars, or imprisonment at hard labor for a period not more than three years, or both, at the discretion of the court.—*Act approved March* 27, 1839.

Electors not to vote in more than one ward.

How ward elections to be conducted

SEC. 10. The said ward elections shall be conducted as heretofore, or as near as may be in all respects, and the said Inspectors shall, on canvassing the votes, certify a full and true return thereof, under their hands, to the Clerk of the said city, carefully sealed up, together with the poll lists and ballots, within twenty-four hours after the closing of the polls; and thereupon the said ward Inspectors, or a majority of them, shall, on the Thursday* next succeeding such charter election, at three o'clock, P. M., meet at the City Clerk's office or Common Council room, and proceed to open and canvass the said returns, and declare the result of said election,—*Act approved March* 27, 1839.

Inspectors to canvass votes and make returns within 24 hours after close of polls.

General canvass.

In cases of tie votes at elections, what to be done.

SEC. 13. If the electors shall, at any charter election, fail to elect any city, district or ward officer, by reason of two or more persons having received an equal number of votes, the Common Council shall, as soon as may be, cause the names of each of such persons to be written on separate slips of paper, and deposited in a box or other proper place, and the person acting as presiding officer of the Council, shall draw out of said box or other place, in the usual manner of determining by lot, one of said slips, and the person whose name is thereon shall be deemed entitled to hold the office for which he received said votes, in the same manner as other officers duly elected; *Provided, however*, That in lieu of the foregoing proceedings, the Common Council may order a new election to be held, and if so ordered, no-

Proviso.

* Hereafter official canvass to be held on *Saturday* after election. See Sec. 1 of Act approved Feb. 12, 1855, *ante*, p. 15.

tice thereof shall be given, and the election conducted, as in other cases.—*Act approved February* 21, 1849.

SEC. 4. That it shall be the duty of the Clerk of said city, so soon as practicable after the closing of the polls of said election, to notify the persons elected to fill the above offices respectively of their election, and that the said officers so elected and notified as aforesaid, shall, within fifteen days thereafter, take an oath or affirmation, before some person duly authorized to administer oaths, faithfully and impartially to execute and discharge the duties of their said offices; a certificate of which shall be given to the person taking the oath, and by him filed with the Clerk of said city. Clerk to notify officers of their election. Officers to take an oath.

SEC. 6. That if any freeman of the said city, who shall be elected as aforesaid to any one of the aforesaid offices, which are elective, by the freemen of the said city, shall, after having notice of his said election, refuse or neglect to take upon himself such office, it shall be lawful for the Mayor, Recorder and Aldermen, of whom the Recorder shall be one, or a majority of them, in Common Council, to impose upon every person so neglecting or refusing, not having a sufficient excuse, such reasonable fine as they shall deem fit, not exceeding twenty-five dollars: *Provided*, That no person be compelled to serve two years successively; and every such fine shall be levied by distress and sale of the goods and chattels, by warrant signed by the Mayor, under the seal of the said city, together with the costs and charges of such distress and sale, rendering the surplus, if any, to the owner; or the same may be recovered by action of debt, in any court within the said city, having cognizance thereof, and shall be recovered and received by the Mayor, Recorder and Freemen for the use of the said city.—*Revised Charter, approved April* 4, 1827. Persons elected refusing to serve may be fined. Proviso. How fine recovered.

SEC. 12. The mode of conducting all state, district and county elections in said city, shall be in the manner herein provided in reference to city officers, except that the returns thereof, by the said ward Inspectors shall be made to the County Clerk, and the same proceedings had, or as near as may be, as are now provided by law for the return of votes by township Inspectors of Election.—*Act approved March* 27, 1839. State, district and county elections—how to be conducted.

SEC. 30. That the Mayor or Recorder and Aldermen, in Common Council, shall have authority to make out and keep, an alphabetical

A list of freemen to be made and kept—and had at the polls.

list of all the freemen in the said city, qualified to vote at any charter election, and any freeman whose name may not at any time be found entered on said alphabetical list, shall have a right to appear at any Council so assembled, or at any session of the Mayor's Court, and show, before such council or court his qualifications as a freeman, and his name shall be entered on such alphabetical list; and it shall be the duty of the Clerk of said city, to have the said list at the polls of every election, and no person whose name is not found on said list shall be entitled to vote, unless he prove his qualifications.—*Revised Charter, approved April* 4, 1827.

PART IV.

RELATIVE TO COMMON COUNCIL.—ITS POWERS, ETC.

Council—of whom to consist.

SEC. 1. *Be it enacted, &c.*, The Common Council of the city of Detroit shall consist of a Mayor, a Recorder and sixteen Aldermen; and the Mayor or Recorder, and a majority of the Aldermen shall constitute a quorum.—*Act approved June* 28, 1851.

Quorum.

In absence of both Mayor and Recorder an Alderman may preside at session of the Council.

SEC. 4. In case of the death or absence from the city of both the Mayor and Recorder, the Common Council may at any regular session or special session, called by three members, and notified to the members of the Council by the Clerk, appoint one of their number to preside at such session, and such session shall be taken to be as legally organized as if the Mayor or Recorder were present.*—*Act approved March* 16, 1847.

Majority of quorum may act.

SEC. 4. In all cases where any act or thing is authorized or required to be performed in virtue of the several acts now in force relative to the city of Detroit, by the Mayor, Recorder, and Aldermen, in Common Council convened, or by the Common Council, it shall hereafter be construed to intend and mean, that such act or acts may and shall be performed by a majority of the quorum present of such members.—*Act approved April* 22, 1833.

---

* This Section taken from the Act of 1847 seems never to have been expressly repealed, and is therefore inserted, though it is evidently in conflict with Sec. 1. of the Act of 1851, cited above. If it is not in force, it should certainly be re-enacted, for the contingency may often arise when it may be necessary to take advantage of its provisions.

SEC. 11. That the Mayor, Recorder and Aldermen of the said city, whereof the Mayor or Recorder shall always be one, shall be called the Common Council of the city of Detroit, and they, or a major part of them, shall have power to make by-laws and ordinances for the preservation of the health of the said city, and for the preservation of the salubrity of the waters of the Detroit River, within the limits of said city; relative to the opening of sluices in all wharves; relative to the filling up of all low grounds or lots, covered, or partially covered, with water; relative to the embanking of the margin of said river, within said limits. And the said Common Council shall have full power and authority, in the manner prescribed by this act, to assess the proportion that each of the owners, occupiers or proprietors of such lots or wharves, adjacent to said river, shall pay for filling up such sunken lot or lots, covered or partially covered by water, or for making such embankments, or cutting such sluices; and if the said owners, occupants or proprietors of said lots, grounds, or wharves, shall not, within ten days after being thereunto required, enter into bonds, with approved security, conditioned for the filling up of said lots, or making the embankments or sluices, agreeably to the directions of, and within a period of time to be specified by, the said Common Council, said Common Council may order and direct such grounds, or lots and wharves, to be sold at public auction, or otherwise, for such number of years or term of time as will pay all expenses of filling up such lots, or of making such embankments or sluices: and such sale shall vest a full and legal title in the purchaser, for such number of years as the same shall have been sold for, and shall be so taken and deemed in all courts of law and equity in this Territory: *Provided, always*, That such sale shall in no case exceed the period of *twenty-five years*:* *Provided, also*, That such grounds or lots, and wharves shall not be leased or sold until the same shall be first filled up, and the embankments and sluices finished and completed, as contemplated in the several provisions of this act: *Provided, further*, That if the owner of any lot so sold, or his attorney or agent, shall within *thirty days** from the time of such sale, pay to the Common Council the charges or expense assessed on his lot so sold, with the interest there-

Mayor, Recorder and Aldermen to be Common Council of Detroit.

Their powers relative to water, sluices low grounds, embankments, &c.

May order lots to be sold, when expense of filling them up has not been paid.

Proviso.

Further proviso.

Owner may redeem within 30 days.

---

* The time limited by the original act thus altered by an amendatory act, approved April 12, 1827.

on, and the cost, it shall be the duty of the Common Council, to order the City Marshal to put the said owner in possession of his said lot, within six days thereafter; and it is hereby made the duty of the said Marshal to execute such order, and to call to his assistance so many citizens as may be necessary for that purpose; and the said Common Council shall have full power and authority, and they are hereby fully authorized and empowered, to pass by-laws and ordinances relative to the duties and powers, and fees of the Marshal, Supervisor, Collector, Assessors, Constables and Clerk of said city, relative to the time and manner of working upon the streets, lanes and alleys of said city; relative to the time and manner of paying moneys and commutation of labor upon streets, lanes and alleys, and the manner of collecting and expending the same; relative to the supplying of the said city of Detroit with pure and wholesome water,* by contract or otherwise, and to grant such exclusive right to any person or persons willing to contract for supplying water as aforesaid; or otherwise to accomplish said object in such manner as to said Common Council may be deemed most advisable; and said Common Council shall also have exclusive power and authority, by by-laws or otherwise, to protect such works for the supply of water as aforesaid, from injury or improper use or application, and also to protect the rights of any such contractor, for supplying water as aforesaid; and the said Common Council, or a major part of them, shall have power to make by-laws and ordinances relative to the public markets within the said city, so as such laws and ordinances shall not extend to the regulating or fixing the price of any articles or commodity which may be brought for sale within the said city; relative to nuisances within the limits of said city; relative to the cleaning of chimneys and protecting the said city from fire; relative to the manner of warning the meeting of the freemen of said city, and the Common Council thereof, and the time and place where they shall be holden; relative to a city watch; relative to the assize of bread, as to the weight of the loaf; relative to bonds and securities and recognizances to be given by Constables, Collectors, Treasurers, or any other officers of the said city, for the faithful discharge of the duties of such officer or officers; relative to the public lights or lamps

Council to pass by-laws relative to the duties of certain officers—relative to work on streets, &c.—relative to supplying the city with water &c.

Powers of Council relative to markets.

Nuisances.

Cleaning chimneys.

Public meetings.

City watch.

Assize and weight of bread.

Bonds of officers.

Public lights.

* The powers of the City in regard to the Water Works have been transferred to the Board of Water Commissioners. See Act approved February 14, 1853, cited among "Acts relative to the city of Detroit."

of said city; relative to the restraining of swine from going at large; relative to the overseeing and support of the poor; and relative to anything whatsoever that may concern the good government and police of the said city: *Provided*, such laws or ordinances shall not be contrary to, or inconsistent with, the laws of the United States, or of this Territory; and the said Common Council may ordain and prescribe such fines and penalties for the breach or non-performance of each and every of the said by-laws and ordinances, as to them shall seem proper.

Hogs.
The poor.
The good government and police of the City.
Proviso.
May fix fines &c.

SEC. 12. That the Common Council shall be summoned and held at such times and places in the said city, as the Mayor, or in case of his sickness or absence, the Recorder of the said city, shall appoint; and the said Common Council shall have the power to impose such reasonable fines for not attending the same after due notice given for that purpose, and without reasonable excuse given for absence, on the officers or members thereof, as to the major part of them shall seem fit, not exceeding two dollars and fifty cents for any one default, to be levied, collected and recovered for the use of the Mayor, Recorder, Aldermen and Freemen, in the same manner as is directed by the sixth section of this act.

Mayor (or Recorder) to fix time and place of meeting, and Council may fine members for non-attendance.

SEC. 13. That the Mayor, Recorder and Aldermen of the city of Detroit, or a majority of them, be, and they are hereby authorized to cause to be surveyed, all that part of the said city lying northerly of Larned street; westwardly of Woodward Avenue; southerly of the outlots, and easterly of the Macomb line, (so called;) and, also, all that other part of the said city lying northerly of Larned street; westerly of the Brush line, (so called;) southerly of said outlots, and easterly of said Woodward Avenue, or so much thereof as they may deem expedient, and to re-lay out and divide the same into lots, streets, lanes and squares, so that every street running easterly and westerly shall be parallel to said Larned street, and every street running northerly and southerly shall be parellel to said Woodward Avenue, or as nearly as practicable.

Power of Council to alter the plan of the city.

SEC. 14. That it shall be competent for the Mayor, Recorder and Aldermen of the said city of Detroit, or a majority of them, and they, or a majority of them, are hereby authorized to provide, by an ordinance to be by them passed, for assessing the value of all the lots,

To assess the value of the lots affected by such alteration, and to assign other lots, &c.

owned by individuals or corporations, or held in trust by the Governor and Judges of the Territory of Michigan, under an act of the Congress of the United States, approved in April, 1806, in that part of the said city which they, or majority of them, shall cause to be surveyed, re-laid out, and divided as aforesaid, and for assigning to the owners of such lots, other lot or lots, to the value assessed, if such owner or owners shall consent to take such lots, and for the payment of said value, or any part thereof, in money: *Provided*, That a right of appeal be allowed to the Circuit Court of the County of Wayne, and said Court shall cause an issue to be made up, and the amount of damages to be assessed by a jury, from the decision on the value of any lot, if the said appeal shall be prosecuted within one year after such value shall be assessed, and not otherwise.

Proviso.

Owner of lots to assign them on payment or tender of value thereof.

SEC. 15. That when the value of any lot or lots ascertained and determined pursuant to the provisions of the ordinance to be passed as aforesaid, or so much thereof as shall be covered by any street or alley, shall be paid or tendered to the owner or owners thereof, or when any other lot or lots to the said value shall be assigned to such owner or owners, the said owner or owners shall thereupon release and quit claim to the Mayor, Recorder, Aldermen and Freemen of the city of Detroit, all title to his, her or their lot or lots, the value of which has been paid or tendered, or some other lot or lots assigned, to the value thereof as aforesaid; and if such owner or owners, after such payment or tender, or assignment, as aforesaid, shall neglect or refuse, for the space of one year, to execute and deliver to the said Mayor, Recorder, Aldermen and Freemen of the city of Detroit, good and valid release and quit-claim, of all his, her or their title, in and to the lot or lots, aforesaid, then, and in such case, the deed and deeds of such owner and owners of the lots shall be void, and shall not be given in evidence of title in any court of law or equity in this territory; and the deed and deeds which may thereafter be executed and delivered for conveying title to the lot and lots, or any part thereof, of such owner and owners, shall be deemed and taken to be, in all courts of law and equity in said territority, conclusive evidence, of legal title in fee of the premises described in such deed and deeds, any law or usage to the contrary notwithstanding: *Provided*, That nothing herein contained shall be so construed as to deprive or debar the owner or owners aforesaid, from having the value of his, her or their said lots so

If not assigned within one year after payment, the title of the owner becomes void

Proviso.

ascertained as aforesaid, and in manner aforesaid: *Provided, also,* That for recording and registering all deeds and other instruments necessary and proper to be recorded and registered in the fulfilment of the change of the plan of the said city in manner aforesaid, the Common Council of said city shall, at the expense of the said city, procure such record books and blanks, as the said Common Council may deem suitable, and the City Register shall be, and he is hereby required, when such record books and blanks shall be procured as aforesaid, to make therein all records and registry of all deeds and other instruments that may be deemed necessary by said Common Council; and the City Register shall receive six and one-fourth cents for every one hundred words actually written, and no more.

Further proviso.

SEC. 16. That all expenses which shall accrue for surveying, relaying out, and dividing said city as aforesaid, for assessing the value of lots, and for making all transfers necessary to give this act effect, and for recording the same, shall be paid by the Mayor, Recorder, Aldermen and freemen of the city of Detroit; and all the lots within the limits mentioned in the 13th section of this act, remaining after all the claims of the owner and owners thereof are satisfied and adjusted in the way and manner as aforesaid, shall become the property, and be and remain to the Mayor, Recorder, Aldermen and freemen of the city of Detroit, and their successors, in fee: *Provided, however,* That a lot of suitable size, to be designated by the Common Council of said City, with the approbation and consent of the Governor of this Territory, shall be reserved around the Court House, and another around the Jail.

Expenses of alteration of plan to be paid by corporation—lots remaining after alteration, to belong to corporation.

Reservation for court-house and jail.

SEC. 17. That it shall be the duty of the Mayor, Recorder, and Aldermen of said city, as soon as convenient after the passage of this act, to make and publish the ordinance prescribed in the 14th section of this act, and thereupon to call a public meeting of the freemen for the purpose of taking the same into a consideration; and a majority of said freemen shall approve of such ordinance, or alter or amend the same until approved of; whereupon the said Mayor, Recorder and Aldermen shall proceed to carry the same into effect.—*Revised Charter, approved April* 4, 1827.

Of the meeting of the freemen to approve the ordinance relative to altering the plan.

SEC. 4. Section twenty of an act relative to the city of Detroit, approved April 4th, 1827, and the act amending the same, approved

April 13th, 1841, are hereby amended by striking out the word "*either*" in the thirteenth line, and the words "*or otherwise, as they may direct*," in the sixteenth line of said section, and by inserting after the provision relative to the establishing a line of buildings, the words "for numbering the same, and establishing a line beyond which docks and wharves shall not be built or extended into the Detroit River," so that said section shall read as follows:—

Council may appoint Street Commissioners.

Sec. 20. That said Common Council shall have full power and authority to appoint Street Commissioners or other officers, to superintend and direct the making, paving, repairing or opening of all streets, lanes, alleys, sidewalks, highways or bridges within said city, with such powers as may be necessary for leveling and graduating the same; for establishing the line thereof, upon which buildings may be erected, and beyond which such buildings shall not extend; for numbering the same; and establishing a line beyond which docks and wharves shall not be built or extended into the Detroit River, within the limits of said city; and generally to do and perform, under the by-laws and ordinances, or other directions of the Common Council, whatever may be deemed conducive to the regularity, public health and convenience of said city; and the Common Council shall have full power and authority to provide funds for defraying the expenses of such paving of streets or sidewalks as may be deemed necessary, by assessment on the owner or occupant of such lot or premises, in front of, or adjacent to, which such streets or sidewalks may be directed to be paved or repaired, and any such assessment hereafter made by authority of the Common Council shall also be a lien, until paid, on such lots or premises in front of which such streets, or sidewalks, may be directed to be paved or repaired; and said assessment shall be collected in the same manner as other assessments or taxes made or laid by authority of the Common Council.—*Act approved Feb.* 12, 1855.

Their powers to establish grades and lines for front of buildings

Numbering buildings. Line of docks and wharves.

Council may provide funds for paving.

Paving assessments to be a lien.

How collected.

Council may permit persons to pave in front of their premises.

Sec. 19. The Common Council of said city may, whenever they deem it for the interest of said city, permit any person or persons to pave the sidewalk and street, or sidewalks and streets, as the case may be, in front of the premises owned or occupied by such person or persons, in said city, under the direction of the Street Commissioner, or any person or committee appointed by said Common Council for that purpose; and whenever any persons, having obtained such permission, shall have paved such side walks and streets, to the satisfaction or said Common Council, such persons shall not be assessed or compelled to pay any road or highway tax on the premises in front of which such pavement shall have been made, so long as such person shall keep the same in repair to the satisfaction of said Common Council; and the said Common Council may make and prescribe such regulations and ordinances in this regard, as may be expedient or necessary to carry into effect the intentions and provisions of this section.—*Act approved April* 13, 1841.

Such persons exempt from highway taxes.

SEC. 21. The said Common Council shall have full power and authority to pass by-laws and ordinances for the abatement of all nuisances within the city, and for the punishment by fine, or otherwise, of all persons occasioning the same; and it shall be the duty of the Marshal and Constables of said city to give information to said Common Council of the existence of any such nuisance, who shall thereupon, or upon complaint of any freeman of said city, make such order for its immediate abatement, as to them the public health or convenience may seem to require: *Provided*, That where damages are claimed by the owner of any building destroyed, removed or injured, on account of the abatement of such nuisance, the Common Council shall proceed to ascertain the damages in the same manner, and the claimant of damages shall be entitled to the same right of appeal as is provided in the nineteenth section of this act;* but no such appeal to the Circuit or Supreme Court, certiorari, injunction, supersedeas, or other process shall prevent the immediate abatement of such nuisance; and when it may become necessary, for the abatement of such nuisance, to fill up or level any lots or other grounds, it shall be lawful for the Common Council to assess the costs or expenses of such filling up, levelling, or removing of buildings, and should the owner or occupant neglect or refuse to pay the full amount of such assessment, the said Common Council shall have full power and authority to sell or lease such premises for the least number of years that will defray

Common Council may pass by-laws and ordinances relative to nuisances.

Marshal and Constables to give information thereof.

Proceedings thereon.

Proviso as to damages.

When nuisances to be abated at expense of owners of lots or buildings.

* The 19th section related, to the assessment and collection of damages, and the right of appeal, in cases of proceedings to open streets. It has virtually been repealed by subsequent acts on the same subject, and is not therefore inserted; still its provisions may be applicable to assessments of damages and appeals, in cases of proceedings to abate nuisances.—See p. 528, Laws of 1827.

such charge or expense, in the same manner as herein provided for the sale of water lots, or wharves, within the limits of said city: *And provided, also,* That the Mayor, Recorder and Aldermen of the said city shall have full power and authority, as is provided for in the eleventh section of this act, for the preservation of the health of the city of Detroit, to remove all nuisances on the margin of the river Detroit, to the distance of half a mile above, and half a mile below the limits of said city.—*Revised Charter approved April* 4, 1827.

Power of Council to remove nuisances.

SEC. 9. The Common Council of said city shall have power, in the manner provided for in the act to which this is amendatory, for the preservation of the public health, to remove all nuisances to the distance of half a mile beyond the limits of said city: *Provided,* That notice shall be first given to the person upon whose premises the same may be, or to the Commissioners of Highways of the township, if it be on public ground or highway, to remove the same forthwith; and if such nuisance shall not be removed by said Commissioners, upon such notice, and said Common Council shall proceed to remove the same, the expense thereof shall be a charge against the township, and shall be audited at such sum as may be justly chargeable by the Supervisors of the county.—*Act approved June* 29, 1832.

Notice of removal to be given.

Powers and duties of the Council in reference to paupers.

SEC. 11. The Common Council of the city of Detroit, are hereby declared to possess, and are hereby granted, the powers and authority, privileges and functions of a Township Board, to all intents and purposes, whenever it may be deemed requisite or proper to exercise the same; and by virtue of this power, to pass all proper ordinances and regulations, for the carrying into effect the powers, authority, privileges and functions, by this section conferred, and to pass all ordinances and regulations relative to the protection, disposal and conduct of paupers in said city, as they may deem requisite; and full power and authority to prevent all persons, vessels and conveyances, from bringing to the city of Detroit, from any other port or place, any paupers, or persons likely to become a charge on said city; to arrest and bring before the Mayor's Court, and on conviction therein, to punish all persons offending in this regard, and to make all needful ordinances in the premises.—*Act approved April* 13, 1841.

Persons, vessels and conveyances.

Common Council may license ferries

SEC. 22. That the Common Council of said city, or the major part of them, shall have the sole and exclusive power, from time to time, to licence, continue and regulate so many ferries from within the said city of Detroit, to the opposite shore of the Detroit river, for the carrying and transporting people, horses, cattle, goods and chattels across the said river, in such manner as shall to them appear most conducive to the public good: *Provided*, That nothing in this section contained shall be construed to deprive any person whatever of the possession or property of the soil on the shore of said river, nor of any right of ferriage under any existing licence.

Taverns, Groceries, Ordinaries, &c.

SEC. 23. That the Mayor, Recorder and Aldermen, in Common Council, shall have the power to license* and regulate all taverns and inns within the limits of said city; also, all keepers of victualing houses, ordinaries and groceries, and also to license all shop keepers and retailers of goods of foreign growth and manufacture, within the limits of the said city; and to demand and to receive, to the use of the said Mayor, Recorder, Aldermen and Freemen of the said city, such sums of money or fees for such license, as may from time to time, be prescribed by said Common Council; exececpting such sums as are now authorized and required by law to be paid to the territorial treasury: *Provided*, That nothing in this act contained shall in any wise limit or restrain the operation of an act, entitled "an act to regulate the assessment and collection of territorial taxes," or any amendment to said act. Proviso.

Of the appointment of firemen.

SEC. 24. That said Common Council or a major part of them, shall have full power and authority to appoint from among the freemen of said city, such number of men, willing to accept, as may be deemed proper and necessary, to be employed as firemen, provided such number does not exceed forty in the management of each fire engine, now provided, or hereafter to be provided, for the use of said city; and each fire company shall have power to appoint their own officers, pass by-laws for the organization and good government of said company, and may impose and collect such fines for the non-attendance or neglect of duty of any of its members, as may be established by such by-laws or regulations of said fire company; and all firemen appointed as aforesaid, shall obtain from the Clerk of said city a certificate thereof, which certificate shall be evidence of their appoint-

Fire companies to appoint their officers, make rules, &c.

Firemen to have certificates, and to be excused from military and jury duty

* So far as this section confers powers upon the Common Council to grant licenses for the sale of intoxicating liquors, it is no longer in force.

ment, and such person shall, in consideration of the faithful discharge of his duties as a fireman, be excused from all duty in the militia in the time of peace, and also from serving upon any jury in any of the courts in this Territory; and it shall be the duty of every fire company to keep in good and perfect repair, the fire engine, hose, ladders and other implements of such company; and upon any alarm or breaking out of any fire, within said city, each member of a fire company shall forthwith repair to the engine house, and from thence proceed without delay, with their fire engines and other implements, to the place of such fire; and the said Mayor's Court shall have power, upon information, to punish any unnecessary or improper delay in the arrival of any fire engine, hose, ladders, hooks or other instruments, by a fine of not more than one hundred dollars, to be levied and collected before said Mayor's Court, of said delinquent fire company, or the officers or members thereof; and the said Mayor's Court may also, upon information or complaint, punish by fine, not exceeding ten dollars, any member of said fire company, for any absence, neglect of duty, or violation of the rules or regulations of such company, or by-laws and ordinances of the Common Council: *Provided*, That it shall be the duty of the Common Council at all times, to provide the engines, hose, ladders, hooks or other instruments for every fire company; and also to pay for the necessary materials and repairs; and it shall be the duty of each fire company to assemble once in each month, or as often as may be directed by said Common Council, for the purpose of working or examining said engine and other implements, with a view to their perfect order and repair.—*Revised Charter, approved April* 4, 1827.

Duty of fire companies.

Com. Council may fine for neglect.

Com. Council to provide engines &c.

Metings of Fire Co's.

Members of hook, ladder, and axe Co's. exempt from military duty and serving on juries.

SEC. 1. That such number of the citizens of Detroit as have been or may hereafter be, organized into a company or companies, by the Common Council of said city, for the purpose of keeping, using and managing hooks, ladders, axes and other implements, for the extinguishment of fires, shall be exempted from military duty in time of peace, and from serving on juries, provided such number does not exceed forty; and the membership in such company or companies shall be certified in like manner, and with like effect, as is provided for firemen in the twenty-fourth section of the act hereby amended.—*Act approved July* 31, 1830.

SEC. 25. That upon the breaking out of any fire within the said city, the Marshal and Constables shall immediately repair to the place of such fire with their staves, and be aiding and assisting, as well in extinguishing such fire as in preventing any goods from being stolen, and also in removing and securing the same, and shall in all respects be obedient to the Mayor, Recorder and Aldermen, or such of them as may be present at any such fire.—*Revised Charter, approved April* 4, 1827.

Duties of Marshal and Constables in case of fire.

SEC. 23. The fourteenth section of an act entitled "an act to amend the charter of the city of Detroit," approved April 14, 1841, is hereby amended by striking out the clause commencing in the ninth line with the word "higher," and ending with the word "building," in the eleventh line, so that said section as amended shall read as follows: "Sec. 14. The Common Council of said city shall have full power and authority to pass such by-laws and ordinances for the prevention and extinguishment of fires in said city, as may be proper and requisite for the public good; and the said Common Council shall have full power and authority to prohibit and forbid any person or persons, to erect or cause to be erected, within such parts, streets or districts of said city, as the public safety may require, any wooden or frame house, store, shop, or other building; and the said Common Council shall have full power and authority to pass such by-laws and ordinances as may be proper and necessary in the premises, and also in regard to the regulation and construction of partition walls, and the construction and location of blacksmith shops and bakeries in said city.—*Act approved February* 22, 1848.

Com. Council may pass ordinances and by-laws for the prevention of fires.

May prevent the erection of wooden buildings in certain parts of the city.

May pass ordinances relative to partition walls, blacksmith shops and bakeries.

SEC. 26. That the Common Council or a major part of them, may establish, keep and regulate one or more markets within such places, within the said city as they shall deem best suited to the public convenience, and shall appoint such proper officer or officers as they shall from time to time deem necessary, to superintend the same; and the said Mayor, with the advice of the Common Council, shall also have power to license, under such regulations as the Common Council shall from time to time prescribe in and for said city, one or more porters, cartmen, and watchmen, when it shall be deemed necessary and beneficial by the Common Council that there should be such appointments made.—*Revised Charter, approved April* 4, 1827.

Council may establish markets.

May license porters, cartmen and watchmen,

Additional powers of Council relative to cartmen, porters and draymen. Council may fix rate of hire of hackney coaches, carriages, &c.

SEC. 1. That it shall be lawful for the Common Council of the city of Detroit to regulate and license porters, cartmen and draymen, owners and keepers of livery stables, hackney coaches, carts, drays, and carriages of every description, used or employed for hire or reward in the said city; and also to fix and regulate the amount and rates of such hire or reward, and to impose and enforce penalties for the violation of such regulations, not exceeding twenty-five dollars, besides costs, on any one person, for any one offence: *Provided*, The said Common Council shall license all persons applying therefor for the purposes mentioned in this act, if they shall be satisfied such applicant is trustworthy, and may at any time revoke such license for any violation of the provisions thereof.—*Act approved May* 16, 1846.

Fine for violation thereof. Proviso.

Council may appoint policemen, &c.

SEC. 5. The Common Council shall have full power to employ and appoint watchmen and policemen whenever they deem it requisite, and to prescribe their duties, powers and compensation; and said policemen, when appointed and qualified, shall possess and exercise all powers, and their acts shall have the same virtue, force and effect as the powers and acts of any Constable in the county of Wayne. —*Act approved February* 12, 1855.

Their powers

Council may regulate vessels, their moorings, ballast, also the disposing of earth from cellars, wells, &c., also, walls, size of brick, sewers drains, firewood, hay, docks and wharves.

SEC. 27. That the said Mayor, Recorder and Aldermen, in Common Council convened, shall have the power, by law, to regulate the stationing, anchoring, and mooring of vessels within the limits of said city, and the laying out of ballast from the same, and for disposing of earth that may be dug from foundations, cellars and wells, and for prescribing the thickness of the walls of houses, and regulating the size of brick; and also to erect, repair, and preserve sewers and drains; also, the measuring of firewood and weighing of hay, and the building of docks and wharves within the said city; and generally, to pass all laws and ordinances, and regulations, necessary to carry the powers by this act granted, into full effect. — *Revised Charter, approved April* 4, 1827.

Powers of Council relative to billiard tables.

SEC. 3. That the Common Council of said city, or a major part of them, shall have power to make by-laws and ordinances in regard to billiard tables, and all other tables kept for hire, gain or reward, within said city; and also, full power and authority to make all such by-laws and ordinances, as may by said Common Council be deemed expedient or necessary, for effectually preventing or suppressing all disorderly houses, and houses of ill-fame, within the limits of said city.—*Act approved June* 29, 1832. Houses of ill-fame.

SEC. 43. That said Common Council, in addition to the powers with which it is already vested, shall have full power and authority to make by-laws and ordinances to restrain swine, sheep, horses, asses, mules, goats, neat cattle and geese, from going at large within the limits of said city, and to provide and maintain one or more sufficient pounds, in which they may be restrained, and to appoint one or more pound-masters, to prescribe their duties and compensation, and the notice to be given, and the final disposition to be made of the property so impounded; and said Common Council may, also, by by-laws and ordinances, restrain dogs from running at large in said city, and may, also, when they deem it expedient, direct such dogs to be killed; and said Common Council may, also make by-laws and ordinances relative to the carrying, keeping and storing of gunpowder within the limits of said city.—*Act approved February* 12, 1855.

Council may pass ordinances to restrain cattle and other animals from running at large.

May establish pounds. Appoint pound masters.

May pass ordinances relative to dogs.

SEC. 3. From and after the passage of this act, no bond or other evidence of debt shall be issued by the said Common Council, except for the completion of works already under contract, or for refunding bonds, or for funding evidences of debt already issued; and any bonds or evidences of debt issued in contravention of this Section shall be absolutely void: *Provided, however*, That the provisions of this Section shall not apply to orders on the Treasurer for the necessary and current expenses of the city.—*Act approved March* 21, 1851.

Council not to issue evidences of debt, except in certain cases.

Proviso.

SEC. 8. Hereafter no contract for building any sewer, or the performance of any public work, in which the Mayor, Recorder, Aldermen and Freemen of the city of Detroit, shall be a party contracting, shall be let to any Member of the Council of the said city; nor shall any person be eligible to a seat in said Council who shall hold any such contract, unless prior to the time for such person to be sworn into office, he shall be released from his contract; and any contract or agreement, between the Mayor, Recorder, Aldermen and Freemen of the city of Detroit, and any member of the Common Council thereof, or in which any such member shall be interested directly or indirectly for the building of any sewer, erection of any building, or the performance of any public work, hereafter made, shall be absolutely void.—*Act approved February* 12, 1855.

Council not to enter into contract with any member thereof

Persons holding such contracts ineligible to seat in Council.

Certain contracts void.

PART V.

RELATIVE TO DRAINS AND DITCHES.

Power of Council relative to drains and sewers.

SEC. 7. The Common Council of said city shall have, and is hereby vested, with full power and authority to enact all requisite and proper ordinances and regulations, relative to the control, regulation, protection and use of drains and sewers in said city.—*Act approved April* 13, 1841.

May assess persons using or benefitted by public drain or sewer.

SEC. 20. The Common Council shall have full power to assess and collect of each individual using or being benefited by any public drain or sewer, as follows, to wit: the sum of one dollar and fifty cents annually, for each cellar drained directly or indirectly by a drain, into any public drain or sewer, which assessment shall be taken to include all other drainage of the premises to which said cellar especially belongs; and the sum of fifty cents annually for each lot or subdivision of lot, being without a cellar, drained as aforesaid into any public drain or sewer; and such sums as may be fixed by the Common Council for all establishments requiring an unusual or extraordinary amount of drainage, drained as aforesaid; which sums, when collected, shall constitute the Sewer Fund, and shall be expended exclusively for the repair and construction of sewers.—*Act approved Feb.* 12, 1855.

Whereas, It is represented and believed by the Mayor, Aldermen and Freemen of the city of Detroit, that great and serious injury to the health of the citizens of said city results from the overflow of water on the low lands in rear of and adjacent to the said city, thereby overflowing a large portion of the lots of ground on which buildings are now being erected; and as the drains constructed, although of large dimensions, are by no means capable of carrying off, at once, the flood of water resulting from sudden rains, or dissolving of snows, it follows that many cellars are filled with water and the debris thus carried into them, from which the injury to health must be apparent; therefore,—

Com. Council to enquire and certify whether marshes and low lands cause disease.

SEC. 1. *Be it enacted, &c.*, That the Common Council of the city of Detroit shall inquire into and certify whether any and what marsh, swamp, or other low lands are a source of disease and injury to the public health of said city, and whether said public health will be promoted by draining the same; and if they shall so certify, shall file said certificate with the Clerk of the Mayor's Court of said city.

SEC. 2. The Common Council shall thereupon issue a summons directed to the Marshal of said city, Sheriff, or any Constable, of the county of Wayne, requiring him to summons nine reputable freeholders of such county, who are not interested in the lands through which any ditch contemplated to be cut shall pass, nor in anywise of kin to the parties interested in the land, to be and appear on the premises, at a certain time to be specified in such summons, not less than fifteen, nor more than twenty days from the date thereof, which summons shall also direct the officer to serve the same, and give six days' notice to the owner of such lands, of the time at which the jury is to appear; and which summons shall be executed and return made thereof, in the manner and with the like authority, as upon services (*summons?*) issued in cases pending before Justices of the Peace, and certify that the notice required has been given.

Proceedings thereupon.

Jury to be summoned.

Owner of land to be notified

Return of summons.

SEC. 3. The Mayor or any Alderman or Justice of the Peace thereto designated and required by the Common Council, shall attend at the time and place specified in the summons, and if it appear that the notice above prescribed has been given, and if six or more, of the nine freeholders, as above specified, shall then and there appear, he shall administer to each of them an oath or affirmation well and truly to examine and certify in regard to the benefits, or damages which will result from the opening of said ditch or ditches.

Jury to be sworn.

SEC. 4. The Common Council shall deliver to the jury a map of the land through which said ditch, or ditches, are proposed to be opened, on which map, the plan, length, width and depth thereof shall be particularly designated, with a space sufficient on each side to receive the deposit of the excavation; and thereupon the Jury shall personally examine the premises and hear any reason that may be offered in regard to the questions submitted to them; and if the jury shall be satisfied that the opening of said ditch, or ditches, is necessary or proper, they shall so certify in writing; and further certify whether the benefits which will accrue to the owner of the lands for the opening of said ditch, or ditches, will, or not, be equal to any damages that he will sustain thereby; and if such benefits are certified not equal to the damages, the jury shall assess and certify the damages which, in their judgment, will be sustained by the owner.

Map to be given to jury.

Duty of jury.

Certificate of jury.

Assessment of damages.

SEC. 5. Such inquisition shall be signed by all the Jurors, and delivered to the Mayor, Aldermen, or Justice in attendance; and for

Jurors to sign their verdict.

Fees of jurors all services rendered, the same fees shall be paid as are allowed for similiar services in cases tried before Justices of the Peace.

Agents of Council may enter upon lands and open ditches on certain conditions.

SEC. 6. Upon the delivery of the certificate of the Jury to the Mayor, Aldermen or Justice in attendance, (which certificate, together with the inquisition and map shall be filed with the Clerk of the Common Council,) and upon payment of costs of proceedings, and payment or tender of the damages assessed by the jury, if any, it shall be lawful for the Common Council to enter, by their agent, teams and necessary implements, upon said lands, and cut and open such ditch, or ditches, designated on said map, as adopted and sanctioned by such Jury, not deteriorating (*deviating?*) materially from the dimensions there laid down.

And keep ditches open from time to time.

SEC. 7. After said ditch, or ditches, shall have been opened, it shall be lawful for said Common Council, their successors, or agents, forever thereafter, from time to time, as it shall be necessary, to enter the lands through which the same are opened, and clear and scour such ditch, or ditches, so as to preserve the original dimensions thereof.

Persons obstructing ditches to pay damages.

SEC. 8. Any person who shall in any way obstruct or injure any ditch, or ditches, so opened, shall be liable to pay the Common Council aforesaid double the damages that shall be assessed by the Jury for such injury, and in case of a second or other subsequent offence by the same person, treble such damages.

Jurors failing to attend liable to a fine.

SEC. 9. If any person, summoned to attend as a Juror, in accordance with the provisions contained in section two of this act, shall fail or neglect to attend at the time and place specified, unless satisfactory excuse be given for such non-attendance or neglect, he shall be liable to a fine of five dollars, which may be imposed by the officer who shall officiate at the swearing of the jury, which officer may order such delinquent juror to be imprisoned until such fine is fully paid.—*Act approved March* 29, 1849.

PART VI.

RELATIVE TO OPENING, ALTERING AND CLOSING STREETS AND ALLEYS.

SEC. 18. That the Common Council of the said city, or a majority of them, shall have full power and authority to lay out, establish, open, and make, such streets, lanes, alleys, sidewalks, highways, watercourses and bridges, within the limits, and agreeably to the plan, of said city, as they may deem necessary for the public convenience : *Provided*, That notice of the intention to lay out, open, establish and make such street, lane, alley or sidewalk, highway, watercourse or bridge, shall be given, either personally to those interested, or by publication in some newspaper in said city, previous to the meeting of the Common Council for that purpose.—*Revised Charter, approved April* 4, 1827.

Power of Council to open and establish streets.

Proviso.

SEC. 1. That the Common Council of the city of Detroit, shall have, and they are hereby vested with, full power and authority to lay out, establish, open, make or alter such streets, lanes, alleys, sidewalks, highways, water-courses, and bridges, within the limits of the said city of Detroit, as the public improvement and convenience shall require.—*Act approved January* 29, 1832.

Power of Council to open and alter streets, &c.

SEC. 5. The Common Council shall have full power to close or alter streets and alleys in the bounds of the city of Detroit, and make such disposition of streets so closed as the public good may require : *Provided*, That nothing herein contained, shall be so construed as in any manner to interfere with private rights.—*Act approved February* 23, 1846.

Com. Council may alter or close streets

Proviso.

SEC. 21. That whenever the Common Council of said city shall deem it necessary to lay out, open, extend, straighten, widen, close, vacate, or in any other manner alter, any street, avenue, square, lane, alley, highway, or other public ground, or any water course or bridge, it shall be lawful for said Common Council to cause a notice to be published for four weeks successively, in any newspaper printed in said city, stating the nature of the contemplated improvement; and where private property is to be taken for the same, specifying and describing as particularly as may be practical, the ground, with the appurtenances which may be required for either of the purposes aforesaid; and the time and place, at which the damages and recompense

When Council proposes to open or alter streets a notice shall be published.

Contents of notice.

which the owner or owners of such ground may be entitled to for the same, or to which any person or persons, may be otherwise entitled by reason of the premises, will be inquired into, and assessed; and such damages and recompense apportioned and assessed among the owner or occupants, of the houses and lots of ground, and other real estate, which are to be benefited by the intended public improvement; and it shall be lawful for the Mayor or Recorder of said city, by a precept under his hand, and the seal of the Mayor's Court of said city, to command the Marshal of said city, to summon and return a jury of twenty-four freeholders of said city, who shall be in no wise interested in the aforesaid questions of damages and recompense, or the apportionment and assessment thereof, as aforesaid, to the Mayor's Court of said city, at the term specified for that purpose in such precept, which shall be the time and place expressed in the aforesaid notice; and that such precept shall be delivered to said Marshal, at least ten days before the return day thereof, who shall by virtue thereof summon and return such jury as aforesaid, twelve of whom shall be chosen by ballot, and constitute the jury for the purposes in said precept specified; and that it shall be the duty of said Marshal, at least six days before the return day of such precept, to serve on the owner or owners of the ground which shall be required as aforesaid for public use, if resident in said city, or the occupant or occupants of such ground, a written or printed copy of the notice to be published as aforesaid, directed to the owner or owners of such ground: And further, that in case the piece or pieces of ground so required, shall be vacant, and the owners thereof shall not reside in said city, or shall be unknown, it shall be a sufficient service of said notice, by said Marshal, to affix the same on some conspicuous part of such vacant premises; and further, that the said jury when balloted for, as aforesaid, in said Mayor's Court, shall be sworn well and truly to inquire whether the public convenience and necessity require the contemplated improvement to be made; and if they find in the affirmative, then to inquire into and assess the damages and recompense, if any, which any person or persons may sustain by reason of the premises; and, where private property is to be taken, to inquire into and assess the damages and recompense, which the owner or owners of the ground, with the appurtenances described and designated in said precept shall be justly entitled to; and in all

Precept to issue for summoning a jury. Qualifications of jurors

Duty of Marshal. How many to form jury.

Marshal to serve on owners of property to be taken copy of notice.

Notice where land is vacant

Jury to be sworn.

cases to apportion and assess such damages and recompense upon the owner or owners of all the houses and lots of ground lying within a thousand feet in any direction of the intended improvement, which will be benefited by the public use of such ground required as aforesaid, or by the making of any of the said contemplated improvements, as nearly as may be in proportion to the advantages which such owner or owners shall be deemed to acquire; and that said jury shall make and return under their respective hands, into said Mayor's Court, their verdict in the premises, specifying the amount of the damages and recompense, which they shall assess as aforesaid, if any, and the person or persons, to whom the same shall be assessed; and also the apportionment thereof, in the manner above directed; and shall also designate and describe the houses and lots included in such apportionment; and it shall also be the duty of said jury to set forth in said verdict and apportionment, the names of the owners, lessees and occupants, of the houses and lots upon which such damage and recompense, or any part thereof, shall be apportioned and assessed, as far as the same can be ascertained; and that the said verdict shall be returned to said Mayor's Court, at the same or any subsequent term thereof; and on being confirmed by said Court shall be binding and conclusive, as well upon the owner or owners, as upon the lessees or occupants, mentioned therein, or intended to be affected thereby, his, her, or their heirs, executors, administrators or asssignees; and that it shall be lawful for said Common Council upon paying or tendering the amount of damages so assessed, if any, to the parties respectively entitled thereto, to enter upon and take possession of the ground, with the appurtenances, as aforesaid, and to convert the same to the public use or uses for which it has been required and assessed; and in any case where private property shall not be taken, but damages shall have been assessed for the proposed improvement in the vacation of streets, public grounds or otherwise, such damages shall be paid or tendered before such improvement shall be consummated.

Damages to be assessed on property benefitted within 1000 ft

Verdict of jury.

Contents of verdict.

Verdict to be returned to Mayor's Court.

Proceedings on confirmation of verdict.

Damages to be paid or tendered before improvement carried out.

SEC. 22. That if said panel of jurors shall be exhausted by challenges or otherwise, or if a sufficient number of them should not attend to form a jury, it shall be competent for said Mayor's Court to direct a sufficient number of talesmen to be summoned to make up

If panel of jurors exhausted, talesmen may be summoned.

the panel: and it shall be competent for any person who may be affected by said proceedings, to object to any of the said jurors at the time of impanneling the same, for any ground which would be sufficient under the laws of this State to disqualify any person from acting as a juror in a civil case. And in the event, at any time, that any such jury may not be able to agree, it shall be competent for said Mayor's Court to discharge such jury and to impannel another, which shall be summoned by virtue of a *venire facias*, issuing from said Court, who shall be duly sworn, and proceed to discharge the duties aforesaid.

Jurors may be objected to.

If jury cannot agree—court may discharge same and impanel another.

Certified copy of assessments to be filed with the Register of Wayne Co.

Assessments to be a lien.

SEC. 23. That a certified copy of the assessment and apportionment of the damages and recompense aforesaid, shall, after having been completed and confirmed, be filed in the office of Register of Deeds for the county of Wayne, and be a lien upon the houses and lots designated in said verdict on which the same has been apportioned and assessed as aforesaid, from the time of such confirmation until the same shall be paid or satisfied.

Parties interested may appear before Mayor'sCourt and object to confirmation of verdict.

New jury to be impaneled if verdict set aside.

Appeal may be taken to Circuit Court.

Appeal may be taken to Circuit Court

Proceedings on appeal.

SEC. 24. Any person whose property is affected by said proceedings, and who is aggrieved thereby, may, at any time, before the confirmation thereof, appear in said Mayor's Court and shew cause against such confirmation, and if said Court shall, for sufficient reasons, either set aside said proceedings or refuse to confirm the same, then a new jury may be impanneled as aforesaid; but if said Court shall overrule all objections to said proceedings and confirm said verdict, then any person whose property is affected by such proceedings and aggrieved thereby, may appeal to the Circuit Court, for the county of Wayne, by filing a written notice of such appeal, and a specification of the alleged error or errors in said proceedings with the City Clerk, within five days after such confirmation; and it shall be the duty of said Clerk to certify all said proceedings to the ensuing term of said Circuit Court: *Provided, however*, that on such appeal nothing but the regularity of said proceedings shall be inquired into, and that such proposed improvement or alteration, shall in no manner be stayed by such appeal.

Power of Circuit Court on appeal.

SEC. 25. The said Circuit Court on such appeal may affirm or reverse said proceedings, and may assess costs in such manner as they shall deem proper; but no reversal shall be granted for matter of form only; and in case of any error in matter of substance, the erroneous proceeding, and all proceedings subsequent thereto, shall be reversed and set aside; and thereafter said Common Council may proceed from the last regular step to a termination; and the same may be so varied that the proceedings shall have reference only to the rights and interest of the appellant merely.

Power of Council on reversal by Circuit Court.

SEC. 26. It shall be competent for said Common Council to abandon or discontinue any proceedings under this act at any time before the same shall be confirmed by said Mayor's Court.

Proceedings may be discontinued any time before confirmation.

SEC. 27. It shall be the duty of said Common Council to cause notice to be given at least five days before such confirmation to every person who shall be assessed for benefits as aforesaid, of the time and place of the application for the confirmation of said verdict, and requiring them to show cause against such confirmation, if any they have; and in the event that the owner of any such property may be a non-resident of said city, or unknown, or such property be vacant, then such notice may be served as is prescribed in the first section of this act; and every such person conceiving himself aggrieved in the premises may appeal to said Circuit Court as aforesaid within thirty days from the confirmation of such apportionment and assessment as aforesaid, in accordance with, and subject to, all the regulations and provisions above made in reference to other appeals.

Persons assessed for benefits to be notified.

SEC. 28. All assessments for benefits shall be paid by the parties respectively to the City Treasurer, on confirmation of said verdict, unless an appeal be taken as aforesaid, and in such case such appellant shall pay such assessment as soon as his appeal shall be disposed of by confirmation in said Circuit Court; and in the event that any person or persons so assessed for benefits as aforesaid shall at any time fail or neglect to pay any such assessment, the Common Council shall cause a notice to be published in any newspaper printed in said city, which notice shall be published for five weeks successively, requiring the owner or owners of the houses and lots, or other real estate, with the appurtenances, upon which such assessments have been mad and apportioned as aforesaid, to pay the Treasurer of said city th amount thereof, with interest from the time of the confirmation, and any costs which shall have accrued, within sixty days from the date of such notice; and that if default shall be made in such payment,

When assessments for benefits to be paid

If persons fail to pay assessments, Council to publish notice.

such houses and lots, and other real estate, will be sold at auction at a day and a place to be specified in such notice, for the lowest term of years for which any person shall offer to take the same for the sum apportioned and assessed thereon, with interest and costs; and if, notwithstanding such notice, the owner or owners shall neglect or refuse to pay such apportionment and assessment, with such interest and costs, then it shall be lawful for said Common Council to cause such houses and lots, and other real estate, to be sold at public auction as aforesaid, on the day and at the place in such notice specified for that purpose, and to give a declaration of such sale to the purchaser thereof, under the common seal of said city; and such purchaser, his executors, administrators and assigns, shall and may by virtue thereof, and of this act, lawfully hold and enjoy the premises so sold for his and their own proper use against the owner or owners thereof, and all claiming under him or them, until his term shall be completed and ended, with full liberty to remove all the buildings and materials at the expiration of the said term which he or they shall have erected thereon.

If assessments not paid in 60 days after notice, premises to be sold.

Rights of purchasers at such sales.

Property under lease to be discharged therefrom on confirmation of assessment

SEC. 29. That in all cases where any part of said real estate required for public improvement as aforesaid, by virtue of this act, shall be subject to a lease, or other agreement, all the covenants and stipulations contained in such lease or agreement shall, upon the confirmation of such assessment as aforesaid, cease, determine, and be absolutely discharged.

Former provisions relative to opening streets repealed.

SEC. 30. That sections five, six, seven, eight, nine, ten, eleven, twelve, thirteen, and fourteen of an act entitled "an act to amend the Charter of the city of Detroit," approved the twenty-second day of February, A. D. one thousand eight hundred and forty-eight, be, and the same are hereby, repealed, saving all rights already accrued under the same, and acts done.—*Act approved Feb.* 12, 1855.

Proceedings only to be reversed in regard to persons taking appeal. Appellant not entitled to damages until appeal decided. Costs.

SEC. 15. If the property of several persons is affected by the proposed measure, the proceedings, if erroneous, shall be considered as reversed only in regard to the person or persons making the appeal, and no appellant, pending the appeal, shall be entitled to any money paid to the City Clerk for his damages; and in case the proceedings are sustained, all costs awarded against the appellant shall be deducted from said damages, and the balance only paid to the appellant.

SEC. 16. The Common Council shall have full power to prescribe the fees to be paid to the jurors and other officers for their services under the foregoing provisions.—*Act approved February* 22, 1848. Council may prescribe fees for jurors and officers.

PART VII.

RELATIVE TO ASSESSMENTS.

SEC. 10. From and after the year 1855, the Assessor of each ward in the city of Detroit shall make the assessment of real and personal property in the ward for which he has been elected Assessor; and no Assessor shall act in any other ward than that for which he has been elected Assessor. Assessors only to act in their own wards.

SEC. 11. The annual assessments in the several wards of said city, after the year 1855, shall be made during the month of March in each year; and the Common Council shall cause proper books, or rolls, to be prepared for the use of the Assessors in making their assessments, (one for each ward,) on or before the first day of March in each year. Annual assessments to be made in March. Council to furnish books for assessors.

SEC. 12. The ward Assessor in each ward is hereby fully empowered and authorized to demand of every person owning, or having charge of, any taxable property, as agent, or otherwise, in the ward, a list of such property, with such description as will enable him to assess the same; and he shall have power, and is required, when not satisfied with such list, to examine the party under oath touching the same. Assessors empowered to demand lists of property of persons to be assessed.

SEC. 13. If any person refuse to furnish a list of his or her property as aforesaid, or to testify under oath concerning property belonging to him or her, or under his or her charge, or to deliver a correct description of his or her property to the Assessor, within ten days after such demand shall have been made, or wilfully omit any such property from the list furnished by him or her, such person shall, upon conviction before the Mayor's Court, or any other court of competent jurisdiction, be liable to a fine not exceeding five hundred dollars, and the costs of prosecution. Persons refusing to furnish lists may be fined in Mayor's Court.

SEC. 14. Each Assessor shall make out and complete the entire assessment roll of the ward in which he is elected, without inter- Each assessor to make out his own assessments.

ference from, or consultation with, the Assessor of any other ward; and after all the Assessors have completed their rolls, and on the first Monday in April in each year, succeeding their election, they shall meet together at the Common Council room in said city, and organize as a Board of Assessors, for the purpose of hearing complaints of any and all persons against any assessments contained in any of said rolls, and making such corrections or alterations of the assessments, whether of real or personal property, as the majority of the Board shall deem proper. Said Board shall continue in session from day to day for the space of two weeks; and any person considering himself aggrieved may lay the cause of such grievance before the Board of Assessors, either verbally or in writing, and on sufficient cause being shown by the affidavit of such person, or by other evidence, to the satisfaction of said Board, they shall review the assessment complained of, and may alter the same, as to the property of any such person, and the estimated value thereof: *Provided, however*, That the Assessor who has made the particular assessment complained of shall have no voice or vote on the decision to be made by the Board on such assessment, and that a concurrence of a majority of the remaining Assessors shall only be required in any case on the question of altering or reducing any such assessment.

Assessors to organize as a Board after rolls are completed.

Board to sit two weeks.

To review assessments complained of.

Proviso.

SEC. 15. The Common Council shall, at its next regular session, after the expiration of said two weeks in which the Board of Assessors are to sit, confirm said assessment lists or rolls: *Provided*, That all persons who consider themselves aggrieved by the assessment of their property, and the decision of the Board of Assessors thereon, may, at said session of the Common Council, appeal to said Council. Every appeal shall be in writing, and shall state specifically the grounds of the appeal, and the matter or the thing complained of; and no other matter shall be considered by the Council. While acting upon said appeals, the Assessors may meet with the Council, and make such explanations as may be requisite in each case. The Council shall hear and determine all appeals in a summary way, and correct any errors which they may discover in the assessment rolls, and may place upon such rolls any property not already listed, and may increase or diminish any assessment as they

Council to confirm assessment rolls.

Persons aggrieved may appeal to Council.

How appeals to be made.

Power of Council on appeals.

may see fit; after which said rolls shall be fully and finally confirmed.

SEC. 16. The City Clerk shall cause a notice to be published in the official paper of the city, and in one other daily paper published in the city, for two weeks prior to the time for the first meeting of said Board of Assessors, informing tax payers of the time and place of the meeting of said Board, and of the objects for which it will meet, and the length of time it will continue its sessions. Such notices shall continue to be published in said papers, on each publication day thereof, until the expiration of the time for said Board to hold its sessions.

Clerk to publish notice of meetings of Board of Assessors.

How long notice to be published.

SEC. 17. Said Ward Assessors shall receive as compensation such sum or sums of money as the Common Council shall prescribe for the time actually employed by them in making their assessments, and while sitting as a Board, payable upon the warrant of the City Auditor.

Compensation of assessors

SEC. 18. So much of the provisions of "an act to amend the charter of the city of Detroit," approved January 30, 1850, as conflicts with the foregoing sections and provisions relative to assessors and assessments, shall be of no force or virtue after the expiration of the present year, 1855, and all laws, or parts of laws, in any way conflicting therewith shall be, and the same are hereby, repealed from and after the present year.

Former provisions relative to assessments repealed.

SEC. 19. After the assessment rolls of the city of Detroit for the present year, 1855, have been made out, according to the provisions of laws now in force, the Assessors of said city shall leave the same at the City Treasurer's office, and shall cause a notice to be published in two of the public newspapers published in said city, (one of which shall be the official paper of the city,) informing the tax payers of the city that the rolls have been made out, and are at the City Treasurer's office, and will remain there for two weeks, for the inspection of all persons interested in the same: and said Assessors shall meet at said Treasurer's office at the hour of 9 o'clock on each day, (except Sunday,) for the two weeks said rolls shall remain in said office, and continue in session as a Board for three hours on each day. All persons aggrieved by any assessment on said rolls may appear before said Board, on any of the days it shall continue in ses-

Provisions relative to assessments for year 1855.

Notice thereof to be published.

Persons aggrieved thereby may lay their complaints before the assessors.

sion, and present to the Board such affidavits, certificates or statements as they may deem proper, relative to any assessments on the said rolls, and said Board, or any two members of the same, on being satisfied, by affidavits or otherwise, that any assessments on said rolls are incorrect, unjust, or excessive, may make all such corrections in regard to names of persons or descriptions of property, and may reduce the amount of any assessment, as to them may seem right. The notice contemplated in this section shall be published ten days before the commencement of the two weeks during which the Assessors are to meet, as herein provided for; and any person aggrieved by the final action of the Board of Assessors, upon any matter submitted to them, according to the provisions of this section, may appeal to the Common Council, at its next session after the Assessors have closed their sittings, and the said Council may examine into the matter of the assessments complained of on such appeals, (but in no other cases,) and make, or cause to be made, such modifications of the same, on the assessment roll, as the majority of the Council may think proper. After the Council has acted upon all cases appealed to that body, from the Assessors, the assessment rolls shall be declared fully and finally confirmed, and shall remain as the basis of all taxes to be collected in the city of Detroit until the assessment for the year 1856 has been made.—*Act approved February* 12, 1855.

Majority of assessors may correct assessments.

Notice to be published two weeks.

Persons aggrieved may appeal to Council.

Council to confirm assessment rolls.

SEC. 18. The Assessors in each ward shall, once in each year, between the first Monday of March and the first Monday of April, make out the assessment roll of all the taxable persons and property in their respective wards, and when any lot or lots shall lie partly in two or more wards, the same shall be assessed in the ward where the greater proportion of such lot or lots are situated; and the said Assessors shall describe all lands, tenements or premises subject to any tax or assessment in said city, by referring to the number and section of the lot, and the owner and (*or*) occupant thereof, if known, and if the number and section of such lot cannot be ascertained, then by such other sufficient description as such Assessors may deem proper; and when by mistake or otherwise, any person may be improperly designated as the owner or occupant of such lot or premises, such tax or assessment shall not, for that cause, be vitiated, but the same shall be a lien on such lot or tenement, and collected as in other cases.

Provisions from act of 1841 relative to assessments.

Where a lot lies in two wards how assessed.

At the meeting of the Assessors, as authorized and required by section six of an act, entitled "An act relative to Ward Elections in the city of Detroit, and for other purposes," approved March 27, 1839, they shall have the same power and authority as the County Commissioners, by virtue of Sections Fourteen and Fifteen, of Chapter Second, Title fifth, Part first, of the Revised Statutes, have or may have to review, correct and equalize said roll.*—*Act approved April* 13, 1841. Powers of assessors relative to reviewing rolls.

PART VIII.

RELATIVE TO TAXES AND TAX SALES.

SEC. 1. That the Common Council of the city of Detroit, shall and may from time to time cause a tax not exceeding one-fourth (*half*†) of one per cent. in any one year, on all the real and personal estate within the limits of said city, to be assessed, collected and paid as they may direct: *Provided*, That a meeting of the freemen of said city be previously called for the purpose, by any three of the members of said Common Council, (of whom Mayor or Recorder shall be one,) and that a majority of the freemen present at any such meeting, consent to the levy of any such tax. And it shall be the duty of the Mayor or Recorder to call a meeting of the freemen of said city, when it shall be requested by petition, for that purpose, signed by twenty-four of such freemen; and the said Common Council, or a majority of them, whenever they may deem it necessary, may also call a meeting of said freemen.—*Act approved April* 22, 1833. Council may levy a tax. Proviso. Meeting of freemen to be called by Mayor.

SEC. 1. *The People of the State of Michigan enact:* That in addition to the tax now authorized to be levied by the Charter of the city of Detroit, the Common Council shall have power to cause to be assessed, levied, and collected, each and every year, upon all the real and personal estate within the limits of the said city, a tax not exceeding in amount a sum sufficient to pay the interest accruing upon the funded debt of the said city for the year for which such tax is Council may levy tax to pay interest on funded debt.

*This section of the act of 1841, seems never to have been expressly repealed, and as it seems in no way to conflict with the act of 1855, relative to assessments and contains provisions on certain points upon which the act of 1855 is silent, it was thought proper to insert it.

†See act approved April 13, 1841.

Also an additional tax not to exceed $5,000. levied and collected, and also an additional tax each year, not exceeding in amount the sum of five thousand dollars

How certain taxes to be appropriated. SEC. 2. That said sums, or any parts thereof, so levied and collected, shall be appropriated as follows, and to no other purpose whatever: Any and all sums levied and collected as aforesaid for the payment of interest, shall be applied to the payment of the interest accruing upon said funded debt of said city for the year for which such tax is levied and collected; the annual tax of five thousand dollars, or any portion thereof, levied and collected as aforesaid, shall, Idem. together with all sums that can be saved from the general tax, and from all other sources of revenue of said city, constitute a sinking fund, which shall, under the direction of the said Common Council be applied exclusively to the payment of the funded debt of said city.

Powers of Council relative to taxes for public works. SEC. 4. The Common Council shall have power, in addition to those already granted, to levy taxes in the manner prescribed in said charter, upon all the real and personal estate within the limits of said city, (*for the construction of public works within said city*:*) Proviso. *Provided*, That no such work shall be contracted for, or commenced, until it shall have been approved by the Common Council, and a tax levied to pay for the same; and no such work shall be paid for or contracted to be paid for, save out of the proceeds of the tax levied especially therefor;. and all contracts made in contravention hereof, shall be absolutely void. All the provisions of the charter of said city, and the amendments thereto, in any way inconsistent or contravening the provisions of this section, and the provisions contained in this act, are hereby repealed.†—*Act approved March* 21, 1851.

Com. Council may direct mode of levying and collecting highway and township taxes. SEC. 5. It shall be competent for the Common Council to direct the manner of assessing, levying and collecting all highway and township taxes, within the limits of said city, where no existing law of this territory may now otherwise adequately provide for the same, and to make all by-laws and ordinances necessary to carry this power into full effect: *Provided*, That such by-laws and ordinances be as near

---

* These words are not contained in the copy of the act as printed in the session laws of 1851, but they were inserted in the original draft of the section, and undoubtedly are in the enrolled copy of the law, and are therefore inserted here.

† See acts relative to Free Schools, cited among acts relative to the city of Detroit, for provisions relative to School Taxes.

as may be in accordance with the provisions and principles of the several acts now in force respecting the assessment and collection of county and township taxes, and highway taxes.—*Act approved April* 22, 1833.

SEC. 18. The Common Council shall have power to pass such ordinances in relation to the assessing of the road tax in the said city, and to the time and manner of applying the same, whether in labor or money, as they may deem expedient.—*Act approved March* 27, 1839. Powers of Com. Council relative to road tax.

SEC. 13. The said Common Council, in addition to the powers which they now have, relative to the assessing of the road tax in said city, and to the time and manner of applying the same, shall also have power to pass all such ordinances and provisions as they may deem requisite, relative to the assessing, levying and collecting of such road tax: *Provided*, That any person assessed for such tax, shall have the right to work out the same on or before the first day of July in each year, if he shall so elect.—*Act approved April* 13, 1841. Idem.

SEC. 8. The said Common Council shall have power to pass such ordinances as they may deem expedient in relation to the assessing of the road tax in said city, and as to the time and manner of applying the same, and providing for the payment and collection of the same, and whether the same shall be paid and collected in labor, money, or otherwise: *Provided*, Such road tax shall not in amount exceed the rates now fixed by law.—*Act approved January* 30, 1850. Idem.

SEC. 20. The Common Council shall have full power to assess and collect of each individual using or being benefitted by any public drain or sewer, as follows, to wit: the sum of one dollar and fifty cents annually, for each cellar drained directly or indirectly by a drain, into any public drain or sewer, which assessment shall be taken to include all other drainage of the premises to which said cellar especially belongs; and the sum of fifty cents annually for each lot, or subdivision of lot, being without a cellar, drained as aforesaid into any public drain or sewer; and such sums as may be fixed by the Common Council for all establishments requiring an unusual or extraordinary amount of drainage, drained as aforesaid; which sums, when collected, shall constitute the Sewer Fund, and shall be expended exclusively for the repair and construction of sewers.—*Act approved February* 12, 1855. Council may assess persons using or benefitted by sewers. Sewer assessments to be a sewer fund.

A capitation or poll tax may be levied

SEC. 46. That it shall and may be lawful for the Mayor, Recorder, Aldermen and Freemen of the said city, at any meeting convened and held by virtue of this act, to levy by a plurality of votes of the qualified voters present, a capitation or poll tax, upon every qualified voter as aforesaid: *Provided*, That the said tax shall not in any one year exceed the sum of one hundred cents on each person to be so taxed. —*Revised Charter, approved April* 4, 1827.

Proviso.

Ward collectors to collect city, school, state and county tax.

SEC. 6. It shall be the duty of said Collectors* respectively, to collect the city and school taxes and the county and State taxes, in and for their respective wards, and account for the same as required by law. They shall be required to give bonds in such manner, and be entitled to such compensation, as may be prescribed by law for township officers doing similar duties: *Provided*, That for the collection of the city and school taxes, they shall be entitled to take and receive only such compensation as may be fixed and allowed therefor by the Common Council. Sections seventeen, eighteen, nineteen, twenty and twenty-one of an act entitled "An act to amend the Charter of the city of Detroit," approved February 22, 1848, are hereby repealed.—*Act approved February* 21, 1849.

To give bonds Their compensation.

Collectors may sell personal property for taxes.

SEC. 2. The several Collectors shall have power to levy upon the personal property of persons from whom taxes may be due, whenever such property may be found within the bounds of the city.—*Act approved January* 30, 1847.

Warrants for collection of taxes may be issued without demand or return.

SEC. 1. The warrants authorizing the collection of any tax or assessment which may be hereafter imposed or laid by the Common Council, of the city of Detroit, may hereafter be issued in the first instance without any previous demand or return, under the corporate seal of said city.—*Act approved February* 16, 1842.

Collectors to pay over moneys to treasurer.

SEC. 29. That all moneys to be raised by tax shall be paid over by the Collector to the Treasurer, at such times, and under such regulations as shall be prescribed by the ordinances of the Common Council. —*Revised Charter approved April*, 1827.

Taxes lawfully imposed to be a lien on lands.

SEC. 2. Every assessment or tax, lawfully imposed or laid by the authority of the Common Council, on any lands, tenements hereditaments or premises whatsoever, in said city, or upon any owner or occupant thereof, shall be and remain a lien on such lands, tenements,

---

* See sec. 2, of act of 1849, cited *ante*, p. 6.

and hereditaments, from the time of making such assessment or imposing such tax until paid; and the owner or occupants of, or parties in interest respectively in, said real estate, shall be liable, upon demand, to pay every such assessment or tax, to be made as aforesaid; and in default of such payment, or any part thereof, it shall be lawful for the Mayor, Recorder and Aldermen of said city, or any three of them, (of whom the Mayor or Recorder shall be one,) by warrant under their hands and seals, to levy the same by distress and sale of the goods and chattels of such owner, occupant, or lessee refusing or neglecting to pay the same, rendering the overplus, if any, after deducting the charges of such distress and sale, to such owner, occupant or lessee; but if goods and chattels cannot be found, or if such person or persons be non-residents of said city, it shall be lawful for said Common Council, to cause a notice to be published in any one of the newspapers printed in said city for one month, (*four successive weeks*,*) if such person be a resident, and for three months, (*four successive weeks*,*) if a non-resident, requiring the owners, occupants or lessees of such lands, tenements, hereditaments and premises, to pay the sum or sums at which the same shall be assessed or taxed, or which may be assessed to any person or persons as the owner, occupant or lessee thereof respectively; and if default shall be made in any such payment, such real estate will be sold at public auction, at a day and place therein to be specified, for the lowest term of years at which any person shall offer to take the same, in consideration of advancing the sum assessed or taxed on the same, with the costs and charges in the premises; and if, notwithstanding such notice, the owners, occupant or occupants, lessee or lessees, shall neglect or refuse to pay such assessment or taxes, with the costs and charges, then it shall be lawful for the said Common Council to cause any such real estate to be sold at public auction for a term of years, for the purpose and in the manner already expressed, and to give a declaration of such sale to the purchaser thereof; and such purchaser, his executors, administrators and assigns, shall by virtue thereof, and of this act, lawfully hold and enjoy the same, for his and their own proper use against every such owner, occupant and lessee thereof, and all claiming under him or them, until his or their term shall be complete and ended, being at

Who liable for such taxes

How collection enforced

Notice of sale of lands for taxes to be published.

Lands, how sold for taxes

* See sec. 7, of act approved January 30, 1850—Post. p. 50.

liberty to remove any building or materials which he or they may erect thereon: *Provided, always*, That when any lands, tenements, and hereditaments, shall be sold in conformity with the provisions of this act, for the payment of any assessment or tax as aforesaid, if the owner or proprietor thereof shall, within the period of one year after such sale, deposit with the Treasurer of said city, for the use of the purchaser, the full amouut of assessment or tax, for which the same was sold, together with interest at and after the rate of ten per cent.* per annum, from the time of sale; then the term for which the same was sold, shall cease, and be determined at the time of making such deposit, any thing herein to the contrary notwithstanding: *And provided further*, That the person in possession of any real estate, at the time any tax is to be collected, shall be liable to pay the tax imposed thereon; and in case any other person by agreement or otherwise, ought to pay such tax, or any part or proportion thereof, the person who shall pay the same, shall or may recover the amount from the person who ought to have paid the same.—*Act approved April* 22, 1833.

Redemption.

Persons in possession of lands liable for taxes.

Rate of Interest that may be charged on redemption of lands sold for taxes.

SEC. 6. The Common Council of the city of Detroit shall have power to charge interest at a rate not exceeding twenty-five per cent. per annum on the amount of any tax or assessment for the non-payment of which, any lands, tenements, or hereditaments may hereafter be returned or sold, and shall have power to pass such ordinances as they may deem expedient, in relation to the apportionment of said interest and the collection of the same, and the amount or rate of interest to be paid upon the redemption of any premises so sold: *Provided*, The same shall not exceed the rate of twenty-five per cent. per annum.

Time notice of sales of lands for taxes shall be published.

SEC. 7. The notice of the sale of all real estate, subject to be sold for the payment of any tax or assessment in said city, shall be published once a week for four successive weeks, in the official paper of said city, which said notice shall be sufficient, and in lieu of any notice or notices now required by the charter of said city, or any of the amendments thereto.—*Act approved January* 30, 1850.

SEC. 2. That it shall be lawful at any time, for the lessee or pur-

* The Council may now direct that the interest on redemptions shall be *twenty-five* per cent. See sec. 6 of act approved January 30, 1850, next cited.

chaser of any lots or grounds and wharves, to remove any building or buildings erected thereon, within six months, (*thirty days**) after the expiration of said lease or time for which said lots or grounds or wharves were sold.—*Act approved April* 12, 1827.

Purchaser of lots for taxes may remove buildings after expiration of lease.

SEC. 2. The Mayor, or in his absence, the Recorder, of said city, under the corporate seal thereof, and in the corporate name, may execute any conveyance or declaration of sales of land hereafter sold for any taxes or assessments, which, when attested by the City Clerk and duly acknowledged, may be recorded as other conveyances of land.

Mayor to execute declaration of sales of lots for taxes.

SEC. 3. It shall be the duty of the City Clerk to bid in for the said corporation, at any sale of land, for taxes or assessments, every lot of land for which no person shall offer to bid, and if any purchaser shall neglect or refuse to pay the sum or sums bid by him within the time and under the regulations prescribed by the Common Council, such bid shall enure to the benefit of said corporation, if the Common Council so elect; and the Mayor, or in his absence, the Recorder, shall convey in his name, in the manner aforesaid, to the said corporation, the lot or lots so bid off by such purchaser, or by the City Clerk.—*Act approved February* 16, 1842.

Clerk to bid off lots for city.

SEC. 9. Whenever the Collector or other officer of said city, shall make return in pursuance of law, or any tax or assessment roll, that the tax or assessment, or any part thereof, as mentioned therein, has not been paid or satisfied, it shall and may be lawful, if the Common Council shall so direct, to commence an action of assumpsit, in the name of the Mayor, Recorder, Aldermen and Freemen of the city of Detroit, for the purpose of recovering such tax or assessment, or any part thereof; and in any such action, or any other cause or proceeding, such tax or assessment roll, and the return of the proper officer, made thereon according to law, shall be taken as *prima facie* evidence of the contents thereof. The provisions of this section shall apply, and be in force in relation to any tax or assessment heretofore imposed or laid by the authority of the corporation of said city, and which remains unpaid or unsatisfied: *Provided, always,* That such action and the proceedings had therein shall not appear so as to release or discharge any lien that has or may attach on any lands, tenements or

City may commence suits for recovery of taxes.

Such suits shall not discharge liens.

* See section 6 of act approved April 22, 1833.

premises, on account of such tax or assessment, until the same shall be paid or collected.

Conveyance of lots prima facie evidence.

SEC. 10. That the conveyance made in pursuance of the sale of any lands, tenements or premises for the non-payment of any tax or assessment in said city, shall be taken and received as *prima facie* evidence of the regularity of the proceedings whereon such conveyance or title is founded.—*Act approved April* 13, 1841.

Writ of possession may be issued by Mayor's court to remove occupant of lands sold for taxes

SEC. 8. Whenever any lands, tenements or hereditaments, shall be sold or leased, pursuant to the provisions of section second of an act entitled "An act to amend the several acts of the city of Detroit," approved April 22, 1833, for the payment of any assessment or tax, imposed by the authority of the said Common Council, and the owner or proprietor thereof, shall not, within one year after such sale or lease, deposit with the Treasurer of said city, for the use of the purchaser or lessee, the amount of the assessment or tax, for which the same was sold or leased, together with interest, at the rate of ten per cent.* per annum, from the time of sale or lease, then, upon the facts being made satisfactorily to appear to the Mayor's Court, at a regular session thereof, the said Mayor's Court may award a writ of possession, directed to the Marshal of said city, commanding him, in the name of the people of the State of Michigan, to take with him the force of the city, if necessary, and cause the owner, proprietor or occupant, as the case may be, of the lands, premises or tenements in question, to be removed therefrom, and to place the purchaser or lessee in peaceable possession thereof, and to make out of the goods, chattels, lands and tenements of such owner or occupant the sum of ten dollars, for costs and trouble in the premises; and the said Marshal shall execute said writ pursuant to the command therein contained.

Costs thereon

When writ to issue.

No writ of possession shall issue, until the person in possession shall have been notified to show cause why the same should not issue.—*Act approved April* 13, 1841.

---

* Now twenty-five per cent. See section 6 of act of 1850, cited, *ante*, p. 50.

PART IX.

RELATIVE TO AN ALMS AND WORK HOUSE.

SEC. 31. The Common Council are hereby vested with full power and authority to provide by ordinance for the organization, regulation, control and support of an Alms House Department, including therein an alms house proper for the support and relief of the poor of said city, hospitals for the care of the sick, asylums for the insane and blind, nurseries for poor and destitute children, houses for the confinement, correction or punishment of males over sixteen and females over fourteen years of age, who shall be convicted, before any court of law, of violating any law of the State of Michigan, or any ordinance of the city of Detroit, for which, under existing laws, or any which may be hereafter enacted, they would be liable to confinement in the city prison, or the jail of Wayne county; houses for the confinement and reformation of males under sixteen and females under fourteen years of age, who shall under existing laws, or those hereafter enacted, be liable to confinement in the city prison or jail of Wayne county, or in the State penitentiary, when in the discretion of the court, or magistrate giving sentence, the public interests would be subserved thereby; houses wherein vagrants, disorderly persons, and persons guilty of petty offences, may, upon conviction before any court of competent jurisdiction, be confined and compelled to labor in such manner as shall be prescribed by ordinance.

Com. Council may establish an alms house, asylum for blind, hospital, &c.

Also work houses.

SEC. 32. The Common Council may from time to time, as in their discretion the circumstances may require, levy and collect taxes, in addition to those heretofore authorized by law, upon all the taxable real and personal estate in the city, in the manner and subject to the limitations prescribed in the charter for levying city taxes, for the purchase of lots, the erection of suitable edifices thereon, and the protection, government and support of said Alms House Department, and for the payment of all legitimate and necessary expenses thereof; and shall from time to time, employ and appoint such and so many officers and assistants as they may deem necessary for the control, management and safety of the different branches of said department.

May levy taxes for such purposes.

SEC. 33. Whenever by the sentence of any Court, any person shall be confined in any branch of said department who would, under existing laws, or those hereafter enacted, have been liable to

Certain expenses to be paid by State

confinement in the State prison or penitentiary, all expenses attending the confinement or maintenance of such person shall be paid by the State Treasurer, quarter-yearly, on the certificate of the City Auditor that such expenses have been incurred; and whenever any person shall be confined, supported or maintained, in any branch of said department, for whose confinement, support or maintenance any township in the county of Wayne, or any county in the State of Michigan, would have been liable, under the provisions of law, all expenses attending such confinement, support or maintenance, shall in like manner be paid quarter-yearly by the Treasurer of such township or county, upon the certificate of the City Auditor that such expenses have been incurred.

Also by counties and townships.

Persons required to labor, who are received into such establishments.

SEC. 34. Every person confined, supported, maintained or relieved in said department, whose age and health will permit, shall be employed in some useful labor, and the officers in charge thereof shall use their best endeavors to provide for all persons under their care, such labor as, on trial, shall be found to suit the capacity of the individual. It shall be the duty of the officers to keep and employ separate and apart from each other, the paupers and criminals, and as far as possible to classify the latter, so that the novice in crime may not be contaminated by the evil example and converse of the more hardened and confirmed. The hours of labor, which shall not exceed ten per day, shall be regulated and fixed by the Common Council. There shall be an accurate account kept with all paupers, charging them with the expenses incurred by the city for their board and maintenance, and crediting them with a fair and reasonable compensation for the labor performed by them; and when they shall leave the department, if any balance shall be found due them, it shall be paid to them in cash at the time of their discharge: *Provided*, That the Common Council may, in their discretion, order said balance to be paid to some discreet citizen, who shall expend or invest the same for the benefit of such pauper, and shall report fully his action in the matter to said Council. And in case any convict or pauper shall refuse or neglect to perform the work allotted to him or her by the person in charge, such convict or pauper shall be punished by solitary confinement, and shall be fed on bread and water only, until they shall comply with the rules of said department, not

Inmates to be classified.

Hours of labor.

Accounts to be kept with paupers.

Paupers or convicts refusing to work may be punished.

exceeding five days at any one time, and such refusal and punishment shall be forthwith reported to said Common Council; and in case any pauper shall refuse or neglect to perform the work assigned to him or her, on three several occasions, such paupers shall be expelled from the Alms House.

SEC. 35. The Mayor, Recorder or any two Aldermen, or any Court or Magistrate of competent jurisdiction, in the city of Detroit, or the county of Wayne, may commit to any branch of said department provided for punishment or reformation, any and all such persons as shall be convicted as vagrants or disorderly persons, or as persons guilty of any offences against any of the laws of this State, punishable by fine or imprisonment in the city prison or the jail of Wayne county; and for whose punishment in the State prison the laws do not provide. And any Court of competent jurisdiction in the State of Michigan may, in their discretion, commit any male under sixteen, or any female under fourteeen years of age, to the work-house branch of said department, who shall be convicted of any crime punishable by confinement in the State prison, whenever in their opinion the welfare of the public and the convict will be promoted thereby. The Director of the Poor of the city of Detroit shall commit to the Alms House all paupers who shall apply to him for that purpose, or for whose support or maintenance the laws authorize him to provide. The officers in charge of said department may receive and provide for, or confine, any insane, or blind or idiotic person, or any male under sixteen, or female under fourteen years of age, who shall be brought to them by the Director of the Poor, or other proper officer of any township in this State, or by the parent, guardian, or friend of any such person: *Provided*, That such officer, parent, guardian or friend shall give ample and satisfactory security for the payment, at least once a month, of all expenses that may be incurred on account of the person so received: *And provided further*, That nothing herein contained shall be so construed as to make any person who may be brought to said department for confinement or maintenance a citizen of Detroit.

Who may commit to alms house department and who to be commited

Idem.

Idem.

Provisions relative to insane, blind or idiotic persons.

SEC. 36. The chief officer of said department shall have full power to indenture and bind out, as apprentices, during their minority, any minor children who may be under their care and control

Minor children in alms house may be bound out

by reason of the provisions of this act, or any other law of this State, in the forms and with the provisions now prescribed by law: *Provided*, That such child shall have been under the care and control of said department for at least three months; and he shall have the same power that is possessed by parents or guardians to cancel such indenture.

Proviso.

Powers of officers of alms house department.

SEC. 37. The officers in charge of said department shall have power to transfer any person committed to their care from any one branch to any other branch of said department. It shall be lawful for said officers, and they shall have full power in relation to all persons committed as vagrants, by reason of their being persons who shall have contracted an infectious or other disease, in the practice of drunkenness or debauchery, requiring medical aid to restore them to health, after the same shall have been, under medical treatment, sufficiently cured to be discharged, or to work or labor, in their discretion, to detain such person or persons, and commit them to the work-house branch of said department, until from the proceeds of their work and labor, there shall have been received by said officers, beyond the charge of their support while in said work-house, a sum sufficient to reimburse all the expenses of their charge and care while under medical treatment as aforesaid: *Provided*, That under this section no person shall be so detained in said work-house for a longer period than six months.

Com. Council to make laws and regulations relative to alms house

SEC. 38. The Common Council shall make all by-laws, ordinances, rules and regulations, necessary to carry into effect the provisions of this act, and shall have full power to change, amend, alter, repeal or annul such ordinances, by-laws, rules, and regulations, from time to time, as they in their discretion shall deem requisite.

Shall appoint committees to visit and inspect same.

SEC. 39. The Common Council shall, by committees by them for that purpose duly appointed, visit and inspect said department and all its branches thereof, at least twice each year, and it shall be made the duty of some city officer to visit and inspect every branch of said department once in each week, who shall report to said committee anything which in his opinion shall require the attention of said committee; whereupon it shall be the duty of said committee to visit said department and correct the evil, if in their power, or to report the same to the Common Council for its action.—*Act approved February* 12, 1855.

Duty of committee.

PART X.

RELATIVE TO MAYOR'S COURT.

SEC. 31. That the Mayor, Recorder and Aldermen, or any three of them,* of whom the Mayor or Recorder shall always be one, shall have full power and authority, and they are hereby vested with full power and authority, to inquire of, hear, try, and determine, in a *summary manner*, all the offences which shall be committed within the said city, against any of the laws, ordinances or regulations that shall be made, ordained or established, by the said Common Council, in pursuance of the powers granted them in this act, and to punish the offender or offenders, as by the said laws, ordinances or regulations shall be prescribed or directed; and to award process and take recognizances for the keeping of the peace and for good behavior, and for appearance or otherwise, or to commit to prison, as occasion shall lawfully require. Power of Mayor, Recorder, and Aldermen to try offences committed in the city.

SEC. 32. That the Mayor, Recorder and Aldermen, * holding such court, in term, and each or every of them, in vacation, shall have the same powers, as conservators of the peace within the limits of said city, as any courts of record have, or any Justice of the Peace has or shall have, by law, in any county of this Territory. Powers in term and in vacation, same as courts of record and justice.

SEC. 33. That for the ends, intents, and purposes, in this act mentioned, the said Mayor, Recorder and Aldermen, * or any three of them, of whom the Mayor or Recorder shall always be one, shall have full power and authority to hold and keep a court of record within the said city, by the name, style, and title of the "Mayor's Court of the city of Detroit:" *Provided*, That in case of the sickness, death, or absence of the Mayor and Recorder, the said court shall be held by the Aldermen.—*Revised Charter, approved April* 4, 1827. May hold a court of record; its style. Proviso.

SEC. 2. The Mayor's Court shall be held by the Mayor, and in case of his absence from the Court, by the Recorder, and in case of the absence of both, by any Alderman previously designated by the Common Council. Who shall hold Mayor's Court.

SEC. 6. All acts and parts of acts contravening the provisions of this act, are hereby repealed.—*Act approved March* 16, 1847.

---

* Court now held by Mayor, or Recorder, alone. See sec. 2, of act approved March 16, 1847.

Terms of court.

SEC. 34. That the said Mayor's Court of the said city shall be held on the second Monday of every month, and the terms of said court may continue for three days, or until all the business of said term shall be disposed of.*—*Revised Charter approved April* 4, 1827.

Special terms

SEC. 3. It shall be competent for the Mayor, Recorder and Aldermen, or any three of them, (of whom the Mayor or Recorder shall always be one,) to hold special terms of the Mayor's Court of said city, as often as they may deem it necessary or expedient, for the despatch of business in such court.—*Act approved April* 22, 1833.

City Clerk to be Clerk of Mayor's Court.

SEC. 35. That the Clerk of the said city shall be the Clerk of the said Mayor's court, and shall perform all the duties of Clerk of the said court, and shall be entitled to demand and receive all the fees and perquisites belonging to said office.

Duties of Marshal, Clerk and Constables as officers of said court.

SEC. 36. That the Marshal, Clerk and Constables in the said city, shall attend the said Mayor's Court, unless such attendance be dispensed with by the Court, and obey and perform all the duties of their respective offices, as well when required by the said Mayor's Court, or any judge thereof, as otherwise; and the said Marshal and other Ministerial officers of said city, shall execute and return all the process of the said Mayor's Court, directed to them respectively, in the same manner as the Sheriff and other officers of any court of record in this Territory.

Of the practice of Mayor's Court.

SEC. 37. That the practice of the said Mayor's Court shall be regulated agreeably to the rules and practice of the Supreme Court of this Territory, where the same are applicable, and until the said Mayor's Court shall have made rules for its practice, which the said Mayor's Court is hereby authorized and empowered, from time to time, to do.

Style and test of process from Mayor's Court.

SEC. 47. That all writs and process from the Mayor's Court shall run in the style of the United States of America,† and shall bear test in the name of the said Mayor, if not interested, but if interested, then in the name of the Recorder; shall be sealed with the seal of

---

* A proviso to this section, contained in the original act, limiting the term of the Court, repealed by act approved April 22, 1833.

† Process now to run in name of "People of the State of Michigan." See sec. next cited from act of 1839.

said Court, be signed by the Clerk, and be dated on the day on which the same may issue.—*Revised Charter, approved Ayril* 4, 1827.

Sec. 16. All process and proceedings in the Mayor's Court, (which is hereby declared to be clothed with similar jurisdiction and powers as heretofore.) shall be in the name of the people of the State of Michigan.*—*Act approved March* 27, 1839.

Process, &c., to be in name of People of Michigan.

Sec. 45. That in all process, prosecutions or proceedings, before the said Mayor's Court, no freeman ef said city, summoned and attending as a witness, shall be deemed incompetent to testify as a witness, on account of the interest such witness may have, as a freeman of said city, in the event of such process or proceedings.—*Revised Charter, approved April* 4, 1827.

Persons not incompetent as witnesses on account of interest as a freeman.

Sec. 1. In no case before any court, nor before any Justice in the State of Michigan, whenever the Mayor, Recorder, Aldermen, and freemen of the city of Detroit are, or may be parties, or interested, shall it be deemed to be ground of objection to jurors, witnesses or court, or to either or any of them, that they are freemen or citizens of said city, nor shall it be a good objection to jurors or witnesses, that they have been subpœned or summoned by an officer of said city, who is a freeman or citizen thereof, on the ground that such officer is therefore interested.—*Act approved April* 13, 1841.

Jurors, witnesses, court or officers not to be objected to because they are citizens of Detroit.

Sec. 41. And to the end and intent that such person and persons, charged with the offence and offences, supposed by such charges to have been committed within the said city, against the provisions of this act, as shall dwell, remain, lurk, or (reside,) without the bounds and limits of said city, may be brought to justice, the said Mayor's Court, in session, and the Mayor or Recorder, or either of the Aldermen of said city, shall and may, in vacation, as often as occasion shall require, issue his or their writ or writs of capias, under the seal of the court, to the Sheriff or Sheriffs of any county or counties, or town corporate, within this territory, directed, commanding him or them to take and bring the body or bodies of such person or persons, as shall be so as aforesaid charged, before him, the said Mayor, Recorder and Aldermen, or either of them, to be dealt with according

Court in session, or Mayor, Recorder or Aldermen, in vacation, may issue capias to apprehend persons charged with offences, wherever they may be found

* The remainder of this section, as contained in the original act superseded by provisions of act of 1848, relative to juries in Mayor's Court.

to law; and every Sheriff or other officer, to whom any such writ or writs of capias shall be directed or delivered, is hereby enjoined and required to use such due diligence to execute the same, under such pains and penalties as are by law incurred by any Sheriff or other officer, for neglecting or refusing to obey and execute any capias or other process to him directed or delivered; and that in case where the person so charged as aforesaid, shall be within the limits of the county of Wayne, and out of the limits of the said city, the writs and process may be directed to the Marshal or any Constable of the said city, who shall be authorized to serve the same within the limits of the said county: *Provided*, That the person or persons, preferring the charge mentioned in this section, shall be responsible for costs and damages, in case of acquittal.—*Revised Charter, approved April* 17, 1827.

Officers to whom writ is directed, to serve the same, or liable to penalty

Marshal or Constables may serve writ in Wayne Co. Proviso.

Council may provide city prison.

SEC. 16. The Common Council of said city shall have power and authority to provide a city prison in said city, where all persons charged with, or convicted of, offences or misdemeanors against the charter, by-laws or ordinances of said city, may be confined or imprisoned, until discharged by authority of law; and the said Common Council shall appoint all officers necessary for said prison, prescribe their powers, and duties, regulate the time and manner such prisoners shall be kept at labor, and make all by-laws, ordinances or orders concerning the good government and regulation of said prison, and for the punishment of such prisoners who may refuse to work therein, as they may deem necessary and proper.

Appoint officers for same.

Persons arrested, confined in county jail.

SEC. 17. Any person arrested by virtue of any process from the Mayor's Court, or by authority of any officer of said city, may be confined in said prison to the same effect as prisoners are or may be detained in the jail of the County of Wayne; and any law of this State prohibiting escape, aiding prisoners to escape, or any other act detrimental to safety of prisoners in a county jail, shall apply to said prison: *Provided*, The Common Council, or the Mayor or Recorder of said city, may at any time direct any or all of such prisoners to be removed from said city prison to the jail of the county of Wayne: *And provided, also*, Such prisoners, or any of them, may at any time, in the first instance, be confined in the said county jail, whenever the same may be deemed necessary by said Common Council; and the keeper of said jail or city prison shall be allowed such compensation for keeping and providing for prisoners confined therein, as the Common Council may determine to be just and reasonable, not exceeding the amount allowed by the County Commissioners for county prisoners.—*Act approved April* 13, 1841. Compensation to prison keeper for keeping prisoners.

SEC. 38. That the said Mayor's Court established by this act, is hereby vested with full power and authority to hear, try and determine, according to the laws of the United States, or of this Territory, and according to the by-laws and ordinances of said Common Council, and according to the course of the common law, all actions, personal or mixed, arising within the limits of said city, and to which the Mayor, Recorder, Aldermen and Freemen of said city, in their corporate capacity, are a party, and especially for the collection of taxes or other debts due, or which may become due to said corporation, for the rents of any buildings, lands or premises belonging to said corporation, and for obtaining possession of lands or tenements belonging thereto, and for eviction of tenants holding over possession, after their leases shall have expired: *Provided*, That no tenant shall be turned out of possession, unless the Marshal or other officer thereto directed, shall have given such tenant six days' previous notice, after the expiration of his lease. Of the jurisdiction of Mayor's Court. Proviso.

SEC. 39. That the said Mayor's Court shall have full power and authority to hear, try and determine, according to the laws of the United States, or of this Territory, and according to the course of the common law, all such offences and misdemeanors, of which this court has jurisdiction or cognizance by this act, although no by-law or ordinance shall have been made or passed relative to such offence.—*Revised Charter, approved April* 4, 1827. Further as to jursdiction.

SEC. 2.* And the said Mayor's Court, when any defendant is found guilty of the complaint or information filed against him, may punish said defendant by fine and costs, and may hold him to bail for good behavior in such security, as circumstances may require, and may further order that such defendant stand committed, and be kept at hard labor, until his sentence be complied with. Mayor's Court may punish by fine, hold to bail, or commit to prison.

---

*The former part of this section, enacting whose duty it shall be to hold the Mayor's Court, being inconsistent with, and consequently repealed by, the act of 1847, is not inserted.

Additional powers of Mayor's Court.

SEC. 3. The Mayor's Court of said city, in addition to the powers it now has, shall have and exercise original jurisdiction in all personal actions and remedies at law, arising within the limits of said city, and to which the Mayor, Recorder and Aldermen and freemen of the city of Detroit, in their corporate capacity, are a party plaintiff. And the said Court shall have and exercise all the powers usually exercised by any court of record, at the common law, for the full exercise of the jurisdiction given to it by law: *Provided*, That when an issue of fact shall be joined in any civil action, in said Mayor's Court, a jury shall not be called to try the same, unless upon the request of either party, and in such case a jury shall be summoned, drawn and sworn, as in other cases provided for in said court. And if, from any cause, the said court shall not be held on the day appointed therefor, all causes or matters therein shall stand continued till the next meeting thereof. —*Act approved April* 13, 1841.

Juries.

SEC. 1. That in all cases where a jury may be required by the Common Council of the city of Detroit, the same shall be obtained in the following manner:

Assessors to make out a list of jurors and return same to Council.

SEC. 2. The Common Council may, at any time, not oftener than once a year, direct the Assessors of the several wards or districts to select from their respective assessment rolls, as last prepared, a list of the names of two hundred persons, who are legally qualified voters and residents of the city of Detroit, and return the same to the Common Council, to serve as jurors in all cases, required as aforesaid, which said returns shall be signed by said Assessors, respectively, and filed with the City Clerk. [But it shall not be necessary to place on said list the name of any person who is exempted by law from serving as a juror.*]

Clerk to deposit names of persons returned as jurors in a jury box.

SEC. 3. When such returns are all made, as above provided the City Clerk shall write the name of said persons so selected on separate strips of paper, and deposit and preserve the same in a jury box, to be kept for that purpose, and such persons so returned shall be liable to serve for the period of at least one year, and until another return shall be made in the manner aforesaid, under the direction of the Common Council.

---

*The words in brackets are added to section 2 and also to sction 4, on next page, by Sec. 41, of act approved February 12, 1855.

SEC. 4. Whenever a jury shall be required at a sitting of the Mayor's court, the City Attorney shall notify the Clerk of the same, who shall forthwith in the presence of the presiding officer of the court, and the Marshal, proceed to draw from said jury box the names of twelve persons, who shall serve as such jurors, and the Clerk shall immediately make out a venire facias, commanding the City Marshal, or any city Constable, to summon the parties so drawn to attend the session of said court, and not depart the same until discharged, under such penalty, not exceeding ten dollars, as the court may impose; and in case of a default in the attendance of such jurors, or in case the number in attendance be reduced by challenge, (the right to which is hereby extended to the parties, as in circuit courts,) the said Mayor's court shall have the power to direct the summoning of talesmen, who shall be subject in case of default, to the penalty in this section provided. [And such jury shall attend the session of said court to which they shall be summoned, until discharged by the court; and they shall be competent to try all issues and cases pending in said court, which may be submitted to them.*]—*Act approved February* 22, 1848.

How jury drawn for Mayor's Court.

How summoned.

Talesmen.

SEC. 40.† It shall be lawful for the said Mayor's Court to punish, by fine or otherwise, any juror for non-attendance, when summoned as aforesaid, in the same manner as the County or Circuit Courts of this Territory, may lawfully do; and no juror summoned and attending as aforesaid, shall be deemed incompetent to serve as a juror, on account of the interest which such juror may have as a freeman of said city, in the event of the cause to be heard and tried; and said Mayor's Court shall have full power and authority to establish, from time to time, the costs and fees of all the officers and witnesses attending said court: *Provided*, That no higher costs or fees shall be at any time allowed than those which are or may be established for similar services in the County Courts of this Territory: *Provided, also*, That said fees shall be demanded, taken and recovered, in the same manner in all respects as is or shall be provided by law for the taxing and recovering of the like fees in the said several County Courts.—*Revised Charter approved April* 4, 1827.

Court may punish jurors for non-attendance.

Juror not incompetent on account of interest as a freeman.

Court may establish fees

Proviso.

---

*See note on page 62, ante.

†The former part of this section, relative to the manner of obtaining juries for Mayor's court, being inconsistent with the provisions before cited from act of 1848, is not inserted.

Further as to costs and fees

SEC. 6. The Mayor's Court of said city is hereby vested with full power to establish, from time to time, the costs and fees of all officers and witnesses attending the said court, but shall not fix them at a higher rate than those which are, or may be, established for similar services in the Circuit Court.—*Act approved April* 13, 1841.

Rules of Circuit Court to apply to Mayor's Court in civil cases.

SEC. 4. Any civil action, of which said Mayor's Court has or may have jurisdiction, may be commenced and proceeded in, in the same manner as is or may be required by the laws of this State in relation to such actions in the Circuit Court for the county of Wayne, so far as the same can apply; and the rules of the said Circuit Court shall, so far as the same can apply, be observed in all cases when the amount of debt or damages exceeds one hundred dollars: *Provided*, That upon all judgments not exceeding one hundred dollars upon civil actions before said Mayor's Court, (except) actions upon recognizances, the defendant shall be entitled to a stay of execution as is provided for in judgments upon actions before Justices of the Peace; and that any party conceiving himself aggrieved by any judgment in any civil actions before said Mayor's Court, may appeal to the Circuit Court for the county of Wayne, by, within five days after judgment, paying all the costs that may have accrued and entering into a recognizance, with at least one surety, in a sum not less than fifty dollars in any case, and where the whole amount of the judgment for debt, and damages, and costs shall exceed twenty-five dollars, in double the amount thereof, conditioned to prosecute the appeal to judgment, at the next term of the Circuit Court, and to abide the order of said court therein, and all proceedings before said Circuit Court, in cases of appeal by virtue of this section, shall conform, as near as may be, to proceedings in cases from Justices of the Peace.

Stay of execution in like manner as in Justices Court; appeal allowed to Circuit Court.

When cases removed by certiorari, recognizance to be given.

SEC. 5. Whenever a writ of certiorari to remove any judgment of said Mayor's Court shall be granted, the same shall not operate as a stay of execution, unless the party suing out the same, his agent or attorney, shall enter into recognizance, with at least one responsible (surety,) to be approved by the City Clerk, in a sufficient sum, not less than double the amount of the judgment and costs, conditioned to prosecute such writ of certiorari to judgment, at the next term of the Supreme Court, and abide such order as the court may make therein.

SEC. 23. The said Mayor's Court shall have full power and authority, and are hereby declared to have full power and authority, to hear, try and determine, pursuant to the provisions of section thirty-one of the "Act relative to the city of Detroit," approved April 4, 1827, all offences which shall committed within said city, against any of the laws, ordinances, or regulations of said city, passed, ordained or made, or which may be passed, ordained or made by the Common Council of said city, in pursuance of authority in such behalf lawfully granted unto them.—*Act approved April* 13, 1841.

Jurisdiction of Mayor's Court confirmed.

SEC. 4. That when any person is convicted of any violation of the ordinances or by-laws of said city, before the Mayor's Court of said city, for which a fine shall be imposed, it shall and may be lawful for said Court, in term time, or for the Mayor or Recorder, in vacation, after such conviction, to discharge such prisoner, upon his giving satisfactory security, by a good and sufficient bond, payable to the Mayor, Recorder and Aldermen of the city of Detroit, conditioned that the amount of his fine and all costs and charges shall be worked out upon the streets of said city of Detroit or otherwise, as may be required, under the authority of the said Common Council, and in the event of a breach of any such bond, a suit shall be instituted thereon, in any court having jurisdiction, and on the rendition of judgment thereon, there shall be no stay of execution allowed.

Mayor or Recorder may discharge a prisoner on certain terms

SEC. 5. That it shall be competent for the Common Council of said city to employ, under the superintendence of any person or persons, to be appointed by said Common Council, any person or persons who may be convicted in said Mayor's Court, and who may not have availed himself, or may not be entitled so to do, of the provisions of the fourth section of this act, to work on the streets of said city or otherwise, as the Common Council may direct, during the period for which such person or persons shall have been sentenced to imprisonment, and until such person or persons shall have paid up, in such work, all costs and charges; and when the sentence of said Mayor's Court may be for fine and costs, then until payment is made as aforesaid, of such fine and costs, and all charges; and on the payment of such fine and costs to discharge and release such prisoner or prisoners; and when the convicts who may be confined in the jail of the county of Wayne, by the judgment or sentence of any other court, or Justice or Justices, in said county, are not otherwise employed under any ex-

Persons convicted in Mayor's Court may be employed on streets.

Convicts in county jail may be employed on streets.

isting provisions of law, the said Common Council are hereby empowered also to employ such convict or convicts to work on the public streets of said city: *Provided always*, That all such convicts to be employed as aforesaid, shall, while at labor, be secured by ball and chain, or otherwise, as the said Common Council may direct, and shall not be suffered to remain out of said jail other than in the day time, and not after sun-set; and the said Common Council are empowered to make such by-laws and ordinances as may be necessary to carry the provisions of this, and the preceding section into effect.—*Act approved June* 29, 1832.

Proviso.

How fines and costs to be disposed of.

SEC. 42. That it shall be the duty of said City Marshal, and of his assistant, if he has any, to pay into the hands of the City Clerk, immediately on receipt of the same, all fines, penalties and costs imposed by said Mayor's Court, who shall forthwith pay over said fines and penalties to the City Treasurer, and pay the costs to the officers entitled thereto; and said Clerk shall make quarterly reports to said Common Council, of all the cases disposed of in said Court, stating the several fines and penalties imposed, the manner in which the same may have been satisfied, and the sums which he may, from time to time, have paid to said Treasurer as aforesaid.—*Act approved February* 12, 1855.

Clerk to make quarterly reports to Council of business of Mayor's Court.

PART XI.

MISCELLANEOUS PROVISIONS.

Printed copies of by-laws and ordinances prima facie evidence thereof in courts.

SEC. 25. The printed copies of all by-laws and ordinances passed by the Common Council, and which shall be published under their authority, shall be admitted as *prima facie* evidence thereof, in all the courts of law in said city, and on all occasions whatsoever; and the Common Council may require the Clerk to preserve, in a sufficient book, all by-laws and ordinances published as aforesaid, from time to time.

Clerk to administer oaths.

SEC. 26. The Clerk of said city is hereby authorized to administer oaths, take affidavits and recognizances, in all matters and things soever, connected with the city corporation, or appertaining to his office, or the duties thereof.——*Act approved April* 13, 1841.

SEC. 7. That it shall be lawful for the Mayor, Recorder and Aldermen, and each of them, while in office, and until their successors are duly qualified, to administer oaths and to take affidavits: *Provided*, They shall receive no fee for administering such oath.

Mayor, &c. may administer oaths.

SEC. 8. That hereafter the Constables in the city of Detroit, while in office, shall be respectively vested with the same power, and perform the same duties, which may be vested in and performed by any Constable of the county of Wayne, and shall be subject to the same fees, and take the same oath : *Provided*, That every such Constable, before entering on the discharge of such duties, shall enter into a bond of the United States in the penal sum of two thousand dollars, with good and sufficient sureties, to be approved of by the Mayor, or Recorder of said city, conditioned well and faithfully in all things to perform and execute the office of Constable, during his continuance in office; and to pay to each and every person such sum or sums of money, as such Constable shall become liable to pay for, or on account of, any execution that may be delivered to such Constable for collection; which bonds shall be filed with the Clerk of the city of Detroit, and shall be liable to be put in suit in the same manner as Sheriff's bonds are by law.*—*Act approved June* 29, 1832.

Power of constables.

To give bonds.

SEC. 42. That all the rights of the corporation known by the name of the "Board of Trustees of the city of Detroit," in and to all lands, tenements, hereditaments, ferries, wharves, market stalls, landing places, goods, chattels, moneys and effects whatever, and all other lands, tenements, hereditaments, rights, franchises, privileges, goods, chattels, moneys, and effects whereof any person or persons, bodies corporate or politic, are seized or possessed, or which they or any of them hold or enjoy in trust for or to the use of the citizens of the said city of Detroit, or which said citizens are in any wise entitled to; and they are hereby severally and respectively vested in the said corporation, heretofore and by this act erected, by the name of the "Mayor, Recorder, Aldermen, and Freemen of the city of Detroit," to and for the use of the same, and their successors forever, saving, nevertheless, to all and every person and persons, bodies politic and corporate, his, her and their just rights therein.

All rights of board of trustees of city of Detroit. vested in the Mayor, Recorder, Aldermen and Freemen of the city of Detroit.

---

*A proviso to this section which is contained in the original act, being inconsistent with the acts of 1839 and 1849, is undoubtedly repealed by those acts, and is therefore omitted.

Persons holding evidences, &c., of said rights, to deliver the same to corporation.

SEC. 43. And to the end and intent, that all and singular the estate and estates, rights, privileges, and interests, aforesaid, may be had and received by the said Mayor, Recorder, and Aldermen, and be by them and their successors faithfully applied to and for the use of the said citizens and their successors forever; that all and every person and persons, bodies politic and corporate, who are or shall be seized or possessed thereof, shall, on reasonable request, deliver the same to the Mayor, Recorder, and Aldermen, together with all deeds, evidences, books and other papers, touching and concerning the same, with proper assignments, when the same shall be necessary and just, or true and fair copies thereof; and whoever shall fail herein, shall be liable for the same, and shall moreover forfeit and pay to the Mayor, Recorder, Aldermen, and Freemen, any sum of money not exceeding one hundred dollars, to be sued for and recovered in any court of record in this Territory.

Account of receipts and expenditures to be published, &c.

SEC. 44. That the said Mayor, Recorder and Aldermen, shall, once in every year, cause to be published, a just and true account of all the moneys which shall have accrued in their corporate capacity, during the year next preceding such publication, and also the disposition thereof, and shall also lay a copy thereof before the Legislature of the Territory, if so required by said Legislature.

This a public act, &c.

SEC. 48. That this act shall be deemed a public act, and shall be construed benignly and favorably, for every beneficial purpose therein intended.

Corporation to have no right to the water or water lots in front of the farms included in the limits of the city; nor to extend lanes and alleys across said farms.

SEC. 49. *Provided, however, and be it further enacted*, That nothing in this act contained shall be construed to vest in said corporation or any officers thereof, any right to the water, or the lands under water, in front of the farms included within the said city, nor any power to erect or cause or authorize to be erected, any wharf or other thing on the said land; but the right of the proprietors of the said farms, to the water and lands in front of said farms, and to fill in the water and erect fixtures thereon, shall remain and vest in said proprietors, the same as if this law had not passed: *And provided, further*, That nothing in this act contained shall be so construed as to authorize the said corporation or other authority created by this act, to extend the lanes, or alleys* of said city across said farms unless by consent of the proprietors thereof respectively.

Legislature may alter this act.

SEC. 50. That at all times hereafter, the legislative authority of the Territory, shall have full power to alter and amend this act whenever it may be considered expedient and necessary.—*Revised Charter approved April* 4, 1827.

---

*The section as originally passed prohibited the extension of "streets" across the farms embraced in the city. It was amended by striking out "streets," and inserting "lanes and alleys," by act approved March 4, 1843.

ACTS
RELATIVE TO THE CITY OF DETROIT.

AN ACT to authorize the Corporation of the city of Detroit to contract a loan.

SEC. 1. *Be it enacted by the Legislative Council of the Territory of Michigan*, That the Mayor, Recorder and Aldermen of the city of Detroit, be, and they are hereby, authorized and empowered to contract a loan for the use of said city of Detroit, not exceeding fifty thousand dollars, at an interest not exceeding six per cent. per annum, and which shall be redeemable in thirty years: *Provided*, That a majority of the freemen of said city, in public meeting assembled, shall, by a vote, authorizing (*authorize*) such loan to be made; and public notice shall be given in all the newspapers printed in said city, not less than ten days before said meeting shall assemble, for the purpose contemplated by this act.—*Act approved March* 30, 1835.

Com. Council authorized to contract a certain loan.

Proviso.

AN ACT to authorize the election of Constables in the city of Detroit.

Be it enacted by the Legislative Council of the Territory of Michigan, That the electors of Detroit, on the usual days of the election for city officers, may elect their city Constables, whose duty it shall be to attend the sessions of the Mayor's Court of said city, and who shall perform the duties of police officers of said city, which Constables, or any of them, may be removed by the Mayor, Recorder and Aldermen, on cause shown; and vacancies may be filled by said Mayor, Recorder and Aldermen to the end of the year.*

Constables to be police officers, and subject to removal by city board.

---

* See further as to the election and duties of Constables, *ante* pages 6, 11, 12, 13, 29, 67.

Duties and liabilities.

SEC. 2. The Constables elected as aforesaid, may also perform the same duties, and shall be subject to the same liabilities as Constables in other townships in this Territory.

To give security.

SEC. 3. The Constables elected as aforesaid, shall qualify and give security according to law, before they can enter upon the exercise of their official duties, which security shall be subject to the approval of the Common Council of said city.—*Approved March* 30, 1835.

SCHOOL LAWS

Of the city of Detroit, as collated and published by the Board of Education of said city, A. D. 1855.*

Detroit to be one school district.

SEC. 1. *Be it enacted by the Senate and House of Representatives of the State of Michigan,* That the city of Detroit shall be considered as one School District, and hereafter all schools organized therein, in pursuance of this act, shall, under the direction and regulations of the Board of Education, be public and free to all children residing within the limits thereof, between the ages of five and seventeen years, inclusive.—*Act of* 1842.

Schools free to scholars of certain ages.

School Inspectors to be elected,

SEC. 2. In lieu of the School Inspectors now required to be elected in said city, there shall be twelve† School Inspectors, to be elected in the manner following: at the next annual charter election, there shall be elected in each ward of said city, two School Inspectors, one of whom shall hold his office for two years, and the other for one year; and at every annual charter election thereafter, there shall be elected in each ward, one School Inspector, who shall hold his office for two years. No School Inspector shall be entitled to receive any compensation for his services.—1842.

Their term of office.

Not to receive compensation.

Vacancy in office of School Inspector, how filled.

SEC. 3. In case of a vacancy in the office of School Inspector, the Common Council of the city of Detroit may fill the same, until the next annual election, when, if such vacancy happen in the first year of the term of said office, the electors of the proper ward may choose

---

* The figures at the end of each section refer to the year in which the several acts were passed.

For the laws relating to the "colored children" of the city, see session laws of 1841, page 48.

† By the increase in the number of wards of the city, the number of School Inspectors has been increased to sixteen.

a suitable person to fill the remainder of such term: *Provided*, The City Clerk shall give notice of such vacancy prior to such election, as may be required in other cases.—1842. Proviso.

SEC. 4. Every person elected to the office of School Inspector, who, without sufficient cause, shall neglect or refuse to serve, shall forfeit to the Board of Education for the use of the library, the sum of ten dollars, to be recovered in an action of debt in some competent court: *Provided*, No person shall be compelled to serve two terms successively; and the said Board shall make all necessary rules and regulations relative to its proceedings, and punish by fine, not exceeding five dollars for each offence by any member of the Board, who may, without sufficient cause, absent himself from any meeting thereof, to be collected as they may direct.

Persons elected School Inspectors refusing to serve, may be fined.

Proviso.

Board may establish rules and regulations and fine its members.

SEC. 5. The School Inspectors, together with the Mayor and Recorder of said city, (who are declared to be *ex officio* School Inspectors,) shall be a body corporate, by the name and style of "The Board of Education of the City of Detroit," and in that name may be capable of suing and being sued, and of holding and selling, and conveying real and personal property, as the interest of said Common Schools may require; and shall also succeed to, and be entitled to demand all moneys and other rights belonging to or in possession of the Board of School Inspectors, or any member thereof, or any real and personal property or other rights, of any such district in said city; and the clear proceeds of all such property which may come into the possession of said Board, as last aforesaid, shall be expended and disbursed by and under the authority of said Board of Education, for the support of said schools, after paying all just and legal demands existing against the several school districts heretofore existing in said city: *Provided*, That said Board shall not be liable to pay an aggregate amount of indebtedness against any one district, greater than the amount received from the same by said Board.—1842, 1843, 1846.

Who to constitute Board of Education.

Board, a body corporate.

Its powers and privileges.

How proceeds of property received by Board to be disposed of

Proviso.

SEC. 6. The Board of Education (six members whereof may form a quorum,) may meet from time to time at such place in said city as they may designate. They may elect one of their own number President, and in the absence of the President at any meeting, a majority of the inspectors present may choose one of their number President *pro tem.*—1842, 1846.

What a quorum of Board

Board to elect a President.

Who to be Clerk of Board.

SEC. 7. The Clerk of the said city shall be *ex officio* Clerk of said Board, and shall perform such duties as the Board of Education may reasonably require. In case of the absence of said Clerk, or for any other cause, the Board may choose some suitable person to perform his duties, either as principal or deputy Clerk.—1842.

Recorder of Detroit may meet with the Board.

SEC. 8. The Recorder of said city shall be entitled to a seat at the meeting of said Board, for the purpose of deliberation, and of acting on committees, but shall have no vote therein.—1842, 1846.

General powers and authority of the Board.

SEC. 9. The Board of Education shall have full power and authority, and it shall be their duty, to purchase school-houses, and apply for and receive from the County Treasurer or other officer, all moneys appropriated for primary schools and district library of said city, and designate a place where the library may be kept therein. The said Board shall also have full power and authority to make by-laws and ordinances relative to taking the census of all children in said city between the ages of four and eighteen years; relative to making all necessary reports and transmitting the same to the proper offices, as designated by law, so that said city may be entitled to its proportion of the primary school fund; relative to visitation of schools; relative to the length of time shools shall be kept, which shall not be less than three months in each year; relative to the employment and examination of teachers, their powers and duties; relative to regulation of schools and the books to be used therein; relative to the appointment of necessary officers, and prescribe their powers and duties; relative to any thing whatever that may advance the interests of education, the good government and prosperity of common schools in said city, and (the) welfare of the public concerning the same.—1842, 1850, 1855.

May make by-laws and ordinances, relative to certain matters.

Mayor's Court to have jurisdiction under by-laws of the Board.

SEC. 10. The Mayor's Court shall have jurisdiction of all suits wherein the said Board may be a party, and of all prosecutions for violation of said by-laws and ordinances.—1842.

Board to publish an annual statement.

SEC. 11. The said Board shall annually, in the month of February, publish in some newspaper of the city, a statement of the number of schools in said city, the number of pupils instructed therein the year preceding, the several branches of education pursued by them, and the expenditures for all things anthorized by this act, during the preceding year.—1842.

SEC. 12. The Board of Education shall establish a district library. and, for the increase of the same, the Common Council are authorized annually to lay a tax on the real and personal property within said city, of a sum not exceeding two hundred dollars, which tax shall be levied and collected in the same manner as the moneys raised to defray the general expenses of said city.*—1842. To establish a library. Tax for, how levied.

SEC. 13. The Common Council of said city are hereby authorized, once in each year, to assess and levy a tax on all the real and personal property in said city, according to the city assessment rolls of that year, which shall not exceed two dollars for every child in said city, between the ages of four and eighteen years, the number of children to be ascertained by the last report on the subject, on file in the office of the Clerk of the county of Wayne, or in the office of the Secretary of said Board of Education, and certified by the President thereof; and the said tax shall be collected in the same manner as the moneys raised to defray the general expenses of said city; all said money shall be disbursed by the authority of said Board, for the maintenance and support of said schools, and for no other purpose. The said Board of Education shall have authority to establish a high school in said city, and also to appoint a Superintendent of the public schools, under the charge of said Board, with such salary and with such powers and duties as shall be prescribed by said Board of Education.—1855. Com. Council may levy taxes for support of schools. How taxes collected and disbursed. Board may establish high school, and appoint a Superintendent of public schools.

SEC. 14. The Treasurer of said city shall be the Treasurer of said Board, unless otherwise directed by said Board; he shall keep all moneys belonging to said schools separate from the moneys belonging to the corporation of said city; and he shall not pay out or expend the school moneys, without the authority of the said Board.—1842. Who to be Treasurer of Board. His duties.

SEC. 15. The Collector of said city, when he shall have paid any school money to said Treasurer or other person, shall take a receipt therefor, and file the same with the Clerk of said Board; and it shall be the further duty of the Collector, when he shall have made his final return concerning the collection of said tax, to make a report to said Board, stating the whole amount of school tax, the amount collected, and the amount returned by him to the Common Council as unpaid or uncollected. If any Collector shall neglect or refuse to Duty of Collectors relative to school moneys.

* As to fines for library: R. S. 1846, chapter 158, section 25, 26.

Collectors refusing to pay moneys collected, how proceeded against.

pay to said Treasurer the sums of money required by his warrant, or to account for the same as unpaid, at the time and in the manner required by law, the Recorder of the city of Detroit, or the President of the Board of Education of said city, shall forthwith issue a warrant under his hand, directed to the Sheriff of said county, commanding him to levy such sums as shall remain unpaid and unaccounted for, together with his fees for collecting the same, of the goods and chattels, lands and tenements of such Collector and his sureties, and to pay the same to the Treasurer of said Board of Education, and return such warrant within twenty days after the date thereof.—1855.

Collectors and Treasurer to give bonds.

SEC. 16. The Collector and Treasurer shall, before they enter on their duties under this act, enter into such bonds to said Board, and with such sureties as may be deemed necessary, conditioned for the faithful discharge of their duties respectively under this act.*—1842.

Prior acts repealed.

SEC. 17. All parts of acts, so far as they relate to the city of Detroit, inconsistent with this act, are hereby repealed. And it shall not be necessary to elect any school district officers in said city, as heretofore required by law.—1842.

School taxes to be placed in separate column on assessment roll.

SEC. 1. That all taxes which have been or may hereafter be assessed and levied by the Common Council of the city of Detroit, under and by virtue of the authority conferred on said Council by the thirteenth section of an act, entitled "An act relative to Free Schools in the city of Detroit," shall be set forth in the assessment roll of said city, in a separate column, apart, and distinguished from all other city taxes; and that the Collector of said city, shall collect, and, is hereby authorized and required to collect said taxes in money, and said Collector shall not be required or permitted to receive in payment of said taxes, any liabilities or evidences of debt against said city.—1843.

What collect or shall receive for school taxes.

Who to collect school taxes.

SEC. 1. That the Collectors of the city of Detroit, elected in the different wards of said city, shall act as Collectors of the school tax assessed and levied in said city in their respective wards, under and by virtue of the provisions of the act to which this act is amendatory; and that each of said Collectors previous to his entering upon his duties, shall, in addition to the bond now required by law, make and

Collectors to give bonds.

---

*See Sec. 1 of act of 1846, cited at the foot of this page, for further provisions relative to bonds of collectors.

execute to the Board of Education of said city of Detroit, a bond with two good and sufficient sureties to be by them approved, in the penal sum directed by said Board, conditioned for the faithful performance of his duties as such Collector; and that, in case of neglect or refusal of any one of said Collectors to execute and obtain such bond according to the provisions of this section, he be subject to a penalty of one hundred dollars, to be collected in an action of debt, which may be brought in any Court in this State, at the suit and in the name of, the said Board of Education of the city of Detroit.—1846. Conditions of bonds.

SEC. 1. That in addition to the taxes mentioned in the act to which this act is amendatory, the Common Council of the city of Detroit is hereby authorized and empowered to levy and collect a tax not exceeding fifteen hundred dollars in any one year, to be expended in the purchase of lots in said city for the use of the public schools thereof, and in the erection and building a school house or school houses, with the necessary outbuildings and fixtures, on any lot or lots which may be so purchased, or any other lots now owned by the Board of Education of said city, or which the said Board may hereafter acquire: *Provided*, That said tax, when so levied and collected, shall be paid to the Treasurer of said Board of Education, and be vested in said Board to and for the purpose hereinbefore stated, and no other, and also that the title to such lots purchased shall also be in said Board for the purpose aforesaid.—1847. Taxes for building school houses and purchasing lots therefor may be levied. Proviso. Title to school lots in whom vested

SEC. 2. Said tax shall not be levied or collected, unless, at a meeting of the freemen of said city, called for such purpose as hereinafter provided, a majority of the freemen present shall assent to the same.—1847. Freemen to vote on taxes for school houses.

SEC. 3. It shall be the duty of the Mayor, or Recorder, in case of the absence of the Mayor, or a vacancy in his office, to call such a meeting of the freemen of said city, for the purpose of giving their assent or dissent to such tax, when it shall be requested by petition signed by twenty-four freemen of said city: which call shall particularly express the object of such meeting, and shall be published in two of the daily newspapers, published in the said city of Detroit, one week previous to such meeting: *Provided*, That the Mayor may call such meeting upon the notice herein mentioned, without such petition at his own option—1847. Mayor or Recorder to call meeting of freemen to vote on taxes. Proviso.

Meeting of freemen may be called by two members of Council in certain cases.

SEC. 4. If the said Mayor or Recorder shall refuse to call such meeting upon the presentation to either of them of such petition, or shall neglect to do so for three days after the presentation of such petition, any two members of the Common Council of said city, may on the like petition, call such meeting upon a like notice and publication thereof, in the manner and for the time hereinbefore specified in the case of a call by the Mayor or Recorder. Such meeting may be adjourned from time to time by vote of a majority of those present.—1847.

How taxes for school houses and lots to be collected.

SEC. 5. The said tax shall be levied and collected in the same manner as the tax provided for in the thirteenth section of the act to which this act is amendatory, and shall be consolidated therewith on the tax rolls; but it shall be the duty of the said Board of Education in each and every year when such tax is levied and collected to separate the amount thereof from the gross amount of money received by said Board for such year, and set it apart as a fund to be reserved for the purposes specified in the first section of this act.—1847.

Board of education may borrow money and issue bonds for payment.

SEC. 6. The Board of Education of the city of Detroit is hereby authorized from time to time, on such term or terms of payment as they may deem proper, to borrow a sum of money not exceeding in all the sum of five thousand dollars, for the purposes specified in the first section of this act, at a rate of interest not exceeding seven per cent. per annum, payable semi-annually, and to issue the bonds of said Board in such form, and executed in such manner as said Board may direct: *Provided*, That said Board shall issue no bond for a less sum than fifty dollars.—1847, 1850.

Proviso.

Bonds to be a lien on property of Board.

SEC. 7. The bonds issued under this act shall be a charge upon all the property of said Board, which shall constiute a security for the payment thereof: *Provided*, That no legal proceedings shall be instituted to enforce such lien, or to sell any property of said Board for the payment of the principal money of any of said bonds, until one year after such principal shall become due, according to the tenor and effect thereof.—1847.

Proviso.

Board to keep interest on Bonds paid and provide sinking fund to pay principal.

SEC. 8. It shall be the duty of the Board of Education, whenever they shall borrow any money under the provisions of this act, annually to appropriate a sufficient sum out of any money which may come into their hands, to pay the interest upon the same; and also in addition thereto, an annual sum equal to five per cent. upon the amount so borrowed to be invested under the direction of said Board in bonds of the city of Detroit, bearing interest at such prices as the same can be purchased, to accumulate as a sinking fund for the payment of the principal of the sum so borrowed; both of which appropriations shall take precedence of all others.—1847.

SEC. 3. The removal of any member of the Board of Education of the city of Detroit, from the ward for which he is elected School Inspector, after such election, shall not operate to vacate his office; but notwithstanding such removal, any Inspector so removing shall continue to hold his said office, and to be a member of said Board, and all provisions of any act or acts which make such removal a vacation of said office, are hereby repealed: *Provided*, The removal of such member shall not be from the city.—1850.

Removal of School Inspector from ward for which he is elected not to vacate his office.

Proviso.

SEC. 137 Any person paying taxes in a school district in which he does not reside, may send scholars to any district school therein, and such person shall, for that purpose, have and enjoy all the rights and privileges of a resident of such district, except the right of voting therein, and shall be rated therein, for teachers' wages and fuel, and in the census of such district, and the apportionment of moneys from the school fund, scholars so sent, and generally attending such school, shall be considered as belonging to such district: *Provided*, That a majority of the qualified voters attending at any regular meeting in the district in which such person resides, shall have determined that no school shall be taught in said district for the year: *Or provided further*, That such person shall not reside in any organized school district—*Revised Statutes* 1846, *p.* 235, *and S. L.* 1850.

Persons paying school taxes in any district may send scholars to the schools therein.

Provisos.

AN ACT to incorporate the Fire Department of the City of Detroit.

Whereas, The members of an Association, known as the "Fire Department of the city of Detroit," have petitioned the Legislature to grant them an act of incorporation, to enable them the more effectually to accomplish the objects of their organization, and to provide means for the relief of disabled firemen and their families; therefore,

Preamble.

NOTE.—The State School money must be distributed on the first Monday in May in each year.—*R. S.* 233, *section* 119, *S. L.* 1847.

Fire Department of Detroit, a body corporate.

SEC. 1. *Be it enacted by the Senate and House of Representatives of the State of Michigan*, That all persons who now are, or may hereafter become, members of the Fire Department of the city of Detroit, and their successors, shall be, and hereby are ordained, constituted, and declared to be, and continue, a body politic and corporate, in fact and in name, under the name and style of "The Fire Department of the city of Detroit," for the purposes recited in the above preamble, and by that name they and their successors may and shall have perpetual succession, and shall be known in law, capable of suing and being sued, of pleading and being impleaded, of answering and being answered unto, of defending and being defended, in all suits, complaints, matters, causes, courts and places whatsoever, and both in law and equity; and capable of having a common seal; of acquiring by purchase, gift, devise, or otherwise, and of holding and conveying any real, personal, or mixed estate, necessary, proper or expedient for the objects of this incorporation; *Provided*, That the amount of said estate shall at no time exceed the sum of thirty thousand dollars.

May have a seal and hold real estate.

Proviso.

May make by laws, &c.

SEC. 2. The members of the Fire Department of the City of Detroit, hereby incorporated, shall have, and are hereby declared to have full power and authority to make and prescribe such by-laws, rules, ordinances and regulations, and the same to alter, amend and change at pleasure, as to them, from time to time, shall seem needful or proper, touching the management and disposition of their funds for the objects aforesaid; touching the regular and special meetings of the Department; the regulation, duty and conduct of their members, delegates and Board of Trustees; the election and displacing of officers and delegates; the admission and expulsion of members; the filling of vacancies in offices; and touching every other matter and thing necessary or expedient for the good government and promotion of this incorporation, or which appertains to the business and objects for which the said incorporation is, by this act, instituted: *Provided*, That such by-laws, rules, ordinances and regulations, be not repugnant to the constitutional laws of the United States, or of this State.

Relative to disposal of funds. Meetings. Conduct of members and officers. Election of same. Admission and expulsion of members. Filling vacancies, &c.

Proviso.

Officers of department.

SEC. 3. The officers of said Department by this act incorporated, shall be a President, Vice-President, Secretary, Treasurer, and Collector, who, together with the Chief Engineer of the Fire Department, and the delegates from the several fire companies, and other bodies, pursuant to the provisions of the Constitution and by-laws of the Department, shall constitute a board of Trustees, a majority of whom shall be a quorum for the transactions of business; and said officers and delegates, separately, and as a Board of Trustees, shall do and perform such duties and things as may be incumbent upon, or required of, them by the constitution or by-laws of the Department.

Board of trustees.

SEC. 4. There shall be an annual meetiug of the members of said corporation on the third Monday of January, in each year, at which the officers shall be elected by ballot, by a majority of the members present, from their own body. And the officers elected shall hold their offices for one year, or until others be chosen in their places; but in case it at any time happens that an election of officers shall not be made or had on that day, the said corporation shall not be dissolved, but it shall and may be lawful to hold such election thereafter, pursuant to public notice given in one or more of the newspapers printed in said city.

Annual meeting of fire department.

SEC. 5. Of the Fire Department of the city of Detroit, Robert E. Roberts shall be President; Frederick Buhl, Vice President; Edmund R. Kearsley, Secretary; Darius Lamson, Treasurer; and Elijah Goodell, Collector; who, together with the Chief Engineer of the Fire Department, duly appointed by the Common Council of the city of Detroit, and the delegates chosen as aforesaid, shall constitute the first Board of Trustees, and shall hold their offices until the third Monday of January next, or until others shall be chosen in their stead.

Names of officers for first year.

SEC. 6. The interest arising from the funds of the said corporation, except sufficient to defray incidental expenses, shall be appropriated to the relief of such indigent and disabled firemen and their families, as may be interested in the fund, and who may, in the opinion of a majority of the Trustees, be worthy of assistance.

Interest of funds appropriated to relief of indigent and disabled firemen and their families

SEC. 7. All certificates now required to be obtained by firemen from the Clerk of said city, pursuant to the provisions of any law of this State, shall hereafter be obtained from the Department by this act incorporated; which certificate, signed by the President and Treasurer of this Department, and countersigned by the City Clerk of said city, and under the seal of this incorporation, shall have the like effect of those heretofore obtained from the said City Clerk, and shall be

Certificates, how obtained

Their effect.

satisfactory evidence of the facts therein contained. And each person applying for such certificate shall pay therefor such sum as the by-laws of the Department shall prescribe, for the benefit of the corporation and the objects thereof.

List of members to be made out yearly and given to City Clerk.

SEC. 8. It shall be the duty of the Board of Trustees to make out and deliver to the City Clerk, once in each year, or whenever he may request it, an accurate list of all the members of this corporation, who are exempt from jury or military duty, that they are or may become entitled to the benefits thereof.

This is public act.

SEC. 9. This act is hereby declared to be a public act, and the same shall, in all courts and places, be regarded benignly and favorably for every beneficial purpose hereby intended.

May be repealed or modified.

SEC. 10. The Legislature may alter, modify, amend or repeal this act by a vote of two-thirds of each House.

Acts inconsistent herewith, repealed.

SEC. 11. All acts and parts of acts which contravene the provisions of this act, are hereby repealed; and this act shall take effect from and after its passage.—*Approved February* 14, 1840.

CHAPTER 48—REVISED STATUTES OF 1846.

OF FIRE DEPARTMENTS IN CITIES AND VILLAGES.

Firemen exempted from militia duty and serving on juries.

SEC. 1. Every person who was a fireman in any incorporated city or village in this State, on the sixth day of February, in the year one thousand eight hundred and forty-three, or at any time thereafter, and who shall have served, and shall continue to serve as such for the term of seven years from that time, or from the time of his appointment, if appointed since that time, and every person who may hereafter be appointed a fireman in any such city or village, and shall serve as such for the term of seven years, shall during the time of such service be exempted from serving as a juror in any of the Courts of this State, and from the performance of all militia duty, and shall forever thereafter be exempted from the performance of all militia duty except in cases of insurrection or invasion.

Money may be raised to compensate firemen.

SEC. 2. It shall be lawful for the qualified voters of any such city or village, at their annual election of officers thereof, to authorize the Common Council or other corporate board of such city or village, to raise a sufficient sum to pay each fireman therein the sum of five dollars; and thereupon such sum shall be levied and collected in the same manner as the other contingent expenses of such city or village are levied and collected.

SEC. 3. Upon such provision being made for the payment of firemen, as provided in the preceding section, each fireman who shall produce a certificate from the foreman of his Company countersigned by the Chief Engineer of the Fire Department of such city or village, stating that he has well and faithfully performed his duties as such fireman, during the year then next preceding, shall be allowed and paid out of the treasury of such city or village, the said sum of five dollars as a compensation for his services.

Payment of compensation—how made.

SEC. 4. The Recorder or Clerk of every such city or village shall keep an accurate record, in a book to be provided for that purpose, of the name occupation and residence of every fireman of such city or village, together with the date of his appointment, and a designation of the Company to which he is attached; and whenever any fireman shall resign or be removed, it shall be so entered upon such record; and the appointment, resignation or removal of every fireman, shall also be entered on the minutes of the Common Council or other corporate board.

Record of firemen to be kept by Recorder or Clerk.

SEC. 5. It shall be the duty of the Recorder or Clerk of such city or village, to deliver to every fireman who shall have served during the said term of seven years, as provided in this chapter, a certificate to that effect, signed by himself, and the Mayor of such city, or President of such village; which certificate shall be received as evidence in any of the courts of this State.

Certificate of service.

SEC. 6. It shall be lawful for the Common Council, or other corporated (*corporate*) board of each incorporated city or village, to levy and collect, by a tax upon all the taxable real and personal property within the limits thereof, in the manner prescribed in the charter of such city or village, for the collection of taxes therein, such sums as may be necessary for the purchasing and repairing of fire engines, and other fire apparatus, and for defraying all other necessary expenses of the Fire Department thereof.

Taxes for purchasing and repairing engines.

SEC. 7. Every Fire Company shall have power to make such by-laws, rules and regulations, not inconsistent with the laws of this State, for their government and discipline, and to prescribe such penalties

Fire companies may make by-laws and impose fines for violations thereof.

for the violation thereof, not exceding five dollars for any one offence, as they may deem necessary to the efficient accomplishment of the object of their organization; and they may sue for and collect such penalties in the name of the Common Conncil or other corporate board of the city or village to which they belong.

Fire engines, apparatus, &c., exempt from execution.

SEC. 8. All fire engines and apparatus requisite for, and ordinarily used by, Fire Companies in the extinguishment of fires, which are now owned, or which may hereafter be purchased and owned by any incorporated city or village, and kept for the use of any Fire Companies therein, and all water-works, with the buildings, machinery, and fixtures, and the ground occupied thereby, now owned, or which may hereafter be purchased and owned by any incorporated city or village, and used or intended to be used for the supplying of water for the extinguishment of fires and the use of the inhabitants, shall be and are hereby exempted from levy or sale for any debt, damages, fine or amercement whatever.

AN ACT to amend the Laws relative to "Supplying the City of Detroit, with Pure and Wholesome Water," and to provide for the Completion and Management of the Detroit Water Works.

Name and style.

SECTION 1. *The People of the State of Michigan enact*, That Shubael Conant, Henry Ledyard, Edmund A. Brush, William R. Noyes and James A. Van Dyke, be and they are hereby named and constituted as a "Board of Water Commissioners for the City of Detroit," who, and their successors in office, shall be kuown by the name and style of the "Board of Water Commissioners of the city of Detroit," and by that name shall have power to contract, sue and be sued, to purchase, hold and convey personal and real estate, to have a common seal, to alter and change the same at pleasure, to make by-laws and ordinances, and do all legal acts which may be necessary and proper to carry out the effect, intent and object of this act.

Powers.

Seal.

Term of office

SEC. 2. The said Commissioners shall hold their offices respectively for the term of three, four, five, six and seven years from the first Tuesday in May, of the year one thousand eight hundred and fifty-three; said Commissions shall, within sixty days after the passage of this act, decide by lot their respective terms, which decision shall be notified by a written statement to the Common Council of said city, which shall be entered of record on the books of the said Common Council; and at their first regular meeting in the month of April, in the year one thousand eight hundred and fifty-six, and annually thereafter, the said Common Council shall elect and appoint a citizen of said city, being a qualified voter and a freeholder, as a Commissioner, who shall hold his office for five years from the first Tuesday in the May next following: *Provided*, That this section shall not be so construed as to disqualify any member of the said Board, for re-appointment. And in case of the death or resignation, or removal from the city, of any of said Commissioners, the Common Council shall, as soon thereafter as possible, appoint to fill such vacancy, for the remainder of the term, some citizen of said city, being a qualified voter and a freeholder.

Vacancy, how filled.

SEC. 3. The said Commissioners shall choose one of their own number as President, who shall hold his office until the first Tuesday of May next ensuing the date of his election; they shall also appoint some suitable person as Secretary, who shall hold his office at the pleasure of the Board. And in case of the death, resignation, or removal from the city, of the President, the said Commissioners shall have power to fill the vacancy so happening, as in the first instance.

President and Secretary.

Vacancy.

SEC. 4. The said Commissioners shall have power to loan, from time to time, upon the best terms they can make, after giving public notice by advertising in the city papers for sixty days, and in one paper in Boston, and two in New York, for such time as they shall deem expedient, a sum of money not exceeding two hundred and fifty thousand dollars, upon the credit of said city of Detroit, and shall have authority to issue bonds pledging the faith and credit of said city for the payment of the principal and interest of said bonds; which bonds shall issue under the seal of said Board of Commissioners, and shall be signed by them, or a majority of them, and bearing interest not exceeding eight per cent. per annum. And it shall be the duty of said Commissioners to cause to be kept an accurate register of all bonds issued by them, shewing the number, date and amount of each bond, and to whom the same was issued; and it shall also be their duty to cause to be furnished to the Auditor of said city a copy of such register, as soon as the same is made, which shall be preserved by said Auditor, and copied into the records of said city.

Power to loan money on bonds.

Registry of bonds.

Copy furnished Auditor.

Supply of water.

SEC. 5. It shall be the duty of said Commissioners to examine and consider all matters relative to supplying the city of Detroit with a sufficient quantity of pure and wholesome water, to be taken from the Detroit river, or such other source as may be deemed expedient, for the use of its inhabitants.

Power to employ Supts., &c.

SEC. 6. Said Commissioners shall have power to employ Superintendents, Clerks, Collectors, Assessors, Engineers, Surveyors, and such other persons as, in their opinion, may be necessary to enable them to perform their duties under this act, and to specify the duties of such persons so employed, and to fix their compensation: *Provided*, That in no case shall said Commissioners receive, directly or indirectly, any compensation for their own services.

Commissioners not to receive compensation.

Power to purchase land, &c.

SEC. 7. Said Commissioners shall have power, and it is hereby made their duty, as soon as may be, after the necessary funds shall have been procured, as herein provided, to purchase such land and materials, and to construct such reservoirs, buildings, machinery and fixtures, as shall be deemed necessary or desirable, to furnish a full supply of water for public and private use in said city.

Reservoirs, Jets, Hydrants, &c.

SEC. 8. Said Commissioners shall have power to construct reservoirs, jets and fire hydrants, at such localities in said city, as they may deem expedient and necessary, and to lay pipes in and through all the alleys and streets of said city; and also to construct in such localities as they may deem expedient, not exceeding one to each block, hydrants for public use, and to keep the same in repair; and, also, with the consent of the Common Council of said city, to construct fountains in the public squares, or such other public grounds of said city as they may deem expedient.

Fountains in public squares.

Assessment of water rates

SEC. 9. Said Commissioners shall, from time to time, cause to be assessed the water rate to be paid by the owner or occupant of each house or other building having or using water, upon such basis as they shall deem equitable; and such water rate shall become a continuing lien, until paid, upon such house or other building, and upon the lot or lots upon which such house or other building is situated.

Lien on premises.

Power to make by-laws

SEC. 10. Said Commissioners shall have full power to make and enforce all necessary by-laws, rules and regulations, for the collection of said water rates, either by the appointment of Collectors to demand the same, requiring payment at the office, shutting off the water, or by a suit at law before any Court of competent jurisdiction, or by sale of the lot or premises upon which such rates shall have become a lien: *Provided*, That such sales shall be conducted in the same manner, and shall have the same force, virtue and effect, of sales of lots delinquent for city taxes: *And Provided further*, That the attempt to collect said rates by any process above mentioned shall not in any way invalidate the lien upon said lot or premises.

Sale of property for non-payment of water rates

SEC. 11. The said Commissioners shall cause to be kept an accurate record of all proceedings, together with a list of all assessments for water rates, which shall be subject to inspection at all times.

Record of proceedings.

SEC. 12. It shall be the duty of said Commissioners to make a report to the Common Conucil of said city annually, which report shall embrace a statement of the condition and operation of the works; a statement of the funds and securities of said Board, and all debts due and owing to and from said Board, together with an accurate account of their expenses; which statement shall be certified by said Commissioners, and shall be entered of record by the Clerk of said city, and published in such manner as said Common Council may direct.

Report to Com. Council.

SEC. 13. Whenever the receipts of said Board from water rates, or other sources, shall accumulate so that there shall be a surplus, amounting to a sum of not less than five hundred dollars, not needed for the payment of the current expenses, or the extension of said works, it shall be the duty of the Commissioners, together with the Auditor of said city, who shall be associated with them for that purpose, to invest the same in some safe stock, or upon other real or personal securities. Such investment shall be made in the name of said Board, and in such manner as to make the same available for the payment of interest and principal of the bonds issued as aforesaid, as soon as may be. It shall be the duty of said Commissioners to pay the interest on such bonds, and as fast as such surplus fund will permit, also the principal as the bonds become due, as funds for such purpose shall, from time to time, accumulate. The said Commissioners may, when they have funds for that purpose, purchase the bonds so issued as aforesaid, whether the same have become due or not; and in case the said Commissioners shall at any time not have funds on hand sufficient to meet any of the said bonds at the time when they shall become due, they shall have the right to issue new bonds, for such amount, and on such

Surplus funds to be invested.

Payment of bonds and interest.

Purchase of bonds.

New bonds may be issued

Old bonds cancelled and new bonds registered.

time as they shall deem expedient, in the place of bonds so becoming due as aforesaid; the said old bonds to be cancelled in the registry thereof, and the said new bonds to be recorded in the manner hereinbefore provided.

Oath of Commissioners.

SEC. 14. Before entering upon the duties of their office, said Commissioners shall each take and file with the City Clerk, an oath or affirmation similar to that provided in the case of other officers of said city.

Materials exempt from execution.

SEC. 15. All materials, procured or partially procured, under a contract with the Commissioners, shall be exempt from execution; but it shall be the duty of the Commissioners to pay the money due for such materials to the judgment creditor of the contractor, under whose execution such material might otherwise have been sold, upon his producing to them due proof that his execution would have so attached, and such payment shall be held a valid payment on the contract.

Commissioners may be removed.

SEC. 16. Any member of said Board of Commissioners, may at any time be removed by a vote of two-thirds of the members elect of the Common Council of said city, for sufficient cause, and the proceedings in that behalf shall be entered on their journal: *Provided*, That the said Common Council shall previously cause a copy of the charges preferred against the Commissioner sought to be removed, and notice of the time and place of hearing the same, to be served on him ten days at least previous to the time so assigned; and in case of such removal, the Common Council shall, at their first regular meeting, or as soon thereafter as may be, appoint some person, being a citizen and a freeholder, to fill such vacancy; and the person so appointed to fill such vacancy, may continue in office for the period his predecessor had to serve.

Copy of charges to be served.

Vacancy to be filled.

Power to enter upon land or water.

SEC. 17. The said Commissioners, and, under their direction, their agents, servants and workmen, are hereby authorized to enter upon any land or water for the purpose of making surveys, and to agree with the owner of any property which may be required for the purposes of this act, as to the amount of compensation to be paid to such owner.

SEC. 18. In cases of disagreement between the Commissioners and the owner of any property which may be required for the said purposes, or affected by any operation connected therewith, as to the amount of compensation to be paid to such owner, or in case any such owner shall be an infant, a married woman, or insane, or absent from this State, the Judge of the Circuit Court of Wayne county, may, upon the application of either party nominate and appoint three disinterested persons to examine such property, and to estimate the value thereof, or damage sustained thereby, and to report thereon to the said Court without delay. In case of disagreement Judge of court to appoint appraisers.

SEC. 19. Whenever such report shall have been confirmed by the Circuit Judge of Wayne county, the said Commissioners shall pay to the said owner, or to such person or persons as the Court may direct, the sum mentioned in said report, in full compensation for the property so required, or for the damage sustained, as the case may be, and thereupon the said Commissioners shall become seized in fee of such property so required, and shall be discharged from all claim by reason of any such damage. Confirmation by judge. Payment. Fee of property.

SEC. 20. And in case of the refusal by any owner or owners, person or persons, to receive such sums awarded to them for property required or damages sustained, then the said Commissioners shall deposit with the City Treasurer the sums so awarded, subject to the draft of said owner or owners, persons or persons; and thereupon the said Commissioners shall become seized in fee of such property so required, and shall be discharged from all claim by reason of any such damage; and said City Treasurer shall keep strict account of all sums so deposited, and shall pay out the same on the drafts of the owner or owners, person or persons, to the credit of whom such moneys may have been deposited. Payment when refused money to be deposited. City Treasurer to pay on draft.

SEC. 21. If any person shall wilfully do or cause to be done, any act whereby any work, materials or property whatsoever, erected or used within the city of Detroit or elsewhere, by the said Commissioners, or by any person acting under their authority, for the purpose of procuring or keeping a supply of water, shall in any manner be injured, or shall willfully pollute the water, shall be deemed guilty of misdemeanor, and, upon conviction, shall be punished therefor as other misdemeanors are punished. Injury to property or pollution of water.

SEC. 22. If any person shall without the authority of said Commissioners as delegated through any of their agents, perforate or bore, or cause to be perforated or bored, any distributing pipe or main or Penalty for boring pipe or connecting logs without permission.

log belonging to the water works of said city, or make or cause to be made any connection or communication whatever with the said pipes or logs, every person so offending shall, for each offence, forfeit a sum not exceeding fifty dollars and costs of prosecution, to be recovered in the Mayor's Court of said city, or other Court of competent jurisdiction.

Power to extend pipes and construct reservoirs beyond limits of city.

SEC. 23. The said Commissioners in their discretion, shall have power to extend the distributing pipes and mains, and to construct reservoirs, hydrants and jets, without the limits of said city; and to regulate, protect and control such portions of said water works without the bounds of said city in and after the same manner that they regulate, protect and control said works within said bounds.

Commissioners to report to Common Council what sum may be required to pay interest, &c.

SEC. 24. It shall be the duty of said Commissioners, at least thirty days before the time fixed by the ordinance of said city for assessing city taxes, to make special report to the Common Council of said city, what, if any, sum will be needed by said Commissioners, over and above the revenue of said Board to meet the payment of interest or principal of the bonds issued as aforesaid; and it shall be the duty of the Common Council to raise said amount by a special tax in the same manner as general taxes, to be designated a water tax; and the said amount shall be paid over to said Board by the Treasurer of said city.

Com. Council to raise sum by tax.

Commissioners not to be interested in contracts or purchases of materials.

SEC. 25. No one or more of the said Commissioners shall be interested, either directly or indirectly, in any contract entered into by them with any other person; nor shall they be interested, either directly or indirectly, in the purchase of any material to be used or applied in and about the uses and purposes contemplated by this act.

Lands &c. of present works conveyed to Board of Commissioners.

SEC. 26. All lands, lots, docks, buildings, machinery, pipes, logs, hydrants, and all fixtures whatsoever, purchased, designated or used for the present water works of the said city of Detroit, are hereby conveyed to and vested in said Board of Commissioners, who shall have full power to regulate, protect and control the same; and all the authority, rights and power heretofore exercised and had by said city over said works, are hereby continued to and vested in said Board of Commissioners.

Power to make by-laws &c.

SEC. 27. The said Commissioners are hereby invested with full power to make and enforce such by-laws, regulations and ordinances, as may be necessary to carry into effect the object and intent of this act, and to supply any power or mode not already specified therein, and shall cause all such by-laws regulations and ordinances, to be entered in a book to be kept for that purpose, and signed by the President and Secretary, which, when so entered and signed, shall be evidence in any court of justice. By-laws &c. to be entered in a book.

SEC. 28. All acts or parts of acts contravening the provisions of this act, are hereby repealed. Acts repealed

SEC. 29. This act may at any time be altered, repealed or amended. —*Approved February* 14, 1853. Act amended

---

AN ACT to authorize the the Water Commissioners of the City of Detroit to loan money for the purpose of extending and improving the Water Works of said City.

SECTION 1. *The people of the State of Michigan enact*, That the Board of Water Commissioners of the city of Detroit shall have power to loan, upon the best terms they can make, and for such time as they shall deem expedient, a sum of money not exceeding two hundred and fifty thousand dollars, upon the credit of said city of Detroit, and shall have authority to issue bonds pledging the faith and credit of said city for the payment of the principal and interest of said bonds; which bonds shall issue under the seal of said Board of Commissioners, and shall be signed by them, or a majority of them, and bearing interest not exceeding eight per cent. per annum. And it shall be the duty of said Commissioners be cause to be kept an accurate register of all bonds issued by them, showing the number, date, and amount of each bond, and to whom the same was issued; and it shall also be their duty to cause to be furnished to the Auditor of said city a copy of such register, as soon as the same is made, which shall be preserved by said Auditor, and copied into the records of said city. And the said sum of money shall be expended by said Commississioners solely for the purpose of extending and improving the Water Works of the city of Detroit. Water Commissioners authorized to contract an additional loan and issue bonds of city for the same. Register of bonds to be kept. How money to be appropriated.

SEC. 2. This act shall take effect and be in force from and after its passage.—*Approved February* 6, 1855.

ACT OF CONGRESS.

[Public No. 74.]

AN ACT supplementary to "An Act to provide for the adjustment of titles to lands in the town of Detroit, and Territory of Michigan, and for other purposes, passed April twenty-one, eighteen hundred and six.

Mayor, Recorder and Aldermen to hear claims against gov. and judges, and receive moneys, &c., to which they were entitled.

Section 1. *Be it enacted by the Senate and House of Representatives of the United States of America in Congress assembled*, That the Mayor, Recorder and Aldermen of the city of Detroit, in the State of Michigan, be, and they, or a quorum of them, in council assembled, are hereby authorized to hear, examine, and finally adjust, all claims arising under the act to which this is supplementary, against the Governor and Judges of the late Territory of Michigan, and receive all moneys, or other rights to property to which the said Governor and Judges were entitled, or became entitled under said act.

Also to receive journals, records, papers, &c., of the gov. and judges.

Sec. 2. *And be it further enacted*, That the said Mayor, Recorder and Aldermen of the said city of Detroit, be, and they are hereby entitled to receive from any person or persons having the possession of the same, the journals, records, papers and books of the Governor and Judges of the late Territory of Michigan, acting as a Land Board under the act of April twenty-first, one thousand eight hundred and six, to which this is a supplement; and that all powers and rights vested by the said act in the said Governor and Judges, for the purposes therein mentioned, are hereby trasfered and vested in the Mayor, Recorder and Aldermen of the city of Detroit, in the State of Michigan. And the said Mayor, Recorder and Aldermen, are hereby authorized to institute proceedings at law or in equity, in any Court of competent jurisdiction, in all cases where it may be necessary to carry into effect the purposes of this act.

May commence suits, &c.

May dispose of land and other property, &c.

Sec. *And be it further enacted*, That any land or other property, real or personal, remaining, except the court-house and jail erected under the act to which this is a supplement, after satisfying all just claims provided for in the first section of the act to which this is a supplement, is hereby vested in the said Mayor, Recorder and Aldermen of the city of Detroit, to be disposed of by them at their discretion to the best advantage; and they are hereby authorized to make deeds to purchasers thereof, or other sufficient conveyances; and the proceeds of the land or other property, effects or claims so disposed of, and of other rights and claims of the said Governor and Judges, shall, after the payment of all necessary expenses incurred in giving effect to said act and to this act, and in the adoption of such measures as they may deem decessary for preserving in proper form the records and other evidences of the proceedings of said Governor and Judges, be applied by the said Mayor, Recorder and Aldermen, to such object or objects of public improvement in said city as the said Mayor, Recorder and Aldermen may, in council, direct. And the said Mayor, Recorder, and Aldermen are hereby required to to take oath or affirmation for the faithful discharge of their duties under this act, and make a report to Congress, in writing, of their proceedings, on or before the first day of January, one thousand eight hundred and forty-four.—*Approved August* 29, 1842.

Must take an oath.

AN ACT amending an act relative to the registry of certain deeds, approved March ninth, one thousand eight hundred and forty-four.

SEC. 1. *Be it enacted by the Senate and House of Representatives of the State of Michigan*, That it shall not be necessary to acknowledge or prove the execution of any deed of land which may have been, or shall be granted by the Mayor, Recorder and Aldermen of the city of Detroit, under the provisions of an act of Congress entitled, " An act supplementary to an act to provide for the adjustment of titles to land in the town of Detroit, and Territory of Michigan, and for other purposes," approved August twenty-ninth, one thousand eight hundred and forty-two, to entitle the same to be recorded: but every such deed which may have been, or shall be, executed by said Mayor, Recorder, and Aldermen under their respective hands and seals, shall be entitled to be duly recorded, and every such deed so recorded, or the record or transcript of such deed, duly certified may be read in evidence in any court within this State, without further proof thereof: *Provided*, That this act shall not be construed so as to affect any proceedings, now pending in any Court of law or equity, in this State, or to affect the rights now vested in any person or persons.

Deeds by Com. Council of Detroit, in pursuance of act of Congress need not be acknowledged.

SEC. 2. This act shall take effect and be in force from and after its passage.—*Approved May* 7, 1846.

AN ACT relative to conveyances in the City of Detroit.

Preamble. *Whereas*, Many or most of the conveyances of lots in the city of Detroit, made and executed by the late Governor and Judges of the Territory of Michigan, were made without any acknowledement by the said Governor and Judges as required by the law of the time, requiring conveyances in general to be acknowledged to entitle them to be recorded:

Idem. *And whereas*, Many or most of these conveyances have been recorded in the proper registry of the county of Wayne, or of the city of Detroit as heretofore existing, and now remain of record in the said County Registry:

Idem. *And whereas*, Many of said original conveyances have, by time, accident or otherwise, been lost, or are out of the possession or control of those owning and claiming the said lots: therefore,

Certain deeds of governor and judges may be read in evidence although not acknowledged. SEC. 1. *Be it enacted, &c.*, That all deeds and conveyances of lots or lands in the city of Detroit by the late Governor and Judges of the late Territory of Michigan, that have heretofore been recorded in the registry of deeds of the county of Wayne, in the city of Detroit, the record of said deeds, or a certified copy thereof by the Register of Deeds of the county of Wayne, may be used and read in evidence in all courts and places with the same force and effect as if the original deeds or conveyances from the said Governor and Judges were produced and proved: *Provided*, It shall first be made to appear that that such original deed or deeds have been lost or destroyed.

SEC. 2. This act shall take effect from and after its passage.—*Approved April* 1, 1850.

AN ACT to incorporate "the City of Detroit Gas Company."

Preamble. *Whereas*, Certain persons have associated themselves under the style of "The City of Detroit Gas Company," for the purpose of carrying on and establishing in said city of Detroit a gas manufactory of the kind now generally used, or any improved gas or inflammable substance, and of supplying the citizens with gas who desire the same, at rates to be agreed upon; the following being the names of the persons who have signed the articles of association, and taken shares of stock, viz: L. C. Rose, Jason Braman, J. M. Slater, Jeffrey Coles, James Cooper, John N. Williams, James Beck, Matthew Anderson,

T. R. Davenport, Henry H. LeRoy, Samuel Howlett, F. F. Parker, and of whom at present, said is President, said Beck, Secretary, said Parker, Treasurer, and said LeRoy, Rose, Braman and Slater, are Directors;

And Whereas, The Common Council of said city have given the necessary permit to said association, to locate said establishment in said city, and to run their pipes through the streets of the same, and have given them the exclusive privileges so to do for the period of ten years, on certain conditions and under certain restrictions, as appears by an agreement in writing signed by a committee of said Council, dated September 29, 1848, and approved by said Common Council, and to which reference is hereby had: *And Whereas*, said persons have applied to this Legislature to be incorporated, the more effectually to enable them to accomplish the said objects of their organization: Idem.

SEC. 1. *Be it enacted by the Senate and House of Representatives of the State of Michigan*, As follows, to wit: That said persons above named, who have signed said articles of association, and all such other persons as shall become stockholders and associated with them for said purpose, and their successors and assigns, shall be, and hereby are, constituted and declared to be, a body politic and corporate, under the name and style of "The City of Detroit Gas Company," for the objects and purposes contemplated and stated in the above preamble, for the period of fifty years from and after the passage of this act: *Provided always*, That within the period of one year they commence operations and continue the same with all reasonable despatch.* Incorporation.

SEC. 2. The corporation hereby created by the name aforesaid, and the successors thereof, shall have continual succession for the period aforesaid, and shall be persons in law, capable of suing and being sued, pleading and being impleaded, answering and being answered unto, defended and defending in all Courts, suits, proceedings, places and matters whatsoever; and capable of having a common seal; of acquiring, holding and conveying estate, real, personal, and mixed, necessary or expedient for the corporation, for the purposes and objects thereof. Powers of company.

---

* Amended. See sec. 1 of amendatory act next cited.

Capital stock and officers.

SEC. 3. The capital stock of said Association shall not exceed one hundred thousand dollars,* which, with the property, affairs and concerns of the corporation, shall be managed and conducted by a Board of officers, to consist of a President, Secretary and Treasurer, and of four other Directors, all of whom shall be stockholders, except the Secretary. The Board of officers named in the above preamble shall constitute the officers of this corporation, until others are chosen in their stead.

Powers of board of directors,

SEC. 4. The majority of the Board of Directors and Stockholders, on account of said corporation hereby created, shall have and hereby are declared to have full power and authority to make, prescribe, and carry into effect all such rules, by-laws and regulations, and the same to alter, amend and renew, as the majority of the Board of officers and stock, at a meeting of the holders thereof, regularly called, shall think proper to make, which are necessary and proper for the purpose of carrying out the true intent and meaning of this act, and among other things, to provide for calling new elections, when any election fails to be made when duly called: and may form, if they think proper, a constitution or articles of agreement, to be signed or to govern them within the provisions of this act. containing the elements of their organization; the rights, privileges, and duties of officers and members; the modes and times of calling elections and holding the same; the amounts of stock and liabilities, and privileges of holders and the exercise of the powers above contained; and concerning all other matters and things in and about the regulation, control and conduct of the corporation, its objects, and all matters pertaining thereto, and for the changing and amendment thereof from time to time, as may be necessary. And for the purpose of commencing to organize and making necessary rules, the said present Board of officers and persons who have signed said articles of association, or a majority thereof, assoon as this act becomes a law, may get together and exercise all and singular the powers aforesaid, necessary or expedient. It being expressly provided that this corporation shall never exercise banking powers or brokerage business, or anything in the nature thereof; that it shall make no regulations or rules contrary to law; that it shall at all times be subject to the inspection of the Legislature, or a committee

---

* The stock may now be increased to five hundred thousand dollars. See sec. 1 of act of 1855 cited post p. 98.

thereof; and shall make a full report of all its affairs and doings, whenever required by said Legislature. All the shareholders shall be jointly and severally liable for all debts and contracts of the company until forty per cent. of the capital stock shall have been paid in, and also for all the debts of the company of every description after the capital stock of the company shall have been exhausted.

SEC. 5. Unless the said corporation shall have established their manufactory, and so far progressed therewith as to begin supplying gas to some portions of the city within twenty-four months from the passage of this act, this act shall cease and become null and void.* Time of commencing operation.

SEC. 6. That the property of every individual, vested in said corporation, shall be liable to be taken on execution for the payment of his or her just debts, in such manner as is or may be prescribed by law.

SEC. 7. That this act be, and the same is hereby declared to be, a public act; and that the same be construed in all courts and places favorably for every beneficial purpose therein mentioned.

SEC. 8. The Legislature may at any time alter, amend or repeal this act for any violation of this charter.—*Approved March* 14, 1849.

AN ACT to amend sections one, five and eight of "An act to incorporate the City of Detroit Gas Company," and to change the title of said Company to that of the "Detroit Gas Light Company."

SEC. 1. *The People of the State of Michigan enact*, That section one of an act to incorporate the City of Detroit Gas Company, approved March fourteen, eighteen hundred and forty-nine, be and the same is hereby amended so as to read as follows: Sec. 1 of act No. 82, of 1849, amended.

"SEC. 1. That said persons above named, who have signed said articles of association, and all such other persons as have or shall become stockholders, and associated with them for said purpose, and their successors or assigns, shall be and are hereby constituted and declared to be a body politic and corporate, under the name and style of the Detroit Gas Light Company, for the object and purposes contemplated and stated in the above preamble, for the period of forty-eight years from and after the passage of this act: *Provided always*, That within the period of three years they commence operations, and continue the same with all reasonable dispatch." Incorporation. Proviso.

---

* Amended. Sec. sec. 2 of amendatory act next cited.

Sec. 5 amended.

SEC. 2. That section five of said act be and the same is hereby amended, so as to read as follows:

Time of beginning operations.

"SEC. 5. Unless the said corporation shall have established their manufactory, and so far progressed therewith as to begin supplying gas to some portions of the city within four years from the passage of this act, this act shall cease and become null and void."

SEC. 3. The Legislature may at any time alter, amend or repeal this act, or the act to which this is amendatory.

Acceptance of act where and when to be filed.

SEC. 4. This act shall take effect immediately, and said company shsll be entitled to its benefits, and subject to its provisions, whenever they shall accept the same, and their acceptance in writing, signed and certified to by the President or Secretary of said company, shall be filed in the office of the Secretary of State: *Provided*, Such acceptance is filed within sixty days from the passage of this act.—*Approved March* 8, 1851.

AN ACT to amend an act entitled an "An act to incorporate the City of Detroit Gas Light Company."

Sec. 3 of act No. 82 of 1849 amended.

SEC. 1. *The People of the State of Michigan enact*, That section three of an act entitled "An act to incorporate the City of Detroit Gas Light Company," approved March the fourteenth, one thousand eight hundred and forty-nine, be and the same is hereby amended so as to read as follows:

Capital stock.

SEC. 3. The capital stock of said Company shall not exceed five hundred thousand dollars, which with the property, affairs and concerns of the said corporation, shall be managed and conducted by a board of officers, to consist of a President, Secretary, Treasurer, and four other Directors, all of whom shall be stockholders, except the Secretary."

Board of officers.

To make annual report to Common Council of Detroit.

SEC. 2. That said Company shall annually, in the first week in January, make an accurate report in writing to the Common Council of Detroit, showing the amount of capital stock paid in; the amount issued; all real or personal estate held or owned by said Company, and the cost of the same; a statement of the extent of pipe laid down; the number of street lamps erected; which report and statement shall be verified by the oath of the Secretary and one of the Directors of said Company.

SEC. 3. The said Company shall not increase the present price charged for gas, without the consent of the Common Council of said city. Price of gas, &c.

SEC. 4. Said Company shall be entitled to all the benefits and subject to the provisions of this act, on filing in the office of the Secretary of State a a written acceptance of this act, signed by its President and Secretary, and sealed with its corporate seal. To file acceptance.

SEC. 5. This act shall take effect immediately.—*Approved February* 13, 1855.

AN ACT ceding to the United States of America jurisdiction over certain lands and appurtenances, situate in the City of Detroit, and for other purposes therein mentioned.

Whereas, The United State have recently appropriated money for the purchase of sites in and near the city of Detroit, for the erection of certain buildings thereon, one to be used as a Marine Hospital, and the other as a Custom House, Post Office and U. S. Court room; Preamble.

And whereas, It is deemed by the Legislature highly necessary to the interest of said city that said buildings should be erected; therefore,

SEC. 1. *The People of the State of Michigan enact*, That jurisdiction of the lands and their appurtenances, that have been or may be purchased in and near said city of Detroit, for the erection of the aforesaid buildings, be and is hereby ceded to the United States of America: *Provided however*, That all civil and criminal process issued under the authority of this State, or any officer thereof, may be executed on said lands and in the buildings that may be erected thereon, in the same way and manner as if jurisdiction had not, been ceded as aforesaid. Cession of jurisdiction. Right to execute process reserved.

SEC. 2. The lands above described, with their appurtenances, and all buildings and other property that may be thereon, shall forever hereafter be exempted from all State, county, and municipal taxation and assessment, so long as the same shall remain the property of the said United States of America.—*Approved February* 12, 1855. Exemption from taxation.

CHAPTER 103—REVISED STATUTES OF 1846.

OF THE RETURN OF JURORS FOR CIRCUIT COURT.

Assessors &c. to make list of persons to serve as jurors.

SEC. 8. The Assessors and Township Clerk of each township, and the Assessor and Alderman of each ward in the city of Detroit, shall at the time appointed by law for said Assessors to review their assessment roll in each year, make a list of persons to serve as (petit jurors, and a list of persons to serve as) grand jurors for the ensuing year.

How selection to be made.

SEC. 9. The said officers shall proceed to select from those assessed on the assessment roll of the township or ward for the same year, suitable persons, having the qualifications of electors, to serve as jurors: and in making such selection, they shall take the names of such only as are not exempt from serving on juries; who are in possession of their natural faculties, and not infirm or decrepid; of fair character, of approved integrity, of sound judgment, and well informed, and free from all legal exceptions.

Number to be selected.

SEC. 10. Such list shall contain not less than one for every one hundred inhabitants of such township or ward, computing according to the last preceding census, and having regard to the population of the county, so that the whole number of jurors selected in the county shall amount at least to one hundred, and not exceeding four hundred, one-half of whom shall be designated as petit jurors, and one-half as grand jurors.

Officers to avoid selecting persons who served the preceeding year.

SEC. 11. In making such selection, the said officers shall avoid as far as practicable, selecting any of the same persons who were actually drawn, and who served as jurors, during the preceding year.

Duplicate lists to be made, &c.

SEC. 12. Duplicate lists of the persons so selected, shall be made out and signed by the officers making such selection, or the major part of them, and within ten days thereafter, one of each of said lists shall be transmitted to the County Clerk, and the other shall be filed with the Clerk of the township or Assesor of the ward, as the case may be.

BOARDS OF HEALTH IN CITIES AND VILLAGES.

REVISED STATUTES OF 1846—CHAPTRR 35.

Mayor and Aldermen a Board of Health.

SEC. 49. The Mayor and Aldermen of each incorporated city, and the President and Council, or Trustees of each incorporated village in this State, shall have and exercise all the powers* and perform all the duties, of a Board of Health as provided in this chapter, within the limits of the cities or villages respectively of which they are such officers.

CITIES OF DETROIT AND MONROE.

REVISED STATUTES OF 1846—CHAPTER 16.

SEC. 104. The cities of Detroit and Monroe respectively shall continue to have and exercise all the powers and privileges, and be subject to all the duties and liabilities conferred or imposed upon them respectively by law; and two additional Justices of the Peace shall contiue to be chosen in the township of Monroe, and two in the city of Detroit, in the same manner, and with like powers, and subject to the same duties and liabilities, as provided in this chapter in relation to the election, powers, duties and liabilties of Justices of the Peace.

Powers and privileges of cities of Detroit and Monroe continued.

Detroit and Monroe may elect 2 additional justices of the peace

---

*See, as to the powers and duties of a Board of Health—Revised Statutes of 1846—pages 162-3-4-5-6-7 and 8.

ORDINANCES AND BY-LAWS

OF THE

CITY OF DETROIT.

REVISED AND PUBLISHED BY ORDER OF THE COMMON COUNCIL.

JULY, 1855.

REVISED ORDINANCES

AND

BY-LAWS OF THE CITY OF DETROIT.

Be it Ordained by the Mayor, Recorder and Aldermen of the City of Detroit, in Common Council convened.

TITLE ONE.

OF THE CITY OFFICERS

CHAPTER I.

Relative to appointment and duties of certain officers.

SECTION 1. That on the second Tuesday next ensuing the charter election in each year, or as soon thereafter as shall be deemed necessary, the Common Council shall appoint the following officers, who shall hold their offices for the term of one year, and who shall be residents of said city, one Pound-Keeper and a City Printer. *Printer and pound keeper when appointed.*

SEC. 2. All officers of the corporation shall, within fifteen days after notice of their appointments, take and file with the Clerk an oath or affirmation, that they will support the Constitution of the United States, and the Constitution of this State, and that they will faithfully and honestly discharge the duties of their offices according to the best of their abilities; and the Attorney, Clerk, Treasurer, Collector, Marshal, Superintendent, Director of the Poor, Supervisors, *Oath of office and bond.*

TITLE I. CHAPTER I.

Market Clerks, Sexton, Inspectors of wood, Weigh-Masters, Pound-Keeper and City Surveyor, and shall each enter into such bonds to the Mayor, Recorder, Aldermen and Freemen of the city of Detroit, and with such sureties, as the Common Council may direct, and conditioned that they will well and faithfully discharge and perform all the duties which the by-laws, ordinances or resolutions of the Common Council may, from time to time, direct or require; and on the determination of their said offices, or in case they shall die during the term, or before the accounts thereof be finally closed, that they, or their respective legal representatives, shall well and truly settle their said accounts, and pay over to the City Treasurer, the balance which shall be found to have been in their hands respectively due to said corporation, and shall deliver up to Mayor or Common Council, all their books of account, and all official papers and vouchers that may have come into their hands: *Provided*, The city Treasurer shall pay all moneys in his hands to his successor in office.

Salaries when and how fixed.

SEC. 3. The Common Council shall, from time to time, by resolution, prescribe the salaries of all corporation officers, for all services rendered by such officers respectively to the Common Council in discharge of the ordinary and usual duties of their offices, but which shall not affect any compensation other than that to be made by the Common Council.

Returs of officers to be evidence of what they set forth, when.

SEC. 4. The returns made by any officer of the corporation in pursuance of any writ to him directed, and the returns or reports made by any such officer to the Common Council or other officer of the corporation in pursuance of the charter of the city, or by-law, ordinance or resolution of the Common Council, shall be taken and received as evidence of the truth of what they set forth.

Officers to pay over moneys and penalty for neglect.

SEC. 5. It shall be the duty of every officer of the corporation, to pay to the Treasurer of the said city, the same money which he may have collected by virtue of his office, excepting therefrom such amount as shall be due him for his salary up to that time, and for which he may have received an order on the City Treasurer; any officer violating the provisions of this section, shall, for every such offence, forfeit a sum not exceeding twenty per cent. on the amount of moneys improperly used or withheld by him.

SEC. 6. It shall be the duty of the Marshal and Constables of this city, to notice all infractions and violations of the laws and ordinances of this city, and make complaint thereof to the City Attorney.

TITLE I. CHAPTER 2. Marshal and constables to notice violations of ordinances.

SEC. 7. The City Printer shall publish the proceedings of the Common Council, the by-laws and ordinances of this city, and all legal notices pertaining to the business of the corporation, unless otherwise directed by the Common Council in extraordinary cases.

Duty of City Printer.

CHAPTER II.

Relative to the City Attorney.

SEC. 1. Must be an Attorney and Counsellor of Supreme Court.
SEC. 2. Duties of.
SEC. 3. To receive and how dispose of moneys collected by him.

SEC. 1. The Attorney for the city of Detroit shall be a person who is an Attorney and Counsellor of the Supreme Court of the State of Michigan, and shall not hold any other office under the Common Council during the period for which he shall be elected.

Must be an Attorney and Counsellor of Supreme Court.

SEC. 2. It shall be the duty of the city Attorney to draft all ordinances, deeds, bonds, contracts and documents of whatever kind which may be required of him by any ordinance or order of the Mayor, Recorder or Aldermen, or of the Common Council, or which by any such ordinances or order are necessary to be done and made by and between the city of Detroit and any person or persons contracting with said city in its corporate capacity, and which the said city is to be at the expense of drawing; he shall prosecute all actions, suits and prosecutions on behalf of the city, in the Mayor's Court, or any other Court in this State; he shall institute and carry on all prosecutions for the recovery of all fines, penalties and forfeitures which have or may accrue for the violation of the by-laws or ordinances of said city; he shall defend all manner of actions brought or to be brought against said city, or any officer thereof in his official capacity, before any court in this State; whenever required he shall render professional advice to the Common Council, or any member, or committee thereof, or any officer of the corporation on all subjects touching the city government; he shall examine and inspect all tax and assessment rolls, and all proceedings predicated thereon, made by the authority of the corporation, and if not correct, to advise the proper officers how to correct the same, and shall do all and every other professional act incident to his office.

Duties of

TITLE I. CHAPTER 3.

To receive and how dispose of moneys collected by him

SEC. 3. The City Attorney shall receive all moneys recovered by any suit instituted by him as aforesaid, and pay the same to the Treasurer of said city at the expiration of every quarter, and also make a written report to the Common Council of all suits instituted by him, showing the names of the defendants, the progress or result of the suits, and the nature thereof, the amount of the money paid to the Treasurer, and from whom the same was received, together with such other general statement of business on his hands as may be necessary.

CHAPTER III.

Relative to City Clerk.

To keep journal of the proceedings of the Common Council.

SEC. 1. The City Clerk shall keep an accurate and correct journal of the proceedings of the Common Council, and file and carefully preserve all papers and documents connected therewith.

Shall keep the accounts of the city and take receipts from officers, when

SEC. 2. It shall be the duty of the City Clerk to keep just and accurate accounts of all matters in which the corporation of said city may be interested and concerned; and whenever any officer of said city shall be authorized to receive or demand from the City Clerk, any accounts, notes, bonds, assessment rolls, or any paper or document whatever, he shall charge or enter the same, in some proper book kept for that purpose, against such officer, and take his receipt therefor.

Shall provide stationery for city business and make quarterly returns of all fees.

SEC. 3. It shall be the duty of the City Clerk to procure all necessary books and stationery for the Common Council and Mayor's Court, and at the expiration of every three months, or sooner if required, report to the Common Council the amount of moneys received and disbursed by him, relative to all matters pertaining to the duties of his office. It shall also be the duty of the City Clerk to keep an account of all Clerk's fees, received by him in the Mayor's Court, and of all other fees received by him as Clerk, and once in each three months to pay the same to the City Treasurer, for the benefit and use of the city, and to take the Treasurer's receipt therefor, and to report the same to the Council.

Shall provide an assessment register

SEC. 4. It shall also be the duty of the Clerk to procure a register, to be denominated the "Assessment Register," wherein shall be registered assessments on any lots or premises on which any tax or assessment has been laid or imposed, but not paid.

Shall inform the Attorney of the filing of assessment rolls and obtain his opinion of their regularity.

SEC. 5. Whenever any assessment roll or any return, or other proceeding relative thereto, shall be left or filed with the City Clerk, it shall be his duty, without unnecessary delay, to inform the City Attorney of the same, and obtain his opinion respecting the regularity of such proceedings; and if there be any irregularity in any matter relative to such proceedings, the Clerk shall inform the officer performing the same, with the view to have any necessary correction made in the premises.

Shall charge expense of making assessments in assessment register.

SEC. 6. When any special assessment shall be made on any lands or tenements by authority of the Common Council, it shall be the duty of the Clerk to ascertain and determine all expenses incurred by the corporation in making the same, and charge the amount thereof in a proper column in the assessment register, which shall be collected together with the amount of said assessment.

CHAPTER IV.

Relative to City Collectors.

Shall collect city tax in several wards.

SEC. 1. The Collectors of the several wards shall collect the city tax within the bounds of their respective wards, and shall be entitled to such rate per cent. for compensation as the Common Council shall from time to time prescribe by resolution or otherwise: *Provided*, The compensation shall in no case exceed five per cent. on the amount collected.

Their compensation.

Bonds of

SEC. 2. The several Collectors shall, before entering on the duties of their office, enter into bonds to the Mayor, Recorder, Aldermen and Freemen of the city of Detroit, with such sureties as the Common Council may direct, in a sum not less than twice the amount of the city tax in the ward for which each Collector has been chosen, and conditioned that they will well and faithfully discharge and perform all the duties which the by-laws, ordinances or resolutions of the Common Council may, from time to time, direct or require, and on the determination of their said offices, or in case they shall die during the term, or before the accounts thereof be finally closed, that they or their respective legal representatives shall well and truly settle their said accounts and pay over to the City Treasurer, the balance, which shall be found to have been in their hands respectively, due to said corporation, and shall deliver up to the Mayor or Common Council all their books of account and all official papers and vouchers that may have come into their hands.

To make deposits of collections once a week and report concerning collections once per month.

SEC. 3. Each Collector shall, at least once in each week, deposit with the City Treasurer all moneys by him collected up to the time of making each deposit, and, as far as practicable, the same money collected, and report to the Common Council all his doings relative to any collections which may be entrusted to him, once in every month, or oftener, if required, and every such report shall be accompanied by the affidavit of the Collector making the same, duly sworn to, that such report contains a true account of all moneys by him collected for said city, during the time embraced in said report.

CHAPTER V.

Relative to City Treasurer.

Duties of—shall open eight different accounts.

SEC. 1. It shall be the duty of the City Treasurer to receive all moneys belonging to the corporation of said city, from whatever sources the same may arise or become due, and once in each week to deposit all moneys so received by him, in such place in said city as the Common Council may by resolution designate. He shall cause to be opened in his books eight distinct and separate accounts, as follows, to wit:

1st. GENERAL FUND.—To which he shall credit all moneys received on account of city taxes proper, sale or rent of city property, lots sold for delinquent taxes, and all other moneys belonging to said corporation received by him, and not hereinafter directed to be credited to some other account.

2d. Fire Department.—To whieh he shall credit all moneys raised, received or appropriated for the benefit or maintenance of said department.

3d. Contingent Fund.—To which shall be credited all moneys received and appropriated from the city tax proper, for contingent expenses.

4th. City Poor.—To which he shall credit all moneys received for grocery or tavern licenses granted by the Common Council.

5th. Road Fund.—To which shall be credited all moneys received on account of road tax.

6th. Interest Fund.—To which he shall credit all moneys raised and appropriated for payment of interest.

7th. Sewer Fund.—To which he shall credit all moneys received on account of sewer tax or assessment.

8th. Mayor's Court Fund.—To which shall be credited all moneys received on account of fines and penalties imposed by said Court.

How to keep his accounts.

Sec. 2. The Treasurer shall keep just and fair accounts of all moneys received and credited by him, in books to be provided for that purpose, showing the amount received and credited on account of each of the funds, mentioned in the preceding section, respectively; and shall once in each week notify the City Comptroller of the amount by him credited to each fund. He shall, once in each month, or oftener, if required by the Common Council, furnish to the said Council, a true and full account of the receipts and disbursements of his office, the amounts due and owing to the city, their nature and condition, and by whom due. He shall at all times keep the books and accounts of his office open to the inspection and examination of the City Comptroller or any committee of the Common Council.

To give receipts countersigned by the Comptroller.

Sec. 3. The Treasurer shall give receipts for all moneys received by him, and said receipts to be countersigned by the Comptroller.

TITLE I.
CHAPTER 6.

CHAPTER VI.

Relative to the City Comptroller.

Term of office

SEC. 1. There shall be appointed by the Common Council to the city of Detroit, an officer to be called the City Comptroller, who shall hold his office for the term of three years from and after the first day of April, A. D. 1850, and until his successor is duly appointed and qualified.

Official Bond.

SEC. 2. Before entering on the duties of his office, said City Comptroller shall take and file with the City Clerk an oath or affirmation similar to that provided in the case of other officers of said city, by section two of chapter one of the Revised Ordinances of 1848, and shall also enter into bonds in the penal sum of thirty thousand dollars, to the Mayor, Recorder, Aldermen and Freemen of the city of Detroit, with such sureties as shall be approved by the Common Council, and with like condition as is provided in said section two, in relation to the bonds of other officers of said city.

All accounts against the city to be filed with and audited by him.

SEC. 3. All accounts against the corporation of said city, shall, in the first instance, be presented and filed with the said Comptroller, and it shall be the duty of the said Comptroller to receive and examine all such accounts, and to report upon the same fully, and with all convenient speed, to the Common Council, and whether in his opinion, said accounts shall be allowed or disallowed; and if allowed, the fund out of which the same should be paid; and once in each month, and oftener if required, furnish to the Common Council a general statement of the business done in his office; the receipts and expenditures of the city government during the preceding month, and an estimate of the probable receipts and expenditures for the succeeding month—distinguishing the receipts and expenditures of each separate fund—the then state of the finances of each fund, and such general suggestions and information in regard to the city finances and government, as he may deem beneficial to the city government; to examine the tax rolls and returns of other city officers; to take general supervision of the acts and accounts of all other officers engaged in the business of said corporation, and generally to act, in all respects, as the business agent of said corporation. The said Comptroller shall keep regular books of account, showing the state of the city finances, and a book of claims, with an index, in which shall be entered a full minute of each claim presented to him, the proceedings had in regard thereto, and its final disposition.

City Clerk shall keep a register of all accounts allowed by Com. Council and file with Comptroller a certificate of the amount of each account

SEC. 4. Whenever any accounts against the corporation of said city shall have been allowed by the Common Council, it shall be the duty of the City Clerk to enter the same in a register, to be by him kept for that purpose, and to file with the City Comptroller, forthwith, a certificate stating each claim so allowed, its amount, and to whom, and out of what fund payable. Upon the receipt of said certificate, the Comptroller shall file the same in his office, and draw his warrant upon the appropriate fund, and no other, for the amount, and it shall then be paid by the Treasurer: *Provided, however*, That all claims shall be paid in the order of priority in which they are allowed; that all warrants shall be drawn upon the fund designated in the certificate of allowance, and that no warrant shall be drawn until there are funds to meet it.

Accounts to be paid out of the fund to which they belong, &c.

SEC. 5. All accounts shall be paid out of the appropriate fund to which they belong: *Provided, however*, That the Common Council may, whenever they deem it expedient, direct that the surplus of any one fund be checked for in the manner provided in the preceding section, and applied to the credit of any other fund.

Salary of.

SEC. 6. The said Comptroller during the time he continues in office, shall be paid a salary at the rate of twelve hundred and fifty dollars per annum, payable monthly, which shall be in full for all services rendered by him to said city.

TITLE I.
CHAPTER 7.

CHAPTER VII.

Relative to Street Commissioner.

To be appointed by and hold his office at the pleasure of the Common Council.

SEC. 1. There shall be appointed by the Common Council of the city of Detroit, an officer, to be called a Street Commissioner, who shall hold his office during the pleasure of the Common Council, from and after the first day of July, in the year in which he is appointed, and until his successor is duly appointed and qualified. Said Street Commissioner shall possess the same qualifications, and take the same oath as other city officers, and before entering upon the duties of his office, give a bond to the city, with one or more securities to be approved of by the Mayor, in the sum of five thousand dollars, conditioned for the faithful performance of the duties of his office.

Oath and Bond of.

Duties of

SEC. 2. Said Street Commissioner shall have full power and authority, and it shall be his duty, to superintend and direct, pursuant to the laws, ordinances, resolutions and orders of the Common Council, the making, paving, repairing or opening of all the streets, lanes, alleys, sidewalks, crosswalks, highways or bridges within the limits of said city, and all expenditures for the above mentioned purposes, shall be made under the supervision and direction of the said Street Commissioner.

Supervisors of several wards to be subject to Commissioner.

SEC. 3. The Supervisors of the several wards of said city shall, in all things pertaining to the duties of their offices, be under the direction and obey the orders of the Street Commissioner; and if any of said Supervisors shall neglect or refuse to perform any such service, when required by said Street Commissioner, it shall be his duty to report such neglect or refusal to the Common Council.

To make assessments of side and cross walks, and to enforce ordinances concerning streets and alleys.

SEC. 4. Hereafter, said Street Commissioner shall make all assessments for the making and repairing of sidewalks and crosswalks, and shall cause to be enforced all the ordinances concerning streets and alleys, and shall make complaint to the Mayor's Court of all persons violating any of said ordinances.

Salary of.

SEC. 5. Said Street Commissioner shall receive as compensation for his services, six hundred dollars per annum.

CHAPTER VIII.

Relative to City Surveyor.

SEC. 1. It shall be the duty of the City Surveyor, when so directed by the Common Council, to ascertain and establish the proper grade to any avenue, street, lane, alley or side walk within the limits of said city, and when required, to run out and stake off the same.

Shall establish the grade of streets, &c

SEC. 2. It shall also be his duty to make all necessary surveys, and superintend the construction, enlargement, or alteration of all drains connecting with the main or lateral sewers of said city, and shall record the same in a book to be provided by said Common Council, and deposit the same with the City Clerk at the termination of his said office.

Shall survey and superintend the construction or alteration of drains.

SEC. 3. He shall also make all necessary surveys, and give such information as may be needed by any committee, or by the Superintendent of the water works in laying down, extending or connecting the water logs or pipes of said water works in said city, and shall at all times, when required, consult and act with any standing or special committee, who may desire any information or assistance in any matter or thing connected with the duties of his office where the city of Detroit is concerned.

Shall make surveys and give information to the Superintendent of Hydraulics, and shall consult and act with committees of requiring official information from him.

SEC. 4. He shall also deliver over to the City Clerk all papers, plans and drafts relating to any survey made by order of the Common Council, and shall also make a written report of his doings and proceedings in all cases when required so to do by the Common Council.

Shall deliver books and papers to City Clerk and when required report to the Council.

SEC. 5. The salary allowed by said Council to the City Surveyor shall be in full for all services rendered, and shall also be in full for all incidental, as well as other labor performed by him as said Surveyor, or by any of his assistants.

Salary of.

TITLE I.
CHAPTER 9.

CHAPTER IX.

Relative to City Historiographer.

Duties of.

SEC. 1. There shall be appointed by the Common Council, an officer to be called the Historiographer, who shall hold his office during the pleasure of the Council.

To collect and keep all books, papers, &c., connected with the History of the city of Detroit.

SEC. 2. It shall be the duty of the Historiographer to collect together, receive and safely keep all such books, papers, documents, and other matters, connected with, and illustrating the history of the city of Detroit, as he may be able to procure without expense to the city.

To make a report annually of the state of his department to the Com. Council.

SEC. 3. It shall be the duty of the Historiographer, to report annually (and at such other time as he shall be required to do,) to the Common Council the state and condition of his department.

To deliver up all books, papers, &c., and penalty for default.

SEC. 4. The Historiographer shall at any time when required by the Council, deliver over to such persons as the Council may direct, all books, papers and documents, and other things that may at any time come into his possession as such officer, and in default thereof, he shall be liable to a penalty of one hundred dollars.

Office honorary.

SEC. 5. The office of Historiographer being honorary, no compensation shall be allowed to said officer.

CHAPTER X.

Relative to City Collector and Special Assessments.

City Collector to be appointed.

SEC. 1. That there shall be appointed by the Common Council an officer to be called the City Collector, who shall hold his office during the pleasure of the Council, from and after the first day of June, in the year in which he is appointed; and until his successor is duly elected and qualified; said City Collector shall have and possess the same powers and qualifications, under the provisions of this ordinance, as the ward Collectors of said city, and take the same oath as other city officers, and before entering upon the duties of his office, give a bond to said city, with one or more securities, to be approved by the Common Council, in the sum of twenty thousand dollars, conditioned for the faithful performance of the duties of his office, and perform all the duties which the By-Laws, Ordinances, or Resolutions of the Common Council may from time to time direct or require; and on the determination of his said office, or in case he shall die during the time, or before the accounts thereof be finally closed, that he or his respective legal representatives shall well and truly settle his said accounts, and pay over to the City Treasurer, the balance, which may be found to have been in his or their hands respectively, due to said corporation, and shall deliver up to the Mayor or Common Council all his books of accounts, and all official vouchers that may have come into his hands. Bonds of.

SEC. 2. It shall be the duty of said City Collector to collect the special taxes or assessments of said city, laid or imposed by authority of the Common Council of said city. The said City Collector shall have full power and authority to collect said taxes or assessments pursuant to the laws and ordinances of said city, and he shall at least once in each week, deposit with the City Treasurer all moneys by him collected up to the time of making each deposit, and, as far as practicable, the same money collected, and report to the Common Council all his doings relative to any collections which may be entrusted to him, once in every month, or oftener if required, and every such report shall be accompanied by the affidavit of the Collector making the same, duly sworn to before the City Comptroller, that such report contains a true account of all moneys by him collected for said city, during the time embraced in said report. Duties of.

SEC. 3. Whenever any special tax or assessment shall hereafter be laid or imposed, by authority of the Common Council of said city, the City Comptroller shall cause the assessment rolls for said special tax or assessment to be delivered to the City Treasurer, who shall give a receipt for the same and be charged therewith. The Treasurer shall retain the said assessment rolls in his office for the space of twenty days from and after the date of such delivery, and during the said period, while said rolls are so retained, any person assessed therein may pay the amount of his or her tax or assessment to the City Comptroller to deliver special assessments to Treasurer, when they shall be delivered to Collector and warrant.

TITLE I. CHAPTER 10.

City Treasurer, who shall receive the same and give a receipt therefor, and mark the same as paid upon the said rolls. Upon the expiration of the said period of twenty days, it shall be the duty of the City Treasurer to deliver the said assessment rolls, or a certified copy of the same, adding thereto the cost of printing or other costs, to the Mayor, Recorder and Aldermen of said city, or any three of them, of whom the Mayor or Recorder shall be one, who shall issue a warrant under their hands and the seal of said city, directed to the City Collector of said city, with a command to levy and collect all sums or assessments then remaining unpaid, with the costs and charges thereon, by distress and sale of the goods and chattels of the person against whom said assessment has been made, or those who may be liable to pay the same, and further commanding the City Collector to make returns to the Common Council, within thirty days thereafter.

How Collector shall proceed.

SEC. 4. Upon receiving the assessment roll, or a copy thereof, and warrant, it shall be the duty of the City Collector to proceed to demand and collect the several sums mentioned therein, and if any person shall neglect or refuse to pay the same, then, if he can find any goods or chattels of the person liable therefor, he shall levy thereon; but before he shall proceed to sell such goods and chattels, he shall give ten days' previous notice of the time and place of sale, by causing the same to be posted up in three of the most conspicuous places in said city, and the property levied upon shall be sold at public auction to the highest bidder; and the City Collector shall render the overplus if any, after deducting the costs and charges of such distress and sale, to the person entitled thereto. The City Collector shall, in all cases, be entitled to demand cents on the dollar on the amount of the assessment, for his services, which the person so assessed shall pay.

Collector to make return.

SEC. 5. The City Collector shall make return of his doings within the time mentioned in said warrant, to the Common Council, if in session; but if not, then at their next ensuing meeting; and in such return describe the goods and chattels sold, and the amount which each article sold for. But if goods and chattels cannot be found, or if such person or persons mentioned in said roll are non-residents of said city, the City Collector shall state such fact, verified by an affidavit taken before the City Comptroller, and annex the same to a list of such lands on which the assessments have not been paid.

Warrant for collection may be renewed.

SEC. 6. Said warrant may be renewed from time to time if the Common Council shall so direct.

Duty of City Treasurer upon return.

SEC. 7. Upon making such return the City Treasurer shall proceed and sell such lots in the same manner as is prescribed for city taxes.

SEC. 8. The following or other sufficient forms may be used in proceedings under this chapter:

Forms.

FORM OF WARRANT.

STATE OF MICHIGAN, }
City of Detroit, } ss.

To the City Collector of the City of Detroit, Greeting:

In the name of the People of the State of Michigan, You are hereby commanded, that you collect from each person or set of persons named in the foregoing tax roll, or of any person liable to pay, the amount of money set opposite his, her or their names, respectively, and on the refusal or neglect of any such person to pay said tax, costs and charges thereon, including per cent. for your services, that you then levy the same by distress and sale of the goods and chattels of such person, according to law, and that you have said roll and this warrant and the receipt of the Treasurer of said city for the amount by you collected, before the Common Council of said city, within thirty days from the date hereof—and fail not, at your peril.

In testimony whereof, we have hereunto set our hands, and [L. S.] caused the seal of said city to be affixed at the city of Detroit, aforesaid, this day of A. D. 18 .

Mayor.

} Aldermen of said city.

Notice of sale of Property.

STATE OF MICHIGAN, }
City of Detroit. } ss.

Notice is hereby given, that, pursuant to law in such case made and provided, there will be sold at public auction, to the highest bidder, at in the city of Detroit, at o'clock in

TITLE I. CHAPTER 10.

the noon of day of A. D. 18 , the following goods and chattels, viz: [here description] or so much thereof as may be necessary to satisfy the amount of a certain assessment made by the Common Council of the city of Detroit, against for defraying the expenses of , together with the legal costs and charges which have accrued in the premises.

By order of the Common Council,

————, City Collector of said city.

Dated at the city of Detroit,
this day of A. D. 18 .

Return on City Collector's Warrant.

STATE OF MICHIGAN, City of Detroit. } ss.

To the Hon. the Common Council of said city:

The undersigned begs leave to submit the following list of lands of residents, (or non-residents,) which were taxed for, (here set forth the object for which the tax was laid,) on the day of A. D., 18 , according to the assessment roll to me heretofore delivered, but which I have not been able to collect.

[Here copy the assessment roll, so far as it relates to unpaid assessments.]

Given at the city of Detroit,
this day of A. D. 18 .

[Let an affidavit of the following form be added:]

STATE OF MICHIGAN. City of Detroit. } ss.

City Collector of said city, being duly sworn, saith that the foregoing return contains the description of all lands, and the names of all persons taxed on the assessment roll of the day of A. D. 18 , and that the several sums mentioned in the foregoing list, remain due and unpaid, and that he has not upon diligent enquiry been able to find or discover any goods or chattels belonging to, or in the possession of the persons charged with or liable to pay the said assessment, whereon to levy the same; and this deponent further saith, that the persons mentioned in said list as non-residents are, as as he believes, non-residents.

————City Collector of said city.

Subscribed and sworn to, this day of A. D. 18 , before me, City Comptroller of said city.

CHAPTER XI.

Relative to Chimney Sweeps.

SEC. 1. There shall be nominated by the Board of Fire Wardens of the city of Detroit, subject to the approval of the Common Council, one Chimney Sweeper for the city, who shall have full power to appoint others under him, according to the subsequent provisions of this chapter.

How appointed.

SEC. 2. No person shall hereafter follow the business or occupation of a Chimney Sweeper, either by himself, or others, within the city of Detroit, unless he shall have been approved in the manner prescribed in section one, and shall give bonds to the Mayor, Recorder, Aldermen and Freemen of the city of Detroit, in the penal sum of fifty dollars, conditioned for the faithful performance of his duties according to the provisions hereinafter contained, and shall have registered his name and the names of all persons employed by him as assistants, with a number affixed to every such name in a book to be kept by the City Clerk, and shall have obtained from said Clerk a certificate of every such registry containing the name of the person and the number affixed in said registry, under a penalty of five dollars for every day he shall follow by himself or others the said business; and the said Clerk is hereby required to make out and deliver to the person so appointed such certificates, for each of which he shall be entitled to demand and receive one dollar.

To give bonds and register their names with Clerk, and Clerk to give them certificates.

SEC. 3. Every person following the aforesaid business within said city, shall wear, and cause to be worn by the persons employed by him, on the front of their caps or hats, in full view, the same figures and numbers respectively as shall be so as aforesaid entered in the said book, and contained in his or their respective certificates, in large figures not less than two inches in length, to be made of durable tin or copper, with the word "Sweep," legibly painted on said badge. Every person who shall violate the provisions of this section shall forfeit one dollar.

To wear a badge and penalty for default.

16

TITLE I. CHAPTER 12.

Duty of. SEC. 4. Every such Chimney Sweep so appointed, who shall not within forty-eight hours after application to him, made by any inhabitant of the district to which he belongs, sweep, or cause to be swept, such chimney or chimneys as he shall be required to sweep, shall for every such offence forfeit and pay the sum of three dollars.

Fees of SEC. 5. Each Chimney Sweeper so appointed shall be entitled to demand and receive for every chimney so swept, the following sums and no more, to wit:—for each chimney with a single flue, the sum of one shilling for every story through which said flue shall pass, and six cents for each additional flue, the same to be paid by the persons respectively owning the same.

Penalty on persons whose chimneys being unswept, take fire. SEC. 6. If any chimney in this city shall sake fire and blaze out at the top, (the same not having been swept within three months next before the time of taking fire,) the occupant of such premises shall forfeit and pay the sum of one dollar and costs. But if the same shall have been swept within three months, then the person having swept the same shall forfeit and pay one dollar and costs.

CHAPTER XII.

Relative to City Scavengers.

To be appointed by the Council. SEC. 1. The Common Council may from time to time license any trustworthy persons to be Scavengers for the city, upon their making application for such license, giving proper security, and paying the sum of one dollar to the City Treasurer for their license.

No person to act as scavenger unless licensed. SEC. 2. No person shall hereafter follow the business or occupation of a Scavenger for hire in the city of Detroit, unless he shall have been licensed by the Common Council, as provided in section one, under a penalty not exceeding fifty dollars for each offence; and each person licensed, as provided in said section one, shall, before entering upon his duties as Scavenger, give bonds to the Mayor, Recorder, Aldermen, and Freemen of the City of Detroit, in the penal sum of two hundred dollars, with such securities as the Common Council may approve, conditioned for the faithful performance of his duties, according to the provisions of this ordinance; and it shall further be the duty of each person licensed as Scavenger, as herein before provided, to register his name in a book to be kept by the City Clerk, and to obtain from said Clerk a certificate of such registry, under a penalty of five dollars for every day he shall follow the business of Scavenger, either by himself or others; and the Clerk is hereby required to make out and deliver to the persons so appointed certificates as aforesaid, for each of which certificates he shall be entitled to demand and receive fifty cents.

To enjoy the exclusive right to clean privies and have the emoluments thereof.

SEC. 3. The persons licensed as Scavengers as aforesaid, and having duly qualified as aforesaid, shall exclusively have the right, and enjoy the emoluments, of cleaning privies in the city of Detroit. They shall, under the direction of the City Marshal, have full power to enter upon any premises in the city, and examine the privy or privies on such premises, and whenever any privy or privies in the city shall be found filled with night soil to a level with the surface of the lot on which they stand, the said Scavengers may, at any time between the hours of ten o'clock in the evening and four o'clock in the morning, clean out such privy or privies, and it shall be their duty to remove all the contents of the same in carts or wagons, to be provided for that purpose, to some point on the Detroit river, and thence convey the same in a scow or other boat provided for that purpose, to the middle of the river, at a distance of at least half a mile below the limits of the city, and then deposit the same in the said river.

What hours to work,

Shall clean privies when requested.

SEC. 4. It shall be the duty of said Scavengers, whenever requested by any of the citizens of Detroit, to clean out the privy or privies of the person or persons requesting the same to be done, between the hours prescribed in section three, and they shall remove the contents of all privies so cleaned out by them, upon request, in the same manner, and to the same place, as provided in said section three.

SEC. 5. It shall be the duty of each and every owner or occupier of a privy within the limits of the city of Detroit, whenever his, her or their privy shall be filled with night soil, within a foot of the sur-

TITLE I. CHAPTER 12.

To be notified of the existance of night soil in privies by the owners—when, and penalty for not so notifying.

face of his, her or their lot, to notify one of the City Scavengers of the fact, and request him to clean out the same, and remove the contents, as hereinbefore provided; and every person neglecting so to notify a City Scavenger, shall be liable to a penalty of not exceeding five dollars for each day he, she, or they shall neglect to give such notice, and make such request: *Provided*, That the fine shall, in no one case, exceed twenty-five dollars, and that all notices for the Scavengers shall be deemed made, according to the provisions of this ordinance, when left at the City Clerk's office in writing.

Fees of.

SEC. 6. The Scavengers shall be entitled to demand and receive a sum not exceeding eight cents for each cubic foot of the contents of any privy by them cleaned out, as hereinbefore provided.

When Scavenger to commence proceedings in Mayor's Court.

SEC. 7. If any person, or persons, whose privy has been cleaned out by a Scavenger, under the provisions of this ordinance, without request, shall refuse or neglect to pay the price charged for the same, (provided that such charge be not above the rate fixed by section six,) it shall be the duty of the Scavenger who has cleaned out his, her or their privy, to commence proceedings in the Mayor's Court, for the recovery of the penalty provided for in section five: *Provided*, That the Scavenger making any complaint, shall receive, in lieu of all claims against the city, one-half of the amount of the penalty collected, upon complaint made, and conviction thereof.

Penalties for breach of duty by Scavengers.

SEC. 8. If any Scavenger licensed, as provided in section one, shall neglcct to take out the certificate provided for in section two, or shall refuse, or neglect to clean out any privy within the city of Detroit, within forty-eight hours after being requested, or when he shall know the same to be full, or shall deposit the contents of any privy by him cleaned out, in any other place than that prescribed in section three, or shall discharge any of his duties in a careless or improper manner, or neglect to repair any damage to the fences, buildings and grounds made in the discharge of his duties, or shall demand any higher price for cleaning out any privy, than that prescribed in section six, he shall for either offence be liable to a penalty not exceeding one hundred dollars.

Proceedings under this ordinance when brought.

SEC. 9. All the penalties provided for in this ordinance, shall be collected by prosecution in the Mayor's Court, with costs of prosecution.

Council make suspend Scavengers' work.

SEC. 10. The Common Council may at any time direct suspension of the work of any of the Scavengers, when it appears that the exercise of the duties may be deleterious to the public health, and for other good causes.

TITLE TWO.

OF TAXES AND ASSESSMENTS.

CHAPTER XIII.

Relative to the Assessment and Collection of City Taxes.

Duty of Attorney relative to general assessment

SEC. 1. It shall be the duty of the City Attorney to meet with the Assessors, and give them all necessary advice relative to the manner of making the general assessment, and if any property belonging to the corporation should be assessed, to request that the same should be stricken from the roll.

Proclamation for public meeting to authorize tax to be published by the.

SEC. 2. That whenever it shall be necessary to call a meeting of the freemen of said city, for the purpose of authorizing the said Common Council to assess or lay a tax on the real and personal property within the limits of said city, the notice or proclamation for convening such meeting shall be left or filed with the City Clerk, who shall cause a copy thereof to be duly published in said city, in one of the city papers and handbills.

SEC. 3. If such meeting shall authorize the Common Council to assess and levy any such tax, the Chairman, or other officer of the meeting, shall certify the same to the Common Conncil, as soon as

TITLE II. CHAPTER 13.

Proceedings of meeting to be filed and recorded. Duty of Clerk or other officer authorized to carry out the amount of tax granted by said meeting.

may be, and such authority so certified shall be recorded in the journal, and filed by the City Clerk. It shall be the duty of the City Clerk, or such other officer as the Common Council shall authorize, to carry out in a proper column of the assessment rolls in each year, the amount of tax, in dollars and cents, agreeably to the authority granted by such meeting of the freemen of said city.

School, highway and sewer taxes to be delivered to Collectors—when.

SEC. 4. All city, school, highway and sewer taxes or assessments not paid to City Treasurer as hereinafter provided, shall be collected by the Collector of the ward wherein the same are assessed and to be collected.

Comptroller cause rolls to be delivered to Treasurer, and how long Treasurer may detain the same.

SEC. 5. Hereafter when the assessment rolls for city, school, highway and sewer taxes or assessments are completed, the City Comptroller shall cause the same to be delivered to the City Treasurer, who shall give a receipt for the same, and be charged therewith. The Treasurer shall retain the said assessment rolls for city, school, highway and sewer taxes in his office until such day as shall be designated by the Council, in each year, and during said periods, while said rolls are so detained respectively, any person assessed therein may pay the amount of their taxes or assessments to the City Treasurer, who shall receive and give a receipt therefor, and mark the same as paid upon the proper roll.

City Treasurer to procure warrant to be attached to tax rolls Contents of warrant.

SEC. 6. When the day designated in accordance with the provisions of the preceding section shall have elapsed, the City Treasurer shall request the Mayor, or in his absence, the Recorder, and at least two Aldermen of said city, to annex to each of the rolls for city, school, highway and sewer taxes, a warrant under their hands and the corporate seal, directed to the Collector for the ward or district in which the said rolls are to be collected, commanding him to collect all sums or assessments then remaining unpaid upon the roll, to which said warrant is annexed, of the person or persons from whom said sums or assessments are due, and if any person or persons from whom such sums or assessments are due as aforesaid, shall neglect or refuse to pay the same, or any part thereof, then that he shall levy the same by distress and sale of the goods and chattels of such person; and further, that he shall make return of his doings under said warrant upon a day to be fixed by resolution of the Common Council, which said warrant may be renewed from time to time as the said Council shall deem necessary; and the said Treasurer shall deliver the said rolls and warrants to the respective Collectors of the wards wherein the same are to be Collected, giving to each collector the roll to be collected in the ward of such Collector.

The amount unpaid on rolls to be charged to the collectors

SEC. 7. Whenever any of said rolls are delivered, as provided in the foregoing section, the Treasurer shall charge the amount unpaid thereon, to the Collector receiving the same, and shall also take the receipt of such Collector therefor.

Collectors to collect and make returns

SEC. 8. Upon receiving the said rolls, the several Collectors shall proceed to collect the amounts appearing unpaid thereon, in the manner provided by the charter and ordinances of said city, and shall proceed and make returns at the times and in the manner in said charter and ordinances prescribed.

Collectors to return taxes unpaid to the Council, &c.

SEC. 9. If any of the taxes mentioned in the tax roll of any ward or district shall remain unpaid, and the Collector for such ward or district shall not be able to collect the same, he shall report and deliver to the Common Council a list of the taxes so remaining due; and on making oath before the City Clerk, or in case of his absence, before any Justice of the Peace, that the sums mentioned in such list remain unpaid, and that he has not, upon diligent enquiry, been able to discover any goods or chattels belonging to or in possession of the persons charged with or liable to pay such sums, whereon he could levy the same, he shall be credited by the City Clerk with the amount thereof, but not otherwise. The Collector shall also designate in such report or list, all persons named in this roll, who are not residents of said city: *Provided*, The Collector may make said return to the Common Council at their meeting next ensuing the time mentioned in said warrant.

SEC. 10. The following or other sufficient forms may be used in proceeding under this chapter:

Forms.

Form of Warrant.

STATE OF MICHIGAN, } ss.
City of Detroit. }

To *Collector of* *Greeting:*

In the name of the people of the State of Michigan, You are hereby commanded, that you collect from each person or set of persons, named in the foregoing tax roll, or of any person liable to pay the amount of money set opposite to his, her or their names respectively, and on the neglect or refusal of any such person to pay such

TITLE II. CHAPTER 13.

taxes, that you then levy the same by distress and sale of the goods and chattels of such persons according to law; and that you have said roll and warrant by you collected, before the Common Council of said city, on the first Tuesday of September next ensuing.

In testimony whereof, we have hereunto set our hands [L. S.] and caused the seal of said city to be affixed, at the city of Detroit aforesaid, this day of A. D. 18 .

Mayor.
Aldermen of said city.

Notice of the Sale of Property.

STATE OF MICHIGAN, City of Detroit. } ss.

Notice is hereby given that on the day of A. D. 18 , at o'clock noon, the undersigned will sell at public auction, at the in said city, the following property, to wit: (here describe the property,) which I have distrained because A. B. hath neglected (or refused) to pay the city tax imposed on him for the year 18 , and which is to be levied by said sale.

Dated at Detroit, this day of A. D. 18 .

Collector for City of Detroit.

Collector's Return.

STATE OF MICHIGAN, City of Detroit. } ss.

To the Hon. the Common Council of the said City:

The undersigned begs leave to submit the following list of the lands of residents and non-residents of said city, which were taxed for the year 18 , according to the assessment roll of said city, to me heretofore delivered to be collected according to law, but which I have not been able to collect.

Names.	Description of lands.	Valuation.		Tax.	
		Dolls.	Cents.	Dolls.	Cents.

Given at the city of Detroit, this day of A. D. 18 .

Collector for city of Detroit.

STATE OF MICHIGAN, } ss.
City of Detroit.

, Collector of in said city, being duly sworn, saith that the several sums mentioned in the annexed list of city taxes for the year remain due and unpaid, and that he has not upon diligent enquiry, been able to find or discover in said city, any goods or chattels belonging to or in possession of the persons charged with or liable to pay the said sums of money, whereon he could levy the same; and this deponent further saith that the persons mentioned in said lists as non-residents are, as he believes, non-residents of said city.

Collector for city of Detroit.

Subscribed and sworn to this day of A. D. 18 , before me.

Clerk of said City..

CHAPTER XIV.

Relative to the Sale of Lands for Taxes and Assessments.

SEC. 1. Whenever the City Collectors, Supervisors, Marshal or other officer of said city, authorized to collect any tax or assessment on any lands, tenements, hereditaments or premises in said city, or on the owners or occupants thereof, shall make due return that such tax or assessment remains due and uncollected, it shall be the duty of the City Treasurer, on behalf of the Common Council, to proceed and sell such lands, tenements, hereditaments and premises in the manner hereinafter prescribed. When lots to be sold for taxes.

SEC. 2. The Treasurer shall make out a list of all such lands, the names, if known, of the owners or occupants, the amount of the delinquent tax or assessment due thereon according to such return; and Treasurer shall give notice of sale the Treasurer on behalf of the Common Council, shall cause such list, with a notice thereto attached, to be published four weeks successively, once in each week, in the official newspaper of said city, requiring the owners, occupants or lessees of such lands, tenements, hereditaments and premises, against whom such assessments may have been made, to pay the same; and further notifying them, that if default shall be made in any such payment, such real estate will be sold at public auction, at a day and place therein to be specified, for the lowest term of years at which any person will offer to take the same, in consideration of advancing the sum assessed or taxed on the same, with the costs and charges in the premises.

Lots to be sold if taxes not paid.

SEC. 3. If, notwithstanding such notice, the owner or owners, occupant or occupants, lessee or lessees, or person or persons liable to pay such tax, shall neglect or refuse to pay the same with the cost and charges thereon, then the Treasurer, on behalf of the Common Council, at the place and on the day mentioned in such notice, shall commence the sale of such lands, and shall continue the same from day to day, (Sundays excepted,) until the same be sold for a term of years, for the purpose and in the manner already above expressed; but each lot or parcel of a lot owned by any one person or set of persons against whom such assessment has been made, shall be sold by itself.

Treasurer to report sale to Common Council, when purchaser entitled to conveyances and on what terms.

SEC. 4. At the close of the sale, the Treasurer shall report to the Common Council the terms for which each lot was sold, the amount bid therefor, and the name of the purchaser; and if there be no sufficient objection, the several purchasers shall be entitled to the necessary conveyances of said premises, when the time of redemption fixed by law shall have fully expired, upon paying for the expense of such conveyance the further sum of fifty cents, unless such lot shall have been sooner redeemed, in which case the purchaser shall be entitled to receive the purchase money and interest.

Treasurer to report to Council neglect of purchasers to pay.

SEC. 5. The purchasers at such sale shall pay the amount of their respective bids to the Treasurer within forty-eight hours after the sale, and if they shall neglect or refuse to pay the same within that time, the Treasurer shall report the names of such persons to the Common Council, who may elect to take the lots bid off by such purchaser.

Attorney to prepare conveyance.

SEC. 6. The City Attorney shall prepare the necessary conveyance and deliver the same to the Mayor, or in his absence, to the Recorder, who shall, under the corporate seal and in the corporate name, execute to the purchaser, his heirs or assigns, a declaration of sale of the land so sold, which shall be attested by the Clerk.

Treasurer to keep a record of land sales,

SEC. 7. The Treasurer shall keep a correct record of all land sales, showing the time when the tax or assessment was levied, and the amount therefor, the cost and charges, the time when the lands were sold, the name of the purchaser or his assignee, the term for which the same were bid off, the time when redeemed, and by whom, with such other entries as may be necessary in the premises. Any person entitled to redeem any such lot, may, within one year from the time of sale, pay the amount due thereon, including all costs and charges, to the City Treasurer, who shall give proper receipts therefor, and shall enter a note of such redemption on said record. Whenever any premises, lands, tenements or hereditaments shall be returned hereafter for the non-payment of any tax or assessment, interest upon the same shall be charged as follows: fifteen per cent. per annum from the date when the same shall be so returned, up to and until the date of the sale of such premises, or the payment of the amount of such tax with interest at said rate, and from and after the sale of any lands, tenements or hereditaments, interest upon the amount for which the same shall be sold, shall be computed and charged at the rate of twenty per cent. per annum, and no person shall be entitled after sale to redeem any premises sold without payment of the said interest and principal in the manner prescribed by law.

How lands so sold may be redeemed.

SEC. 8. The following or other sufficient forms may be used in proceedings under this chapter:

Forms.

Notice of Tax Sale.

STATE OF MICHIGAN, } ss.
City of Detroit. }

Notice is hereby given, that pursuant to law, there will be sold, at the Common Council Hall in the city of Detroit and State of Michigan, between the hours of and , in the forenoon of the day of , A. D. 18 , at public auction, the several premises hereinafter described, each parcel separately, for the lowest term of years at which any person will offer to take the same, in consideration of advancing the sum or sums which were asssessed or taxed by the

TITLE II. CHAPTER 14.

Common Council of said city for the year one thousand eight hundred and, (or on the day of one thousand eight hundred and to defray the expenses of paving or planking side walks, or otherwise as the case may be, in front of or adjacent to the several premises; together with costs and charges in the premises;) unless the said sum or sums, with the costs and charges thereon shall before that time be paid and satisfied, which the owners or occupants of said premises, against whom said sum or sums have been assessed, are hereby required to do. [Here insert an accurate description of the several premises, and add to the description of each, the amount assessed, the name of the individual or individuals against whom the same is assessed, and also the amonnt of the costs and charges, if any up to that time.]

Names.	Description of lots.	Amount of Tax.	Costs of Assessment. *

Dated at the city of Detroit, this day of A. D. 18 -

By order of the Common Council,

City Treasurer.

Form of Declaration of Sale.

This indenture made the day of in the year of our Lord one thousand eight hundred and , between the Mayor, Recorder, Aldermen and Freemen of the city of Detroit, in the State of Michigan, of the first part; and of the second part: *Whereas*, in pursuance of, and in conformity with, the provisions of the laws of said State, relative to the city of Detroit aforesaid, providing for the assessment and collection of taxes and assessments imposed and laid by the authority of the Common Council of the city of Detroit, the lot of land hereinafter described, was, on the day of in the year one thousand eight hnndred and , duly sold for the payment

* This column is unneccssary except in cases of special assessments.

of the assessment (or tax) imposed thereon by the Common Council for the year one thousand eight hundred and , [if it be a special tax, say after the word "Council,"—on the day of , in the year, etc., for the expense of constructing a sidewalk in front of, and adjacent to, the said lot or premises; or other special assessment, as the case may be,] to the said party of the second part, for the sum of dollars and cents, it being the amount of the taxes and costs, and charges on said lot, for the term of years which was the least term for which any person offered to take the same, in consideration of advancing the said sum of money; and the said party of the second part having advanced and paid said sum of money as required by law.

Now, therefore, this indenture witnesseth, that the said party of the first part, in pursuance of law, and in pursuance of the sale aforesaid, and also in consideration of the premises, and of the said sum of money being duly paid and advanced as aforesaid, by the said party of the first part, the receipt whereof is hereby confessed, do by these presents declare, that they demise and lease unto the said party of the second part, executors, administrators and assigns, all that said piece or parcel of land, situate in said city of Detroit, and State of Michigan, known and described as , together with all and singular, the benefits, liberties and privileges to said premises belonging; to have and to hold the said demised premises with the appurtenances, unto the said party of the second part, executors, administrators and assigns, for and during the full end and term above mentioned, fully to be completed and ended; (and if the above lot shall not be redeemed according to law, within one year from the day of these presents will become absolute.)

[L.S.] In testimony whereof, I Mayor of said city of Detroit, and on the behalf of the said parties of the first part, have hereunto set my hand, and caused to be affixed hereunto the corporate seal of said city, at the city of Detroit, the day and year first above written.

The Mayor, Recorder, Aldermen and Freemen of the city of Detroit,

By ————, *Mayor of said city.*

Attest:

————, *Clerk of said city.*

TITLE II.
CHAPTER 15.

CHAPTER XV.

Relative to paving Sidewalks, Avenues or Streets, and constructing Crosswalks.

Side walks, cross walks and streets to be paved or planked.

SEC. 1. That the side and crosswalks of all streets and avenues, which are or shall be graded, and all streets and avenues, shall be paved or planked with such materials as the Common Council may direct.

Persons paving, &c., in front of their premises exempted from tax.

SEC. 2. If the owner of any lot or premises has or shall have paved or planked the street in front of his premises to the centre thereof, according to the provisions of this chapter, and shall keep the same in good repair, such premises shall be exempt, and the owner thereof shall not be liable to pay any assessments for highway labor, upon his producing satisfactory evidence to the Supervisor that such person has or shall have so paved or planked such streets, or paid therefor, and shall have kept the same in good repair; and no such exemption shall be allowed to any person or persons except in the manner, and on the terms and conditions above expressed.

SEC. 3. The owner of all lots on streets which have been graded and prepared for the laying down of sidewalks, under the direction of the Common Council, are hereby authorized to pave or plank in front of their lots, under the direction of such officer or committee as the Common Council may direct.

Owners may pave or plank in front of their lots.

Sidewalks.

SEC. 4. Whenever the Common Council of said city shall deem it necessary to provide funds for defraying the expenses of paving or planking any sidewalks within the limits of said city, they shall do so by assessment on the owners or occupants of the lots or premises in front or adjacent to the sidewalks paved or planked, or directed so to be; and whenever it may be necessary to provide for the expense of constructing any crosswalks in said city, the assessments for the same shall be made in accordance with the provisions of this chapter, particularly relating thereto.

How money raised for sidewalks.

SEC. 5. Whenever the said Common Council shall have paved or planked any sidewalks in said city, or shall direct the same to be paved or planked, the City Surveyor shall make an assessment on the owner or occupants of the lots or premises in front of or adjacent to said sidewalks paved or planked, or directed so to be.

Surveyor to assess expense.

SEC. 6. The said City Surveyor shall, with all due diligence, ascertain from the best evidence in his power, all the necessary facts, and shall then make out a written report or assessment roll, stating therein the names of the owners or occupants of the lots or premises in front of, or adjacent to which such sidewalks may be paved or planked, or directed so to be; describing by itself, with sufficient accuracy, each lot or portion of a lot owned by any one person or company of persons, and also the names of such owner or several owners; and when he cannot ascertain the names of any such owners or occupants, or either of them, he shall state such fact in his report, and he shall therein state who of such owners are residents of said city, and who are non-residents; and said City Surveyor shall also, in as accurate a manner as possible, ascertain, and in said report set forth the space or number of square yards or feet paved or planked, and the quantity of curbing placed, or to be placed in front of or adjacent to the lots or premises owned or occupied by any one person or set of persons, the sum of money which such person or set of per-

Mode of assessment.

TITLE II. CHAPTER 15.

Contents of Surveyor's report to be presented to the Council.

sons shall be assessed at and pay for such paving or planking, and also five cents for each description to defray the expense of making such assessment which report the said City Surveyor ; shall present to said Common Council.

Clerk to notify owners of lots assessed by public notice.

SEC. 7. The City Clerk shall then make out a notice, directed to the several persons in said report named and proposed to be assessed, notifying them that they are about to be assessed, to defray the expenses of paving or planking the sidewalks adjacent to certain premises owned or occupied by them in said city, and that a report or assessment roll made out in the premises is on file in the office of said Clerk, for inspection, and further notifying them of the time and place when the Common Council will meet and review said report or assessment, on the request of any person conceiving himself aggrieved; which said notice shall be published in some daily newspaper printed in said city, four times during ten days.

Collector to serve notice of assessment on certain persons. Contents of notice.

SEC. 8. In addition to the printed notice provided for in the last preceding section, the City Collector, as soon as any such assessment shall have been made, shall forthwith serve or cause to be served upon all persons therein interested, who are residents of the city, a written or printed notice, by delivering the same to them personally, or leaving it at the party's usual place of abode or business, which said notice shall fully set forth the place where said sidewalk, paving or planking is ordered, and that said party is allowed ten days within which to construct the same; and if completed within that time to the satisfaction of the City Surveyor, that no expense of proceedings to collect the same shall be incurred by them ; and upon the expiration of said thirty days, the Collector shall make a full return to the Council of his doings, under this section, and state fully whether such notices have or have not been complied with by said parties ; and if from such return it appears that said sidewalks, paving or planking have not been constructed within the ten days prescribed, by the parties notified ; then the amount of such assessment, together with all costs and charges incident to the collection thereof, shall be collected by warrant issued for that purpose by the Common Council, according to the provisions of chapter ten of these ordinances "relative to a City Collector."

Council to examine and approve assessment.

SEC. 9. The said Common Council shall, at the time and place in said section specified, or at some session thereafter, take said assessment into consideration, and if no person appears to object to said report or roll, and no good cause to the contrary appears, and an affidavit of publication of the requisite notice having been made by some one acquainted with the facts, they shall, by a written resolution to be entered on their journal, declare that they approve of said report or assessment roll; that they receive as correct the description of the premises and the names of the individuals therein contained, and that the sum which said report states to be the correct one, which each individual or set of individuals should be assessed at and pay, be the assessment, and be collected from the respective persons liable, according to law; but if any sufficient cause appears, or is shown to said Common Council, they shall review said report or roll, and make such an assessment as may be just and right in the premises; and said Common Council may, if necessary, adjourn from one time to any reasonable time, for the purpose of finishing said review of said assessment.

Plank Side Walks.

When plank walks may be laid.

SEC. 10. The Common Council may from time to time authorize that good and substantial plank sidewalks shall be laid down and constructed in any street or part of a street, whether graded or not, as hereinbefore described, and under the direction of the City Surveyor.

How plank walks constructed.

SEC. 11. Such sidewalks shall be constructed of good pine or oak plank, which shall not be less than two inches in thickness, nor more than twelve inches wide, on oak, cedar, or hemlock sleepers, not less than four inches square, to be placed not more than three feet apart, the plank to be nailed with nails not less than forty penny, with at least three in each end of each plank, and not less than two at any other bearing, and said walks shall be of the following width: On Jefferson and Woodward avenues, six feet; and on all other streets, three feet; *Provided, however*, That the Common Council may at any time direct that such sidewalk on any street or part thereof, be of more or less width than is hereinbefore described, and all crosswalks shall be constructed of oak plank, not less than two and one-half inches thick, and twelve inches wide, to be laid and fastened as in this section above prescribed for sidewalks; such crosswalks to be of such width as shall be ordered by the Common Council.

TITLE II. CHAPTER 13.

Assessment for plank walks, how made.

SEC. 12. When the Common Council shall direct the construction of any such plank sidewalk, the City Surveyor shall proceed and make an assessment therefor, showing the names of the owners or occupants, (residents or non-residents,) of the premises in front of which such sidewalk is required, with a description of such premises, the length and width of such walk, and the sum of money to be assessed for constructing the same; and when any such assessment shall be completed, the same shall be reported to the Common Council, and such further proceedings had as are required by sections seven, eight and nine of this chapter.

Persons may construct their own walks.

SEC. 13. Any parties interested shall have the privilege of constructing a plank sidewalk in front of their respective premises after the same shall have been ordered by the Council, within the time and after the same manner as is hereinbefore provided in section eight, and shall be entitled to all the rights and privileges secured by said section.

When Council to construct walks. Who liable for expense thereof.

SEC. 14. Whenever an assessment has been duly levied, according to the provisions of this chapter, and a return of the warrant issued for the collection of the same by the City Collector, under the provisions of section eight, has been made, the Common Conncil shall proceed to the construction of the sidewalk as ordered, and the property of all persons whose assessments have not been paid shall be held liable for all costs, charges and interest incurred on their behalf in the construction of said sidewalks, and may be sold for the same, as in the case of delinquent taxes.

Certain mistakes not to vitiate assessment.

SEC. 15. Whenever by mistake or otherwise, any person may be improperly designated as the owner or occupant of any lot or premises in proceedings under this chapter or any other ordinance of said city relative to taxes or assessments, the tax or assessment shall not for such cause be vitiated, but the same shall be a lien on such lot or premises, and collected as in other cases.

Streets and Avenues.

Funds to plank or grade or pave streets—how raised.

SEC. 16. Whenever the Common Council of said city shall deem it necessary to provide funds necssary for defraying the expenses of grading, paving, or planking any alley, avenue or street of said city, or any portions thereof, they shall cause an assessment to be made by the City Surveyor on the owners or occupants of premises in front of or adjacent to avenue or street directed to be graded, paved, or planked.

Assessment for cross streets.

SEC. 17. The said City Surveyor shall make a separate assessment on the lots or premises so assessed, as aforesaid, for the grading, paving or planking any cross street or avenue, in such proportions as he shall deem just and equitable, provided each block shall only be assessed to the centre of such cross street or avenue, each way.

How assessment for paving and planking made.

SEC. 18. The manner of making said assessments, and all other subsequent proceedings in the premises, shall be the same as are required under the provisions of sections six, seven and nine of this chapter, except that the notice be given by the City Clerk, under the provisions of section seven, shall notify persons to be assessed that they are about to be assessed to defray the expenses of grading, paving or planking the street or streets and alleys adjacent to certain premises owned or occupied by them, &c.

Collection of assessments.

SEC. 19. If the owners or occupants shall omit to grade, pave or plank said avenues or streets in front of or adjacent to their respective lots or premises, or pay their proportion of the assessment for grading, paving or planking any cross street, avenue, or alleys, so that the expenses of all grading done shall be assessed upon the property fronting the same, within such time as the Common Council may by resolution direct, then the said Common Council may issue their warrant for the collection of said assessment, and all costs and charges thereon, and on failure of the proper officer to collect the same, the said lots or premises shall be sold agreeably to the provisions of chapter eighteen of these ordinances, "Relative to the collection of special assessments."

Of what materials plank roads to be constructed.

SEC. 20. Such avenues or streets, or such portions thereof as the Common Council may direct to be planked, shall be done with good sound pine, oak or hemlock plank, not less than four inches in thickness, nor more than ten inches in width, said planks to be spiked or pinned down solid, on timbers not less than four inches in thickness, nor eight inches in width, of the same material, and firmly imbedded in the earth, so that the lower surface of the plank shall rest on the earth as well as the bed timbers, which shall be put down not more than four feet apart, said planks to be laid crosswise in the said avenues or streets, and the ends placed firmly against the curb-stones of the side-

TITLE II. CHAPTER 15.

walks, so as to leave the upper surface of the planks five inches below the top of the curb-stones, and the corner to be filled with one-half of a stick of timber five inches square, sawed through the extreme corners, the back well fitted to the curb, and spiked down solid to the plank, so as to prevent the water from washing the sand from between the curb-stones and pavement. All planks to be laid according to the established grade of the avenue or street. The work to be done to the satisfaction of the Common Council, or such committee as they shall appoint to inspect the same.

Cross Walks.

Assessments for repairing and constructing cross walks.

SEC. 21. The expense of construction and the repairs of all crosswalks over the streets and alleys of the city, hereafter to be made, and not already provided for, shall be defrayed by a rateable assesssment upon the real property of one-quarter of each of the blocks so to be connected, and being that half respectively which lies in the line of direction of the crosswalk; and said assessment shall be taken from the general assessment roll of the city for the current year.

When Council to direct construction of crosswalks

SEC. 22. Whenever a majority of the taxable inhabitants of each of any two blocks to be connected, shall petition the Common Council to have a crosswalk constructed to connect said blocks, the Common Council will order the construction of such crosswalk at such point or points of connection as the petitioners may designate, and of the width prayed for; and whenever a less number than such majority shall so petition, or the Common Council shall direct without petition, the construction of such walk shall not be ordered except upon a report thereon by the Committee on the Streets of said city.

Street Commissioner to construct crosswalks and warrant to issue for collection of assessment for the same.

SEC. 23. As soon as a crosswalk shall be ordered, in pursuance of the foregoing provisions, the Street Commissioner shall proceed without delay to construct the same, but at a rate not exceeding the usual relative rates paid by the city for similar constructions; and the City Surveyor shall report the assessment for constructing the same at the next succeeding meeting of the Common Council, for confirmation, and upon such confirmation, a warrant shall issue for the amount of said assessment, and the Street Commissioner shall proceed at once to collect the same.

Repairs.

SEC. 24. All planked or paved streets, sidewalks and alleys in the city of Detroit, shall be kept in good repair by the owner or occupant of the house, lot or premises adjoining or fronting on such street, and whenever any street, sidewalk or alley within the limits of said city shall require repairing it shall be the duty of the Mayor, Recorder, Aldermen, Street Commissioner, or Marshal, or any or either of them, to notify verbally, or in writing, or by a printed notice, the owner or occupant of such house, lot or other premises, adjacent to or fronting on such parts of said street, sidewalk or alley needing such repairs, to repair the same forthwith; and if the owner or occupant of such property refuse or neglect to repair the same for the space of two days, after being served with such notice, it shall be the duty of the Street Commissioner and Marshal, or either of them, to enter a complaint before the Mayor's Court against such owner or occupant, and on conviction before the Mayor's Court, the person so refusing or neglecting to repair such street, sidewalk or alley, shall pay a fine of twenty dollars, in the discretion of the Court and costs of prosecution for every time he shall be so convicted. On conviction before the Mayor's Court as provided in the preceding section, in addition to the fines therein provided, the Common Council may order such street, sidewalk or alley to be repaired, and the expense of so doing shall stand as an assessment against the owner of such property, and be collected accordingly.

When Street Commissioner to notify owners to repair &c.

SEC. 25. All expenses for making assessments under this chapter or any other ordinance, together with the expense of printing notices, and all other charges relating to such assessments, shall be justly apportioned by the City Clerk to the persons liable to pay said assessments, and shall be collected at the same time.

Expense of making assessment to be paid by the person assessed.

SEC. 26. The Common Council may at any time, by resolution, to be entered on their journal, authorize or require any person or officer of the corporation of said city, to perform the same duties which are hereinbefore required to be performed by the Street Commissioner, or other officer.

The Council may authorize any other person to do the duty of Street Commissioner.

SEC. 27. Any person or persons who shall in any manner be guilty of a wanton injury to any side or crosswalk, paving or planking, within the limits of the city, by impairing, destroying, or removing

Penalty for injuring streets, &c.

TITLE II. CHAPTER 15.

the same, or any part thereof, shall, on conviction thereof, in the Mayor's Court, be subject to a fine not exceeding fifty dollars.

SEC. 28. The following or other sufficient forms shall be used in proceedings under the provisions of this chapter.

Forms of proceeding under this chapter.

No. 1.

RESOLUTION..

Resolved, That a plank sidewalk, (or a brick or stone sidewalk, as the case may be,) be constructed on street in this city, between and , and that the City Surveyor make an assessment of the expense of the same, according to the ordinance in such case made and provided.

No. 2.

Assessment Roll for Constructing a Plank Sidewalk from to in the City of Detroit, on the year A. D. 18 .

Names of Residents	Names of Non-Residents.	Description of lots.	Width of walk.	length of walk.	Am't of tax.	Costs of ass't.	Final costs	Total.

To the Hon. the Common Council:

I herewith report to your Hon. body the foregoing report or assessment as correct and just.

Dated at Detroit, this day A. D. 18 .

City Surveyor.

[Let the assessment roll be filed by the Clerk.]

No. 3.

Notice to Persons to be Assessed.

STATE OF MICHIGAN, }
City of Detroit, } ss.

To (here insert the names of those to whom directed, and add,) *or to any other person interested in the premises, within the limits hereafter mentioned:*

You are hereby notified that assessments are about to be made, upon you to defray the expenses of constructing plank sidewalks, (or paving the sidewalks, or streets, as the case may be,) in front of, or adjacent to certain premises or lots of land owned or occupied by you respectively, on street, in the city of Detroit, State of Michigan: and also, that a report or assessment roll has been made in the premises, which is on file in the office of the Clerk of said city, where it will remain open for your inspection until the day of A. D. 18 , when and where you may appear and show cause before the Common Council, in the Common Council house in said city, why the said assessment should not be made and collected according to law.

By order of the Common Council,

———, *City Clerk.*

Dated at the city of Detroit, this day of A. D. 18 .

[After the time mentioned in the notice, and on filing affidavit thereof, let a resolution of the following form be entered on the journal:]

Whereas, It appears by affidavit on file, that due notice has been given to the owners and occupants of premises fronting on street in the city of Detroit, that the Common Council would, on the day of A. D. 18 , meet and review the report or assessment roll filed by the City Clerk on the day of A. D. 18 , for the expense of constructing in front of said premises: *And whereas,* No person has appeared before the Common Council, to object to said assessment, or the confirmation thereof; (if there be any objection, say after the word "whereas"—all objections thereto have been duly considered,) therefore

Resolved, That said assessment roll is hereby approved and confirmed; that the description of premises and the names of persons contained therein, are received as correct; and that the sums which the said assessment roll states to be the correct ones which each individual, or set of individuals, should be assessed at and pay, be the assessment, and be collected from the several persons liable to pay the same according to law.

[Then let the Clerk endorse on the roll, the words: "Approved and confirmed by the Common Council, this day of A. D. 18 ."]

TITLE II. CHAPTER 16.

CHAPTER XVI.

Relative to Road Tax.

Eight road districts established, to consist of one ward each. Qualifications of Supervisors.

SECTION 1. The city of Detroit shall continue as at present, to be divided into eight road districts, each district being composed of and comprehending one of the wards of said city, and each of said districts shall be numbered in accordance with the number of the ward composing the same respectively. At each charter election a Supervisor shall be elected by and for each district, who at the time of his election shall be a freeholder and a resident of the ward composing the district for which he is elected, who shall hold his office for the term of one year, and until his successor is duly elected and qualified.

Supervisors to make a list of persons liable to work on highway by law—shall file said list in office of Comptroller, and thereupon to prepare duplicate assessment rolls for road tax.

SEC. 2. It shall be the duty of said Supervisors respectively, between the first Monday in April and the first Monday in May in each year, to make or cause to be made, a list of all free male persons in the district for which he is elected, who are liable by the laws of this State, to work on the highways, and file the same, together with an affidavit that it is correctly made out, according to the best of his knowledge and ability, in the office of the City Comptroller, who upon receiving said list, shall forthwith, from said list and from the assessment roll of the city for the same year, prepare duplicate assessment rolls for road tax or highway labor on all property in each of said districts, in the manner hereinafter prescribed.

Said rolls to be divided into parts: part 1st residents, part 2d non-residents

SEC. 3. Each of said rolls shall be divided into two parts; the first part shall embrace all assessments upon residents of said city having property subject to be taxed, and shall contain in one column in alphabetical order, the name of each person liable to the payment of a road tax in the district within the same year; one column for the description of the real estate; one column for the valuation thereof; one column for the number of days' work assessed thereon; one column for the amount of personal property; one column for the number of days' work assessed thereon; one column for the day's work as a poll tax, according to the laws of this State; one column showing the total number of days' work for which each person is taxed; and one column showing the amount in dollars and cents. The second part of said roll shall embrace the assessments on the real estate of non-residents of said city, having property situate in the district; and shall contain in one column the names of non-residents, if known; one column showing the description of the property; one column showing the valuation thereof; one column showing the number of days' work taxed to such non-resident; and one column showing the amount in dollars and cents; and when said rolls are prepared, the City Comptroller shall report the same to the Common Council.

Comptroller to report said rolls to Council.

A roll for each district to remain in Clerk's office one day for inspection. What parties aggrieved may do.

SEC. 4. One roll for each district shall remain in the Clerk's office open to the inspection and examination of all persons interested, and if any person or persons consider himself or themselves aggrieved thereby, he or they may, within ten days after depositing of said rolls, appeal to the Common Council to alter or remit any part thereof, by filing with said Clerk a notice of his intention, and his reasons for so doing.

Clerk shall present roll Mayor and at least two Aldermen, who shall annex a warrant thereto.

SEC. 5. It shall be the duty of the Clerk to present the other duplicate assessment rolls to the Mayor, or in his absence, to the Recorder, and at least two Aldermen of said city, who shall annex their warrant thereto, under their hands and the seal of said city, directed to the Supervisor of the proper district and commanding him to require the several persons therein named to pay the amount of tax set opposite their names respectively, according to law; and in default thereof, then that he shall levy the same on the goods and chattels of such persons, and that the Supervisor make a return of his doings to the Common Council, as hereinafter required.

Duplicate and warrant annexed deposited with Comptroller and by him delivered to Supervisors. Supervisors charged with amount of tax.

SEC. 6. Said duplicate, with the warrant annexed, shall be by the Clerk deposited with the City Auditor, who shall deliver the same to the proper Supervisors, and who shall open an account with and charge each Supervisor with the amount of tax contained in his roll.

Supervisors to demand payment of tax, and notice to non-residents, how given.

SEC. 7. Upon receipt of said duplicate with the warrant annexed, it shall be the duty of each of said Supervisors to call upon each person resident in said city, whose name appears upon his roll, and demand the amount of his assessment or commutation, and also upon the agent, (if resident in said city,) of any non-resident, whose lands or property is assessed in his district, and make like demand: *Provided*, That if the Supervisor cannot ascertain that any such non-resident has an agent in said city, he shall affix a written notice on the outer door of the City Hall of said city, and and also insert a notice in the official paper, containing a list of the names of such non-residents, when known, and a description of the lots assessed to them, together with the number of days' labor assessed upon each lot, and the amount of commutation money therefor.

Supervisors to add to rolls names of persons not assessed.

SEC. 8. The names of all persons left out of said rolls, and of new inhabitants of either of said districts, who have not been personally assessed for the same year, and who are liable to pay road tax, shall be added to the assessment roll by the Supervisor of the proper district, subject to an appeal to the Common Council within ten days after notice.

Persons to be assessed sixty cents per day.

SEC. 9. Hereafter the number of days for which any person or property shall he assessed for highway labor, shall be charged at the rate of sixty cents for each day, and the same shall be collected and paid in money, and not in labor or otherwise.

When Supervisors may distrain for amount of tax.

SEC. 10. In case any person shall neglect or refuse to pay the amount of the said road tax, three days after the demand made upon him or his agent by the Supervisor; or in case of non-residents who have no resident agent, for twenty days after said notice has been given, the said Supervisor shall levy the same by distress and sale of the goods and chattels of the person or persons so neglecting or refusing, wherever the same may be found in the said city; and if the Supervisor shall be unable to find any goods and chattels whereon to levy and satisfy said assessment, then the person liable therefor may be sued, and the amount recovered in the corporate name of said city, in the Mayor's Court, in the same manner as in other cases of debts due to the corporation.

To give ten days notice previous to sale of property destined.

SEC. 11. Whenever any property shall be levied upon as provided in section ten, the Supervisor shall give at least ten days previous notice of the sale thereof, by posting up a written or printed notice of the time and place of sale, and the property to be sold, in at least three public places in said city, and the sale shall be by public auction.

When and how Supervisors shall return taxes as unpaid.

SEC. 12. Whenever either of the Supervisors shall not be able to collect the amount of highway labor assessed on the lands and tenements of any person residing in said city, such Supervisor shall return the same as directed in the following section.

SEC. 13. Each of said Supervisors shall, on or before the first Tuesday in September in each year, make out and deliver to the Common Council, if then in session, but if not, then at their next ensuing session, a list of all the lands of residents, non-residents, and persons unknown, who were taxed on his roll, on which the labor assessed has not been paid, and the amount of labor unpaid; and the said Supervisor, previous to delivering such list, shall make out and subscribe an affidavit thereon, before the City Clerk, or other person authorized to administer oaths, stating therein that he has given the notice required in the ordinance, that he has not, upon diligent enquiry and attention thereto, been able to find any person or persons who would pay, or of whom he could collect the amount of said highway tax or taxes, or any goods or chattels of the person liable to pay the same, on which he could lawfully levy and sell for said highway labor; that the account thereof is just and true, as contained in said list, and that the said tax remains unpaid.

Supervisors subject to fine for neglect to make return.

SEC. 14. If either of said Supervisors shall refuse or neglect to deliver such list, or make such affidavit thereon, he shall, for every such offence, forfeit the sum of five dollars, and also the amount of taxes for labor remaining unpaid, at the rate of seventy-five cents for each day's labor: *Provided, however,* The Common Council may authorize such Supervisor to make such return and affidavit at any

TITLE II. CHAPTER 16.

time after the said first Tuesday of September: *Provided, also,* That if any of the duties required by this chapter to be performed on a certain day be not performed, the Common Council shall have power to appoint another day for performance of any such duties.

The assessment returned to be levied on lands and tenements on which they are assessed.

SEC. 15. The amount of such assessment returned unpaid, shall be levied on the lands and tenements so returned, and collected in the same manner and at the same time that lands and tenements are sold for the non-payment of city taxes, unless the Common Council otherwise direct.

To deposit the amount of tax collected once in two weeks

SEC. 16. Each of said Supervisors shall, once in each two weeks, pay to the City Treasurer all money by him collected on account of road tax; and the Treasurer shall give him a receipt therefor, and credit the road fund with the amount paid in.

To render an account to Comptroller once a year, and what to contain.

SEC. 17. Each of said Supervisors shall, on the first day of October in each year, render to the said Auditor and account in writing, verified by his oath, and containing—

1. The number of days' work contained in his assessment roll, and the amount of the tax in dollars and cents.

2. The names of all persons added by him to the assessment roll, and the number of days and the amount of their assessment.

3. The names of all who have paid their assessment, and the amount paid by each.

4. The names of those from whom he has been unable to collect, and the amounts.

5. The amount of money drawn from the Treasury, and expended on the highway; how, and to whom paid, &c.

6. The number of days said Supervisor shall have actually been engaged in working, or superintending work on the highways of his district, and the amount of his compensation: *Provided*, The Common Council may, at any time, require the said Supervisors, and each of them, to report their doings under this or any other ordinance respecting them.

General duty of Supervisors.

SEC. 18. It shall be the duty of the Supervisors to examine into the condition of the streets, lanes and alleys, in their several districts and to report upon the same to the Street Commissioner whenever any repairs or improvements are necessary; and to superintend and direct, under the control of said Street Commissioner, all things in any manner pertaining to the making and improving of the highways in his district, according to the best of his ability. It shall also be the duty of the Supervisor of each district to keep a book, in which he shall record the name of every person in his employ on the highway of his district, and the number of days which each person so employed shall actually work, together with the number of days which such Supervisor may actually work; and it shall be the duty of the Supervisor of each district in the city to report to the Street Commissioner on the last Saturday of every two weeks, in each month, the names of all persons who have actually worked in his employ on the highway of his district; and also the number of days which such Supervisor shall have so actually worked, together with the number of days each person shall have worked on the highway of the district to which such Supervisor shall belong.

Pay of Supervisors.

SEC. 19. Each Supervisor shall be allowed the sum of one dollar and fifty cents for each day he shall actually be employed, and work on the highways of his district, and also five per cent. on all moneys collected by him, which shall be in full for all services: *Provided*, The time occupied in collections shall not be computed in the time for which he is allowed a per diem.

Treasurer to inform Comptroller of amount deposited by each Supervisor or how amount deposited to be drawn from the Treasury.

SEC. 20. It shall be the duty of the Treasurer, from week to week, to keep the Comptroller informed of the amount collected and deposited on account of each district, and the same shall be drawn out in the manner following. Whenever it shall appear to the Aldermen of the ward that any repairs or other improvements are necessary in the district composing their ward, they shall so represent to the Common Council, specifying the repairs and amount of expenditure necessary; whereupon, the Council shall, if right, order the allowance of so much money from the amount collected by such district, which shall be certified by the Clerk to the Comptroller, the same as other claims allowed. The Comptroller upon receiving the certificate, shall draw a warrant for the amount, as in other cases: *Provided*, That it shall be the duty of the Comptroller, before drawing his warrant, to ascertain that there are funds collected in such district, on deposit, to meet it, so that the money collected in each district may be reserved exclusively for, and expended therein, and not in any other.

SEC. 21. If any Supervisor shall neglect or refuse to perform the duties enjoined by this chapter, or shall wilfully permit or suffer the

TITLE II. CHAPTER 16.

Penalty for Supervisors refusing to perform duty

roads, streets or alleys in his district, to remain without the necessary repairs, or shall neglect or refuse to expend moneys in the manner hereinbefore prescribed, or do any act contrary to the provisions of this chapter, he shall for every such offence, when no penalty is prescribed, forfeit and pay a sum not exceeding one hundred dollars and costs of prosecution.

Fees in certain cases.

SEC. 22. Whenever the Supervisor shall levy and sell personal property by virtue of this chapter, he shall be entitled to the same fees as may be allowed the City Marshal for similar services.

Sec. 23. The following or other sufficient forms may be used in proceedings under this chapter.

Forms.

Assessment roll for highway labor in district No.   in the city of Detroit, in the State of Michigan, for the year A. D. 18   .

Names.	Description of lots.	Valuation of lots.	No. of days.	Valuation of personal property.	No. of days.	Poll Tax.	Total No. of days	Total amount.	
								Dollars.	Cts.

To the Hon. the Common Council:

The Committee on Streets for District No.   of this city, report the foregoing assessment as correct.

Dated at Detroit, this   day of   A. D. 18 .

} Committee on Streets, District No.

Form of Warrant.

STATE OF MICHIGAN, } ss.
City of Detroit. }

To   Supervisor of District No.   of said city:

In the name of the people of the State of Michigan, you are hereby commanded to require the several persons named in the foregoing assessment roll to pay the amount of commutation money for road tax set opposite their respective names, according to law; and you are hereby authorized and required in case any such person shall neglect or refuse to pay his, her or their tax, to levy the same by distress and sale of the goods and chattels of such person; and you are further commanded that on or before the first Tuesday of September next ensuing, you make a true return to the Common Council of said city, of all lands on which the taxes have not been paid; and, also, that on or before the first day of October next, you make a final return to said Common Council of your doings in the premises, as required by law.

In testimony whereof, we have hereunto set our hands [L. S.] and caused the seal of said city to be affixed, at the city of Detroit aforesaid, this day of A. D. 18 .

Mayor.
Aldermen of said city.

Notice of Sale of Property.

STATE OF MICHIGAN, City of Detroit. } ss.

Notice is hereby given, that on the day of A. D. 18 , at o'clock in the noon, the undersigned will sell at public auction, at the in said city, the following property, to wit: (Here describe the property,) which I have distrained, because N. B. hath refused (or neglected) to pay the highway tax imposed on him for the year , and which is to be levied by said sale.

Supervisor of District No. of said city.

Dated at the city of Detroit, this day of A. D. 18

Notice to Non-Residents.

STATE OF MICHIGAN, City of Detroit. } ss.

The undersigned, Supervisors of Road District No. of said city, cannot ascertain that the non-resident land holders, whose lands hereinafter described, as assessed for highway labor for the year year 18 , have any agent within said city: Notice is therefore hereby given, that the number of day's labor set opposite to the description of each of the following lots, has been assessed thereon, to wit:

TITLE II.
CHAPTER 16.

Names of non-residents.	Description of lots.	No. of day's labor assessed.	Dollars.	Cents.

Given at the city of Detroit aforesaid, this day of A. D. 18 .

Supervisor of District No. in said city.

Return of Delinquent Taxes.

STATE OF MICHIGAN, City of Detroit. } ss.

To the Hon. the Common Coucil of said city:

The following is a list of all the lands of residents and non-residents, which were taxed on the roll of the undersigned, Supervisor of Road District No. in said City, on which lands the tax assessed for the year has not been paid, to wit:

Names.	Description of Lots	Valuation.	No. of days.	Amount.

Made at the city of Detroit aforesaid, this day of A. D. 18 .

Supervisor of District No. in said city.

(This list to be delivered on or before the first Tuesday of September, to the Common Council, and previous to such delivery, the Supervisor must make or subscribe before the City Clerk, or some Justice of the Peace, an affidavit whereof the following is a form:)

STATE OF MICHIGAN, City of Detroit. } ss.

A. B., Supervisor of Road District No. of said city, being duly sworn, saith: That the foregoing return contains the description of all lands which were taxed on the assessment roll of District No. in said city, for the year A. D. That he has given the notice required by the ordinance of said city, entitled "relative to road taxes;" that he has not, upon diligent inquiry and attention thereto, been able to find any person or persons who would pay, or of whom he could collect the amount of said highway tax, mentioned in the annexed list as unpaid, or any goods or chattels of the person liable to pay the same, in said city, whereon he could lawfully levy and sell for the assessment of said highway tax; that the account thereof as contained in said annexed list, is just and true, and that the said tax remains unpaid as set forth in said list.

Supervisor of Road District
No. in said city.

Subscribed and sworn to
this day of
A. D. 18 , before me.

Supervisor's General Return.

STATE OF MICHIGAN.
City of Detroit. } ss.

To the Hon. the Common Council of said city:

The undersigned, Supervisor of Road District No. of said city, begs leave to submit to your honorable body a final statement and account of the highway labor assessed in said district the present year.

Names of persons.	No. of Days.	Commuted.	Collected.	Not Collected.

Dated at the city of Detroit, this day of A. D. 18 .

Supervisor of District
No. in said city.

Let those added to the list be marked (A.) and those sued be marked (S.)

Let an affidavit that the statement and account is true and correct in all its particulars be attached.

TITLE II.
CHAPTER 17.

CHAPTER XVII.

Relative to Assessment Districts.

SEC. 1. Assessment Districts, how many of them.

Assessment districts, how many of them.

SEC. 1. That for the purposes of assessments the city of Detroit be and the same is hereby divided into three assessment districts, numbered respectively one, two and three. Assessment district number one shall comprise and consist of the first, second and eighth wards of said city; assessment district number two of the third, fourth and seventh wards of said city; and assessment district number three of the fifth and sixth wards of said city.

CHAPTER XVIII.

Relative to the manner of obtaining possession of Lots sold for Taxes.

SEC. 1. Possession of lots under tax title how obtained.
SEC. 2. Person refusing to deliver possession may be cited before Mayor's Court.
SEC. 3. Proceedings to obtain possession of lots leased by the city.

Possession of lots under tax title, how obtained

SEC. 1. Whenever the title of any person shall become absolute by virtue of the sale or lease of any lot or parcel of land in said city, in pursuance of the second section of an act, entitled "An act to amend the several acts relative to the city of Detroit," approved April 22, 1833, such person, his legal representative or attorney, shall make demand in writing of the person in possession, and notify him that he claims possession of such lot, by virtue of a sale or lease under said section.

Persons refusing to deliver possession may be cited before Mayor's Court.

SEC. 2. If the person in possession shall neglect or refuse for the space of six days after such demand, to give up possession of such lot, then the person claiming the same may present a petition to the Mayor's Court of said city, verified by his own oath, or by some person for him, setting forth his right to such possession, and praying that a citation may issue, directed to the person in possession; upon filing such petition, the Court may order that a citation issue accordingly, which shall be issued, and be returnable in the same manner as a summons: *Provided*, The petitioner enter into a bond to the Mayor, Recorder, Aldermen and Freemen of the city of Detroit, with such sureties as the Court shall direct, conditioned to pay all costs that may accrue in such proceedings.

Proceedings to obtain possession of lots leased by the city.

SEC. 3. If the defendant appears, he may plead the general issue, and give notice of any special matter which he intends to give in evidence.

Forcible Entry and Detainer.

TITLE III. CHAPTER 19.

Whenever, according to the laws of the State, relative to forcible entry and detainer, the corporation of said city are entitled to the possession of any lands and tenements, the same proceedings shall be had in such case in the Mayor's Court of said city, so far as the same apply, as are authorized before Justices of the Peace: *Provided*, That in all cases the Marshal of said city shall give notice in writing to the persons in possession to quit the same, and in default thereof, for the space of six days thereafter, the Marshal shall make report thereof to the City Attorney.

TITLE THREE.

OF STREETS AND ALLEYS.

CHAPTER XIX.

Relative to the use of Streets and Alleys.

SEC. 1. No person shall leave any wagon, cart, carriage, sleigh or any vehicle, standing or remaining in any of the public streets of said city, the same not being in use at the time, under a penalty not exceeding ten dollars and costs for every offence.

No vehicle to be kept in the streets.

TITLE III. CHAPTER 19.

No horses to be kept in the streets; carts to have lock chains.

SEC. 2. No person shall leave any horse or horses in any of the public streets of said city, without being sufficiently tied; nor shall any person be permitted to use a cart within the limits of said city, unless such cart is provided with a chain to lock the wheel; any person offending against either of these provisions shall be subject to pay a fine not exceeding five dollars and costs, for every offence.

Certain obstructions unlawful.

SEC. 3. No person shall place or cause to be placed any stone, timber, lumber, planks, boards or other materials in or upon any of the public streets, lanes or alleys of said city, unless for the purpose of building; and then only for a period of time not exceeding four months, without leave had of the Mayor or Common Council; any person offending against either of these provisions, shall, for every offence, be subject to pay a penalty not exceeding fifty dollars and costs.

Penalty for.

Obstructions occasioned by buildings.

SEC. 4. No person so building shall obstruct the gutters or more than one-half of the sidewalk, and one-quarter of the carriage way of said street opposite the lot owned by such person, under a penalty not exceeding twenty-five dollars, and a further penalty not exceeding five dollars for every forty-eight hours that any such sidewalk, gutter or street shall afterwards remain obstructed.

Penalty for.

Building materials to be removed when building is finished.

SEC. 5. After the completion of any building, but within the period of four months aforesaid, (unless otherwise permitted by the Mayor or Common Council,) all building materials and rubbish arising therefrom, shall be removed from the street; and any person offending in the premises, shall be liable to pay a penalty not exceeding five dollars for every forty-eight hours such materials or rubbish shall be or remain in such street after the time limited aforesaid and costs.

Penalty for not removing

How drains, water pipes, &c., laid, penalty.

SEC. 6. It shall not be lawful for any person to make or construct any drain or sewer, or lay down any water pipes in any of the public streets of said city, within at least four feet of the curb stone of the sidewalks, unless it shall be the side drain, sewer or water-pipe, leading to or from the building or lot for which it is designed; any person offending against this provision shall be liable to be fined a sum not exceeding twenty dollars and costs.

Damages occasioned by excavations to be repaired.

SEC. 7. Whenever it shall be necessary for any person, with a view to construct or make any such drain or sewer, or lay down any water pipes, or for any other purpose whatsoever, to tear up any pavement, side or crosswalk, or to dig any hole, ditch or drain, in any of the public streets of said city, it shall be the duty of such person, as speedily as practicable, to repair and put all such pavements, side or crosswalks, and streets in as good order and condition as the same were in previously; to pound down the earth so as to make it firm and solid; and as often as the earth shall settle to repair the same; but it shall not be lawful for any person or persons (except the Board of Water Commissioners, by consent of the Committee on Streets and Sewers,) within the limits of said city to excavate, dig or take up any pavement or paved street, side or crosswalk, or to dig any hole, ditch or drain upon any of the public pavements or paved streets, or for any other purpose whatsoever in said city, without having obtained the written consent of the Street Commissioner, upon written application to said Street Commissioner, signed by the person or persons making application for the same; any person offending against any of the provisions of this section shall be subject to pay a penalty for every offence not exceeding twenty dollars and costs.

Owner, or occupants to clear gutters.

SEC. 8. It shall be the duty of every owner or occupant of any house or other building or premises, in the city of Detroit, at all times to keep the drain or gutter in front of the same clear and free from any obstruction that may hinder the free passage of water; any person offending in the premises, shall be liable to pay a fine not exceeding ten dollars for every offence, and costs.

Rubbish, &c., not to be throw into gutters, and no drains shall lead into streets and allies.

SEC. 9. No person shall cast or throw, or cause to be thrown into any of the drains, sewers or gutters within said city, any straw, shavings, wood, stones, rubbish, or any filth or other substance, or cause any obstruction, nuisance or injury in or to the same, by diverting or stopping the water course thereof, or otherwise, under a penalty not exceeding ten dollars and costs for every offence; nor shall any person drain, or permit to be drained, from any lot or cellar owned or occupied by him or her, within the limits of this city, into, or on the surface of any streets or alleys of said city, the water from his or her lot or cellar, under a penalty not exceeding one hundred dollars and costs of prosecution.

Nuisances not to be placed in streets.

SEC. 10. No person shall throw, place or deposit, or suffer his or her servant, child or family, to throw, place or deposit any dung, dead animal, carrion, putrid meat or fish, entrails or decayed vegetables, or

TITLE III. CHAPTER 19.

nuisance of any kind, nor shall he knowingly suffer the same to remain in any street or lane of said city, and any person who shall violate any of the prohibitions of this section, shall forfeit and pay a fine not to exceed five dollars for each offence, and costs of prosecution. The finding of any of the articles named in this section, in front or rear, or side of any lot, shall be *prima facie* evidence that the same were placed there by the occupant or occupants of said lot; and the burden of proof shall rest on the defendant.

Excavations when made—how protected. Penalty.

SEC. 11. No person shall hereafter be permitted to make any excavation in any of the streets or alleys of this city, for any purpose whatever, between the fifteenth day of October and the fifteenth day of April thereafter, unless by special leave of the Common Council; and no excavation in any of the streets or alleys of the city shall be made at any time, unless the person or persons making the same, or causing the same to be made, shall erect a suitable guard or fence about such excavation, and shall, during the night time, cause lights to be attached and maintained to and upon such guard or fence, proper and sufficient to warn all persons passing by or near the same, or approaching the same, of the existence of such obstruction or excavation. Any person or persons violating the provisions of this section, shall forfeit a sum of not exceeding one hundred dollars and costs of prosecution, to be recovered in the Mayor's Court, and shall also be liable for damages to any person or persons injured in the premises, in their person or property.

Streets and alleys not to be used for labor.

SEC. 12. It shall not be lawful for any carpenter, stone mason or other person, to use or occupy any street, lane or alley in the said city, for the purpose of framing timber, or for cutting, sawing or dropping stone, unless by permission of the Common Council of said city, and all persons offending against the provisions of this section, on conviction thereof before the Mayor's Court, shall pay a fine not exceeding twenty-five dollars for every such offence.

Penalty.

No obstructions to be left in the streets at night.

SEC. 13. It shall not be lawful for any person to leave any cart or carriage or sleigh, wood, timber, or any other incumbrance or obstruction, in any of the lanes or alleys of the said city, during the night season, and any person offending herein, on conviction before the Mayor's Court, shall pay a fine not exceeding twenty dollars, and it shall be the duty of the Marshal to remove all such obstructions.

Rate of driving.

SEC. 14. No person or persons shall run or race any horse or horses, or drive any carriage or vehicle of any kind within the limits of the city of Detroit, at a faster rate than six miles per hour, under a penalty for each offence not exceeding ten dollars and costs.

Cattle.

SEC. 15. It shall not be lawful for any person to drive, herd together, or detain in any of the streets, lanes or alleys of this city, any cattle, horses, sheep, hogs, or goats, for any purpose whatever, under a penalty for each offence, not exceeding twenty dollars and costs: *Provided*, That this section shall not extend to sales at auction, under the laws of this State.

Stud horses, penalty for displaying.

SEC. 16. No person shall display and detain for public exhibition, in any of the said streets, lanes or alleys, any stud horse, under a penalty for each offence not exceeding twenty dollars and costs.

Flying kites prohibited.

SEC. 17. No person or persons shall raise or fly any kite in any of the streets or alleys aforesaid, or within the limits of the said city, under a penalty for every offence not exceeding twenty dollars and costs of prosecution.

Earth not to be removed from streets.

SEC. 18. No person or persons shall, unless authorized specially by the Common Council, dig, remove or carry away any earth, loam, sand, gravel or sod, from any of the public grounds within the limits of the city of Detroit, under a penalty for each offence not exceeding fifty dollars with costs of prosecution.

Parents and employees liable for certain offences

SEC. 19. In all cases where any hired servant, apprentice or minor shall be guilty of any breach of the foregoing sections, the master, mistress, employer, parent or guardian of such person so guilty, shall be responsible for the aforesaid penalty.

Marshal and constables to arrest under this chapter.

SEC. 20. That the Marshal and all the Constables of this city are required and directed to notice all infringements of this chapter, and forthwith to arrest and bring before any member of the Common Council all persons guilty of any breach thereof, who shall thereupon give sufficient bail for their appearance at the ensuing term of the Mayor's Court, or on default thereof, to be committed to custody until the holding of said court.

Not lawful to occupy the streets with shantees &c.

SEC. 21. It shall not be lawful for any person or persons to occupy any portion or part of the public streets or sidewalks with any tent, shantee, shop, table or building, wagon or cart, wheelbarrows and horses, for the retail sale of any liquors, groceries, cakes, pies or merchandise. And any person offending against the provisions of this section, shall on conviction be fined in a sum not exceeding five dollars and costs of prosecution ; and it shall be the duty of the Marshal to remove such tent, shantee, shop, table, or building, cart or wagon as a public nuisance: *Provided*, Nothing in this section contained, shall be construed to interfere with the ordinances relative to markets, or bakers supplying their regular customers.

Vehicles not to block side walks.

SEC. 22. It shall not be lawful for any person to have or keep for an unreasonable time, any cart, wagon, dray or other vehicle, on any of the crosswalks in any street or alley of said city, under a penalty for each offence not exceeding fifty dollars and costs of prosecution.

No nuisance permitted in the streets.

SEC. 23. No person shall knowingly permit or suffer his property to be and remain in any street or alley of said city, so as to become a nuisance, under a penalty for each offence not exceeding fifty dollars and costs of prosecution, together with the expense of removing such nuisance.

CHAPTER XX.

Relative to Cleaning Streets.

Committee on streets and City Comptroller authorized to contract with suitable persons to clean streets.

SEC. 1. The Committee on Streets and the City Comptroller are hereby authorized to contract with the lowest bidder, who shall propose to clean such portions of the paved or planked streets, squares or alleys, as the corporation are liable to clean.

Such persons to furnish security.

SEC. 2. The said lowest bidder or person contracting with the corporation as aforesaid, shall furnish satisfactory security for the performance of such contract, provided notice shall be published for one week, in the city paper, previous to receiving proposals for said work.

CHAPTER XXI.

Relative to Sidewalks.

SEC. 1. That the following be established as the width of all sidewalks within the limits of the city of Detroit: Upon streets of one hundred and twenty feet and upwards in width, the sidewalks on each side of the street shall be of the width of twenty feet throughout, exeepting Washington Avenue, which shall be fifty feet; and also excepting that portion of Jefferson Avenue, which lies between Beaubien street and the eastern line of the said city, which shall have on each side of said portion of said avenue, a sidewalk twenty-five feet wide; on streets of one hundred feet, the sidewalks shall be seventeen feet; on streets of eighty or ninety feet wide, the sidewalks shall be fifteen feet wide; on streets of seventy or seventy-two feet, the sidewalks shall be fifteen feet; on streets of sixty feet, the sidewalks shall be ten feet; on streets of fifty feet, the sidewalks shall be nine feet; and on streets of forty feet, the sidewalks shall be eight feet. Dimensions of sidewalks.

SEC. 2. No person or persons shall place or cause to be placed upon any of the sidewalks of this city, any box, barrel, article of merchandize, or other obstructions whatsoever, except so far as the same be necessary and unavoidable in transporting such articles across the sidewalk; nor shall any person be allowed to place or cause to be placed on any stone pavement or flagging within the limits of said city, (except for the purpose of transporting the same across said walk,) any barrels, kegs or boxes of salt, or of any other substance or material, by which said pavement or flagging may in any wise be injured, defaced or destroyed, under a penalty of twenty dollars for each offence. No obstructions to be placed upon side walks penalty for so doing.

SEC. 3. It shall be the duty of the Marshal, upon knowledge or information that any of the sidewalks of the city are in any manner obstructed or incumbered, to require the occupant or occupants, owner or owners, of the lot or premises in front of which such incumbrance exists, to remove it; every such occupant or owner neglecting Marshal to require persons to remove obstructions.

TITLE III. CHAPTER 21.

for the space of twenty-four hours to comply with such requisition, and every person wilfully offending against this section shall, on conviction thereof, be punished by fine not exceeding twenty-five dollars and costs.

When Marshal shall remove obstructions.

SEC. 4. It shall be the duty of the Marshal to remove all obstructions from the sidewalks in front of unoccupied lots or premises.

Awning posts permitted.

SEC. 5. The restrictions above written shall not extend to posts for awnings, shade trees, or the boxes to protect them, which are now standing, nor ladders which are necessarily used in the building or repair of houses, nor be construed so effect the ingress and egress to and from the yards of houses across said walks, unless otherwise ordered by the Common Council.

Horses to be kept off walks.

SEC. 6. Except for the purposes of ingress and egress, no person whatever shall drive, ride or lead any horse, cart or carriage of any kind on any of the sidewalks within this city, under a penalty not exceeding ten dollars for each offence, and being liable to repair and make good all damages caused by him or them, and if the party offending herein shall neglect to get the same repaired within twenty-four hours after the damage, it shall be the duty of the Supervisor for the district to get said repairs made, and the expenses attendant thereon, with a sufficient recompense to the Supervisor, shall be recovered of the party offending in the same manner as the said penalty.

Side walks and gutter to be cleaned.

SEC. 7. From the first day of April to the first day of November in each year, every owner or occupant of any house or lot in any of the streets in which the sidewalks are now made or which shall hereafter be made (excepting such lots whereon buildings may be erecting, and on which materials for building are laid,) shall cause the sidewalk as well as the gutter to be swept or otherwise cleaned on every Saturday during the period aforesaid, under a penalty of one dollar for every omission.

Mayor to appoint persons to clean streets.

SEC. 8. The Mayor shall from time to time appoint so many persons as he may think proper, who shall exclusively have the right and enjoy the emoluments of cleaning on each Monday, or as soon thereafter as is practicable, such parts of the sidewalks and gutters as shall not have been cleaned on the previous Saturday; and the Mayor shall designate to each person so appointed, what part of the city it shall be his duty to attend, for the purpose aforesaid.

SEC. 9. In case the owner or occupant of any house or lot shall neglect to sweep or otherwise clean such sidewalks and gutters on the day directed by this chapter to be done by him or her, it shall be lawful for the person or persons whom the Mayor shall appoint for that purpose, on every succeeding Monday to sweep or otherwise clean such sidewalk and gutter, and for which he shall he entitled to demand twenty-five cents from the owner or occupant of such house or lot, who, on paying said sum, shall be exonarated from the payment of the penalty incurred as aforesaid; but if the said owner or occupant of any such house or lot shall neglect or refuse to pay the said twenty-five cents to such person appointed, it shall be the duty of the Marshal immediately thereafter to cause such owner or occupant to be prosecuted for the penalty aforesaid.

To be cleaned at the expense of occupant or owner.

SEC. 10. The owner or occupant aforesaid shall cause the sidewalks fronting their respective premises, between the first day of November and the first day of April, to be kept free and clear from snow and ice, by sweeping or otherwise removing the same, within twenty-four hours after the said snow shall have fallen, or the ice formed; and in case of any omission the same penalty shall attach, and the same remedy be applied, as is provided in the preceding sections for sweeping and cleaning the sidewalks and gutters.

Snow to be removed from walks.

CHAPTER XXII.

Relative to Awning and Sign Posts.

SEC. 1. No post, except for the purpose of supporting awning or telegraph wires, or hitching horses, shall be erected or put up in any paved street, road, lane or alley of the city of Detroit, unless under the direction of the Street Commissioner, under a penalty of five dollars, in the discretion of the Court, and costs of prosecution, for each offence.

Posts for telegraphs, &c., to be put up under the direction of Street Commissioner. Penalty.

SEC. 2. No wooden post, for the purpose of supporting any awning, shall be erected, or placed upon or before any paved street, lane,

TITLE III. CHAPTER 22.

No wooden posts allowed in certain places. Penalty.

road or alley in this city, under a penalty of ten dollars, in the discretion of the Court, and costs of prosecution, for each day such post shall be suffered to remain after notice to the owner or occupant of the premises from the Mayor, Committee on Streets, Street Commissioner or Marshal, to remove the same.

Awning posts on paved streets of what made and how.

SEC. 3. All posts erected or fixed in any paved street, lane, road or alley, for the purpose of supporting any awning, shall be of iron and of a uniform style, to be made after a certain pattern to be kept in the office of the Street Commissioner, and approved by the Common Council: and such posts shall be placed next to and along side of the curb stone, and be not less than eight feet in height, or of such height as may be determined on by a resolution of the Common Council. Nor shall any person or persons, place or cause to be placed, or suffer to remain across any of the sidewalks within the limits of the city, (except as hereinafter provided in section 4,) rails, or strips of boards, or bars, connecting any posts placed along side the curb stones, with buildings, or any posts, or erection, by the side of any building or buildings, from which any awning or awnings may be suspended, on which to roll up such awnings, or for any other purpose, unless the same be removed when the awning is taken down. Any person violating the provisions of this section, shall pay a fine of not more than ten nor less than three dollars, in the discretion of the Court, and costs of prosecution, for each day he shall so offend.

Penalty.

Rails connecting Awning posts with building prohibited.

SEC. 4. No person shall place, or cause to be placed, any rails or bars connecting said iron posts with buildings, except so far as may be necessary to brace said posts, under the supervision of the Street Commissioner, and said rails or bars shall be removed when the awnings are taken down, under penalty of five dollars for each offence, and costs of prosecution.

Penalty.

Awning cloths not to hang.

SEC. 5. No portion of any awning cloth or canvass used as an awning, shall hang loosely down from the same, within eight feet of the sidewalk or crossing, under a penalty of ten dollars, in the discretion of the Court, and costs of prosecution, for each day that the provisions of this section shall be violated.

Penalty,

SEC. 6. No person shall place or cause to be placed, or shall suspend or cause to be suspended, from any house, shop, store, lot or place, over any street, any sign, lamp, goods, clothes, wares and merchandise, or wares or any other obstructions whatsoever, except frames for the support of awnings, so that the same shall extend or project from the wall or front of such house, shop, store, lot or place, more than three feet towards or into the street. No canvass, for the purpose of an awning, shall hereafter be erected or suspended from any store, house, building, or lot, alongside of, or adjacent to any paved street, lane or alley, unless the same shall be of sufficient length to project from the front of the building to the outer curb stone of said walk, under a penalty of ten dollars, in the discretion of the Court, and costs of prosecution, for each violation of the provisions of this section.

Certain obstructions prohibited.

Penalty.

SEC. 7. No person shall lay or place, or cause to be laid or placed, any coal, wood, merchandise, box, barrel, or other obstruction, upon any sidewalk or crossing, unless for the purpose of removing the same into or out from some store, shop, house, lot or place, and then the same shall not remain upon such sidewalk or crossing for a longer time than six hours, under a penalty of ten dollars, in the discretion of the Court, and costs of prosecution, for each violation of the provisions of this section.

Certain articles not to be placed upon the walks.

CHAPTER XXIII.

Relative to Digging Cellars.

SEC. 1. It shall not be lawful for any person to make and keep open in the front of any building on the line of the streets, any excavations for cellars, doors, windows or areas to any cellar or basement story, of a greater width, including the front wall and ashlar, than seven feet, in streets of the breadth of one hundred feet and upwards, or of a greater width than one-third of the breadth of the sidewalks as established by the existing ordinances of the said city in all other streets.

How cellars may be dug.

SEC. 2. It shall be the duty of the owner of any building in the front of which any excavation or opening shall be made, or if such owner be a non-resident, of his agent or attorney, and also of the per-

TITLE III. CHAPTER 23.

Areas to be closed while cellars are being dug. When finished to be closed permanently.

son or persons contracting or undertaking to execute the same, to cause such excavation to be well secured by a railing or covering, to the satisfaction of the Mayor, Recorder, or any of the Aldermen of the said city, during the prosecution of the work, and within thirty days after the completion of the same, to cause such excavation or opening to be secured by a substantial and permanent railing or enclosure, and all persons offending against the provisions of this chapter hereinbefore contained, on conviction thereof before the Mayor's Court, shall pay a fine not exceeding fifty dollars for every such offence.

Penalty.

Cellars in lanes, direction for digging.

SEC. 3. It shall not be lawful for any person to dig or cause to be dug, or to keep open, any cellar way or other opening in any lane or alley exceeding the width of three feet from the outer line or side of such lane or alley, and it shall be the duty of the person digging or causing to be dug such cellarway or opening, within five days after commencing the same, to cause it to be completed and secured with a substantial hatch or covering, laid even with the surface of said lane or alley, and all cellarways or openings already made in any lane or alley shall be secured in like manner; and all persons offending against this section of this chapter, on conviction thereof before the Mayor's Court, shall pay a fine not exceeding twenty-five dollars for every such offence.

Excavations not in accordance with this chapter nuisances.

SEC. 4. All excavations or openings in any of the streets, lanes or alleys for the purpose aforesaid, which shall not be secured by a railing, hatch or covering as hereinbefore directed, or which shall hereafter be made or dug, contrary to the provisions and the true intent and meaning of this chapter, shall be taken and considered to be a common nuisance, and may be abated by order of the Mayor or Common Council of the said city at the expense of the said person or persons causing or suffering the same to remain.

Persons taking up pavements to relay the same.

SEC. 5. It shall be the duty of any person or persons taking up any pavement or sidewalk, or causing the same to be done in any street, lane or alley for the aforesaid purposes, to replace and repair so much of the said pavement or sidewalk as is not included in said excavation or opening for cellar doors, windows or areas as aforesaid, in as good order and condition in all respects as they were in previously; and in case of the neglect or refusal of the person or persons whose duty it shall be to replace and repair the same, so to do, the said pavements or sidewalks may be replaced by order of the Mayor or Common Council of the said city, at the expense of the person or persons refusing or neglecting as aforesaid.

CHAPTER XXIV.

Relative to Numbering Buildings.

SEC. 1. Whenever the Common Council shall, by resolution, direct the public streets or avenues, or any part of said streets or avenues, to be numbered, said streets or avenues shall be numbered as hereinafter provided, and the owners or agents of the said buildings or premises so directed to be numbered, lying alongside said streets or avenues, shall pay the costs of numbering the same; and any owner or agent refusing or neglecting to have his premises or buildings so numbered, whenever a public street or avenue is directed to be numbered as aforesaid, such person or persons shall, for every such offence, on conviction before the Mayor's Court, forfeit a sum of five dollars and costs of prosecution.

Streets to be numbered when Council shall direct.

Penalty.

SEC. 2. That the numbering on Jefferson Avenue, Woodbridge street, and Atwater street, commence at the western termination of each of said streets, and that the numbers one, three, five, seven, &c., be used on the left hand of each of said streets, and the numbers two, four, six, eight, &c., be used on the right hand side of each of said streets, and proceed easterly as far as it may from time to time be deemed necessary or expedient.

How numbered.

SEC. 3. That on all streets parallel to Jefferson Avenue the numbering shall commence where such street crosses Woodward Avenue and proceed easterly and westerly, as far as necessary, using the odd numbers one, three, five, seven, &c., on the left, and even numbers, two, four, six, eight, &c., on the right hand side of each of said streets.

Idem.

SEC. 4. That on Woodward Avenue, and all streets running parallel to it the numbering shall commence at the channel of the Detroit river and proceed northerly as far as may be required, using the numbers one, three, five, seven, &c., on the left, and the numbers

Idem.

two, four, six, eight, &c., on the right hand side of each of said streets respectively.

Vacant lots how numbered.

SEC. 5. That whenever there are vacant lots along the line of said streets, one number shall be allowed to every twenty feet of such vacant lot.

CHAPTER XXV.

Relative to Wharves.

SEC. 1. To be kept in repair—Marshal to notify to repair. | SEC. 2. Penalty for not repairing.

To be kept in repair. Marshal to notify to repair.

SEC. 1. It shall be the duty of the owner or owners, occupant or occupants, lessee or lessees, of any of the wharves of this city, bordering upon the Detroit river, and which are not fenced in, or otherwise enclosed, so as to prevent the passage of travelers or others over or across them, to keep the same in good order and condition; and whenever any of the plank, boards, timber, or other materials composing or forming a part of any of the wharves of said city, shall from any cause become loose, or be removed, or whenever any of said wharves shall in any manner, and from any cause whatever, be out of repair, it shall be the duty of the City Marshal to notify either the owner or owners, occupant or occupants, lessee or lessees, of any such wharf or wharves, to immediately replace and securely fasten the plank, board, or other material so removed as aforesaid, or otherwise to repair such wharf or wharves as to the Marshal may seem necessary: *Provided*, That the notice so to be given may be either a verbal or written notice, and may be given by either of the Constables, or by the Mayor or any of the Aldermen, or other officers of the city; and if a written notice, it may be either served personally upon, or left at the place of business or residence of, the person or persons notified.

Penalty for not repairing.

SEC. 2. In case the person or persons so notified, as provided for in the preceding section, shall neglect for twenty-four hours after such notice, to comply with the requisitions thereof, he, she or they shall, on conviction thereof before the Mayor's Court, be liable to a fine of not less than five, nor more than fifty dollars for each and every day he, she or they shall neglect to comply with the requisitions of said notice.

TITLE FOUR.

OF DRAINS AND SEWERS.

CHAPTER XXVI.

Relative to public and private Drains and Sewers.

SEC. 1. That no person or persons be permitted to connect any drain from his, her or their premises, with any public drain or sewer, now made or constructed, or hereafter to be made or constructed, in said city, nor with any private drain, whereby his, her or their premises, will be drained into any public drain or sewer, except on previous application in writing to, and permission by, the Common Council, or some Superintendent by them appointed for that purpose, and the payment of the assessment hereinafter mentioned.

No lot to be drained without application to the Common Council and payment of assessment.

SEC. 2. All private drains to be hereafter made by individuals in any public atreet, lane or alley in said city, and connecting with any public drain or sewer, shall be of such size, dimensions and materials, and constructed and laid, as directed by the Common Council or City Surveyor, and shall enter such public drain or sewer under and according to the personal supervision and direction of said Surveyor, nor shall any person or persons enter any public drain or sewer at any other places than those designated and fixed for that purpose in the construction thereof.

Council to determine the size of drains and to be entered under supervision of City Surveyor.

SEC. 3. The amount which individuals using, or being benefitted by any public drain or sewer, shall pay for such use, is hereby fixed

Assessment for draining cellars.

TITLE IV. CHAPTER 26.

as follows, to wit: the sum of one dollar and fifty cents annually, for each cellar drained by box directly or indirectly into any public drain or sewer, which assessment shall be taken to include all other drainage of the premises to which said cellar especially belongs: And the sum of fifty cents annually, for each lot or subdivision of lot being without a cellar, drained by box, as aforesaid, into any public drain or sewer. And such sums as may be fixed by the Common Council for all establishments requiring an unusual or extraordinary amount of drainage, drained as aforesaid, upon actual inspection of, and report thereon by the assessors.

When to be paid.

SEC. 4. That said assessment shall in all instances, be paid when the city and school taxes are collected.

Persons using drain or sewer liable to assessment.

Assessment lien on lots. How collected. Drain may be cut off.

SEC. 5. Any person whose premises are drained directly or indirectly, into any public drain or sewer, or any person using said premises thus drained, or for whose benefit or family the same is used shall be liable to the payment therefor, and in addition said assessment shall become, and be a charge and lien on the premises thus drained, and be recovered, and the same proceedings had in every respect for the recovery thereof, as are provided for the recovery of other special assessments, and the corporation may also, at their option, stop such private drain, and prevent any person from draining his premises into any public drain or sewer, where such assessment shall not be paid in advance, on the second application, and said privilege shall not be restored unless on the payment of the tax and a forfeiture of double the amount of the assessment.

Penalty for injuring drain.

SEC. 6. Any person who shall remove any grate from the pool, over which it is placed, or in any way, directly or indirectly, injure any public drain or sewer, or any part thereof, shall, on conviction thereof before the Mayor's Court, be liable to a penalty, for each offence, not exceeding one hundred dollars and costs.

Penalty for connecting with drains without permission. How to enter drains. Drain not to be placed by public drain.

SEC. 7. Any person who shall connect any drain from his premises with any public drain or sewer, or who shall drain his premises into any private drain which enters into any public drain or sewer, without first making the application, procuring the permission and paying the assessment, provided for in the first section of this chapter, shall, on conviction of each offence nefore the Mayor's Court, be liable to a penalty not exceeding one hundred dollars and costs; and any person who shall construct and lay any private drain, connecting with any public drain or sewer, or who shall enter any public drain or sewer, in any other manner except as is provided for in the second section of this chapter, shall be liable for each offence, on like conviction, to a penalty not exceeding one hundred dollars and costs: and any person who shall enter any public drain or sewer at any other place than is designated and fixed for that purpose in the construction thereof, shall be also liable to pay for each offence, on like conviction, a penalty not exceeding one hundred dollars and costs; and if any person shall drain his premises along the side of any public drain or sewer, he shall also be liable to pay a penalty, not exceeding one hundred dollars and costs, on like conviction: *Provided*, That this section shall not be construed to extend to any case where a private drain has heretofore been laid down along the side of any public drain or sewer; but such private drain shall not be repaired by any person without having received from the Common Council, or some authorized officer of said city, a certificate that such repair will not endanger the safety and preservation of any public drain or sewer along the side thereof.

When sewers may be entered.

SEC. 8. That no person be permitted to connect any drain from his premises with the grand sewer, nor enter the same, between the first day of December and the first day of April in each year, and any person offending against this section, shall, on conviction of such offence before the Mayor's Court, be liable to pay a fine of one hundred dollars and costs.

What drains are public.

SEC. 9 That all drains now made and constructed, or which shall hereafter be made and constructed by the corporation, shall be deemed to be public drains or sewers within the purview of this chaper; and all sums of money received under the provisions of this chapter shall be stated and kept in a separate account, and are hereby specifically pledged and appropriated to the following uses and objects, and no other, to wit: 1st, to defray the expense of indispensable repairs of existing sewers; 2d, to defray the cost of additional public sewers and their repairs; 3d, to apply on the interest of the city debt accruing on account of the cost of construction and maintenance of such sewers.

How sewer assessments to be appropriated.

How sewer assessments may be collected.

SEC. 10. The assessment provided for in this chapter shall be collected in the manner prescribed by the chapter, "relating to the

TITLE IV. CHAPTER 26.

collection of special assessments," the provisions of which are made applicable hereto, except that the time of the warrants and provision, of per centage shall be made to correspond with the terms of the warrants and the provisions for per centage in the collection of the city and school taxes.

Private Drains.

Certain portion of expense to be paid before connection with drains.

SEC. 11. That no person be permitted to connect any drain from his, her or their premises, with any drain or sewer made by one or more individuals in any street, lane or alley as aforesaid, unless on payment to the proprietors of such drain or sewer of a rateable proportion of the expense of making the same, the amount to be ascertained and determined by the Marshal or Surveyor, with the right of appeal to the Common Council; nor shall any person make or construct a sink, drain or sewer leading into any other drain or sewer, without putting a sufficient strainer at the head of it, under a penalty not exceeding ten dollars and costs, for each offence.

How expense of repairs asscertained.

SEC. 12. Every person having any drain from his, her or their premises, that shall be connected with any drain or sewer now made, or that shall hereafter be made as aforesaid, shall pay a rateable proportion of all expenses necessary for maintaining and keeping such drains or sewers in repair, such proportion to be ascertained and determined in the manner provided for in the foregoing section, and if any person shall neglect to pay the same, when so ascertained, such person shall forfeit and pay the sum of two dollars and costs, for every week during which the same shall remain unpaid.

Penalty.

Marshal to notify persons to repair.

SEC. 13. In all cases where drains or sewers shall be obstructed so as to become, in the opinion of the Marshal, a nuisance, it shall be his duty to give notice to the persons using the same, to repair such drains or sewers, and if the same be not forthwith repaired, it shall be the duty of the Marshal to cause the necessary repairs to be made, and to charge the said persons with a rateable proportion of the expense incurred, including a reasonable allowance to the Marshal for his own services, subject to an appeal to the Common Council, as is provided in the tenth section; and all such appeals shall be made within the time in which such person is required to pay the sums above required; and if any person shall refuse or neglect to pay their proportion of the charges for the space of ten

Proceedings in case of neglect.

days after notice, he or they shall be liable, upon conviction before the Mayor's Court, to pay a fine not exceeding fifty dollars and with costs of suit.

No connection to be made until Surveyor shall have ascertained the grade.

SEC. 14. No connection with public or private sewers or drains shall be made under the provisions of this chapter, until the Surveyor shall have designated the grade therefor, under the penalty of twenty dollars.

CHAPTER XXVII.

Relative to Lateral Drains.

Com. Council may direct owners to construct lateral sewers.

SEC. 1. That the Mayor, Recorder and Aldermen of the city, of Detroit, in Common Council convened, may, by resolution, in all cases direct every owner of lots or land, or his or her agent, or tenant, adjoining any street or alley in said city, to build lateral sewers or drains, to make a sufficient drainage from his house, yard, or lot, whenever in their opinion the same shall be necessary; provided said Common Council, by resolution, shall direct lateral sewers or drains to be laid or constructed through or in said streets and alleys, and shall thereupon give such owner or agent notice thereof in writing, specifying the time within which said lateral sewer or drain shall be completed; and in case the said owner, agent, or tenant, shall neglect or refuse to construct the same, and complete the same within the time specified, the Mayor, Recorder, and Aldermen of said city, shall cause the same to be done at the cost of said owner, agent, or tenant, and shall recover the whole amount of the expense thereof, upon complaint in the Mayor's Court, and the costs of prosecution.

Proceedings in case owners neglect.

To be built under direction of the Council.

SEC. 2. All lateral sewers and drains which hereafter shall be built, and entered into any public sewer of said city, shall be built of such materials as the Mayor, Recorder, and Aldermen of said city shall direct, and be laid or constructed in such direction, of such size and width, such descent, and with such strainers, as said Common Council shall require.

TITLE IV. CHAPTER 27.

To be repaired and cleaned at expense of owners.

SEC. 3. All owners, agents, or tenants of land or lots lying alongside or upon any street or alley in said city through which the Common Council of said city shall order or direct lateral sewers or drains to be built, communicating with any public sewer, laid or constructed, relaid, repaired, or cleansed, shall make, repair, relay, or cleanse such lateral sewer or drain at their own expense and cost, in the manner and within the time prescribed by resolution of said Common Council, upon written notice of the same to said owner, agent, or occupant or tenant to the effect thereof, and if not done within the time prescribed, and in the manner directed, said Common Council may cause the same to be constructed, repaired, relaid, or cleansed, and the City Surveyor shall assess the expense of constructing the same in a rateable proportion to said owners, agents, or tenants of land or lots adjoining said street or alley; and the said sum of money so assessed on such lot or land shall be a lien thereon, and upon suit being commenced in the Mayor's Court of said city, said sum of money so assessed to said owner, agent, or occupant, may be recovered, together with the costs of prosecution.

Thirty days notice to non-residents of drainage of premises.

SEC. 4. Whenever the owner of any lot or piece of land adjoining any street or alley through which the Common Council shall direct lateral sewers or drains to be built or constructed as aforesaid, shall be a non-resident of said city, said Common Council in such case shall give thirty days public notice, in the official paper of said city of the order of said Common Council for the construction of said lateral sewer or drain upon said street or alley, and after the expiration of said thirty days it shall be lawful for said Common Council to build said sewer, pursuant to said public notice, in case said owner has neglected so to do, at the cost of said owner, as aforesaid; and the cost of construction of said sewer or drain shall be collected, together with costs of prosecution, in the Mayor's Court.

To deduct from assessment when premises have been before properly drained

SEC. 5. Whenever it shall appear to the satisfaction of said Common Council that any lot or piece of land adjoining any street or alley in said city through which the Common Council of said city shall direct lateral sewers or drains to be built, said premises having been properly and sufficiently drained, at the expense of the owner or agent of said premises, it shall be in the discretion of the Common Council to make such deduction from the assessment for said sewer or drain for said drainage as they shall deem reasonable and just to said owner or agent.

TITLE FIVE.

OF MARKETS AND SALES.

CHAPTER XXVIII.

Relative to Public Markets.

SEC. 1. All public markets in the City of Detroit shall be held in such places as the Common Council shall from time to time designate and license, and in no other. *Markets held where Council shall designate.*

SEC. 2. The Mayor shall, from time to time, issue licenses to so many and such persons as the Common Council may direct, to sell fresh meat in such places within the limits of the city, as may be designated in such license, but not elsewhere. *Mayor to issue licences to sell fresh meat.*

Said licences shall expire first Monday in April, after they are granted.

SEC. 3. All licenses so issued shall expire and cease on the first Monday of April after the granting thereof, unless sooner revoked by the Common Council, and shall be renewed by the Mayor, under the direction of the Common Council, on application.

Fifty dollars to be paid for licences.

SEC. 4. For each license issued as aforesaid, the sum of fifty dollars shall be paid or secured on the granting of the same, and a like sum for the renewal of the same.

Shops where fresh meat and fish are sold to be under the supervision of the Clerk of the market

SEC. 5. All shops, cellars, stalls, and other places, within the limits of the city, where fresh meat and fish are sold, shall be under the supervision of the Clerk of the City Hall market, and subject to all the regulations which are established by law, for the cleanliness and good government of the public markets.

How stalls in markets to be used and occupied.

SEC. 6. No person shall use or occupy, or cause to be used or occupied, any stall or stalls in the public market house belonging to the Corporation, unless he shall have paid for, or secured the payment for the same, as hereinafter provided, and when so paid or the payment thereof secured, such person shall keep such stall or stalls well supplied with good and wholesome meat, to be sold therein.

Common Council to determine the minimum rents of stalls, and Marshal to offer stalls to highest bidders.

SEC. 7. The Common Council shall, from year to year, determine the minimum rents of all stalls in the public markets belonging to the Corporation, and it shall be the duty of the City Marshal to offer for rent at public auction, to the highest bidder, all such stalls at such time and place as the Common Council shall designate; but no stall shall be rented for a less sum than the minimum price, determined as aforesaid: *Provided*, That no bid shall be received from any person, at such auction, who is in arrears to said Corporation.

One fourth of rent to be paid in advance and the rest secured.

SEC. 8. When any person shall rent a stall in the public market houses belonging to the Corporation, he shall pay to the City Marshal one-fourth of such rent in advance, and shall give security satisfactory to the Committee on Markets, for the remainder thereof, to be paid in three instalments, on the commencement of each quarter of the year then next ensuing.

When markets shall be kept open.

SEC. 9. The market houses belonging to the Corporation shall be kept open every day (Sundays excepted) from daylight till the hour from time to time fixed by resolution of the Common Council, and not otherwise: *Provided*, The provisions of this section shall not apply to markets other than belonging to the Corporation.

TITLE V.
CHAPTER 28.

Meats not to be sold except in market house or places designated by Council.

SEC. 10. It shall not be lawful for any person or persons to sell or expose for sale any fresh meat, (poultry and venison excepted,) in any quantity, at any time, or in any building, or street, or other place whatever within the limits of this city, excepting in the stalls in the respective market houses rented from the Corporation, according to existing regulations, and such other places as may be designated by the Common Council, as hereinbefore provided: *Provided*, That nothing herein contained shall prevent any person or persons from selling or exposing for sale in the streets, in the immediate vicinity of the public markets, or elsewhere, fresh meat by the carcass or quarter, according to the provisions of the next succeeding Chapter of these Ordinances, relative to sale of fresh meat by the quarter, within the bounds of the City of Detroit.

Persons occupying stalls to keep a tub for offal, and to remove the offal one hour after market closes. Certain hides not to be brought to markets.

SEC. 11. Every person occupying a stall in any of the public markets, shall procure and place in such markets a suitable cask or tub, in which he shall deposit, or cause to be deposited, the offals of all slaughtered animals, brought or caused to be brought by him, therein, and such person shall within one hour after the closing of the market house, remove, or cause to be removed therefrom, all such offals as aforesaid; but no person shall bring, or cause to be brought into any public market house, any hides or skins of slaughtered animals, except on calves, sheep, lambs or hogs.

When sales may be out of market hours.

SEC. 12. If any person who may have rented a stall from the Corporation, as aforesaid, shall, within the ordinary hours of business, make application to the Clerk of the City Hall market for the privilege of selling meat after the time the market house is required to be closed, and can satisfy the Clerk that it is for the sole purpose of supplying some boat or vessel about to sail from said city, or traveler about to leave the city in the cars, but in no other, the Clerk may grant such privilege.

All provisions affered shall be sound; if not may be seized and venders punished.

SEC. 13. All provisions opened or exposed for sale in said markets shall be sound and wholesome, and of pure and good quality, and if otherwise, shall be seized, and the sellers or manufacturers thereof, and each and every person engaged in such manufacture, shall be liable for each offence, to a penalty not exceeding one hundred dollars; and all weights and measures used in said markets shall be in conformity with the standard weights and measures regulated by the laws of

TITLE V. CHAPTER 28.

this State; and any person who shall within the limits of said city, sell, or offer to sell, or exhibit for sale, any article which shall be deficient in the weight or measure for which he sells the same, or offers or exhibits the same for sale, shall, upon conviction before the Mayor's Court, forfeit a penalty of not more than one hundred dollars and costs of prosecution.

Markets to be kept clean and clear of obstructions

SEC. 14. Said markets, and a space twenty feet without them and adjacent thereto on every side, shall be kept clear during market hours, of carts, wagons, carriages, wheelbarrows and other vehicles, and of all animals and other obstructions whatsoever, and also of all offals and offensive substances of every kind; and all stalls and meat blocks and benches shall be within the said market houses and not elsewhere, and shall be kept clean: *Provided, however*, That this section shall not be so construed as to prevent the ordinary travel of the highway.

Bad conduct prohibited in markets.

SEC. 15. That within the space of twenty feet aforesaid, and within said market houses, there shall not be any lewd, lacivious or disorderly conduct, nor loud or boisterous noises made, nor any profane or vulgar language used, nor any act done or committed tending to a breach of the public peace, or to disturb the decorum of the place.

Duty of Clerk of market to enforce the provisions of this chapter in Mayor's Court.

SEC. 16. It will be the duty of the Clerk of the City Hall market, and he is hereby authorized and empowered to attend all said markets and enforce the due execution of the provisions of this Chapter, and make complaint to the Mayor's Court, of each and every infringement of this Chapter, and also to remove from the said markets all offensive substances or offals, and all obstructions before mentioned.

Vegetable market designated.

SEC. 17. That the ground enclosed by a railing, beginning at the east end of the City Hall, and extending along Michigan Grand avenue to Randolph street, and all other yards, grounds or enclosures that have been or may hereafter be designated by said Common Council as places of holding vegetable markets, be, and the same are hereby declared public markets, and that the provisions of this Chapter, for the prevention of disorderly conduct, shall apply to said vegetable markets, and to a place twenty feet without them and to the adjacent streets on every side.

What may be sold in vegetable market

SEC. 18. All fresh fish, poultry, eggs, butter, fruits or vegetables of any kind, may be sold within the limits prescribed in the next preceding section of this Chapter, or any grounds that have been or may hereafter be designated as vegetable markets, and on no other public grounds or streets in said city during the hours the market houses are required to be kept open: *Provided*, That nothing herein contained shall prevent the sale of the above articles from wagons within the immediate vicinity of said vegetable markets.

How vegetables &c., exposed; if unsound, Clerk shall order them removed.

SEC. 19. All provisions or vegetables offered for sale at any of the public markets shall be placed on stands elevated from the ground, in such a manner, and shall remain stationed at such place or places as the Clerk of the respective markets shall direct, and if any of such provisions or vegetables shall be deemed by such Clerk to be unwholesome or unfit to be consumed or used, he shall order owners thereof to remove the same immediately from the public markets; and if such owner shall neglect or refuse to remove such provisions, or vegetables as aforesaid, it shall be the duty of said Clerk to remove the same without delay.

No public market house to be used save for sale of meat.

SEC. 20. No person shall use or occupy any public market house, or any part thereof, but for the sale of meat, or cutting, or salting the same, except when permission shall have been obtained for that purpose, as hereinafter provided.

Hucksters, forestallers and grocers prohibited from occupying certain places in vegetable market.

SEC. 21. It shall not be lawful for any huckster, forestaller, grocer, or other person, to occupy the spaces on either side of the platform extending back from the rear of the City Hall vegetable market, for the purpose of vending any meats, butter, vegetables, fruits or other articles of merchandise previously purchased by them.

Penaly for violations.

SEC. 22. If any person shall violate any of the provisions of this Chapter, he or she shall, on conviction before the Mayor's Court, for every such offence, be subject to pay a fine not exceeding one hundred dollars and costs of prosecution.

CHAPTER XXIX.

Relative to Forestalling.

SEC. 1. Forestalling defined, prohibited, and how punished.

SEC. 1. It shall not be lawful for any person who follows the business of huckster, forestaller, grocer or seller of any articles of provision at second hand, to purchase or offer to purchase, either personally or by his or her agent, within the limits of said city, during the hours the public markets are required to be kept open each day,

TITLE V. CHAPTER 30.

Forestalling defined, prohibited and how punished.

any fresh venison, fresh fish, poultry, game of any kind, eggs, butter, fruit, or vegetables of any kind, from any person bringing or having brought the same to said city for sale or barter. And the possession of any such article by any such huckster, forestaller, grocer, or other seller thereof, which may have been previously in the possession of any farmer or other person, within the limits of the said city, during the hours aforesaid, shall be deemed prima facie evidence of a violation of this ordinance. Any person violating the provisions of this ordinance shall be subject to a fine of not more than fifty dollars and costs of prosecution, to be recovered in the Mayor's Court.

CHAPTER XXX.

Relative to the Sale of Meat by the Quarter.

SEC. 1. Persons may be licensed to sell meat by the quarter.
SEC. 2. To give bonds.
SEC. 3. No person to sell by the quarter unless licensed—penalty.
SEC. 4. Farmers not prohibited from selling by the quarter, when.
SEC. 5. Drovers not to sell by the quarter.

Persons may be licensed to sell meat by quarter.

SEC. 1. The Common Council in session, or the Mayor in vacation, may hereafter license any person who is a resident of the State of Michigan, and of the age of twenty-one years, to buy and sell meat by the carcass or quarter, from shops, wagons, carts, or other vehicles within the limits of the city of Detroit, upon the payment at the rate of one hundred dollars per annum, for each and every shop, wagon, cart, or other vehicle to be used for that purpose, and that no license be granted for a less term than three months.

To give bonds.

SEC. 2. Every person so applying for such license, shall first execute a bond to be approved by the Council, in the penal sum of two hundred dollars, conditioned that he will at no time offer for sale or suffer to be offered for sale, any unwholsome meats, of any kind or description, and that he will occupy such place or stand, in the vicinity of the market, or elsewhere, as shall be assigned to him by the Common Council, and that he will preserve order about his shop, or vehicle, while occupying such stand.

No person to sell by the quarter unless licensed. Penalty.

SEC. 3. No person, unless licensed, as hereinbefore provided, shall hereafter peddle, sell, or offer for sale, from any shop, wagon, cart or other vehicle, used for that purpose, in or about the markets of said city, or in any of the streets thereof, any beef, pork, mutton, or other meats by the carcass or quarter, under a penalty not exceeding fifty dollars for every such offence, to be recovered in the Mayor's Court with the costs of prosecution: *Provided*, That it shall not be considered a violation of the provisions of this section for drovers or others to sell any such meat as aforesaid, either by the carcass or the quarter, to any or either of the regular butchers of this city occupying stalls rented of the city of Detroit, in either of the public markets of said city.

Farmers not prohibited from selling by the quarter, when.

SEC. 4. The foregoing provisions shall not be so construed as to apply to any farmer who shall offer for sale any meat which may have been fatted and killed by him; but shall be applied only to such persons as may offer such articles for sale—the same having been previously purchased by them for that purpose; and for the purpose of a conviction under this chapter, the possession of such articles by such party shall be deemed *prima facie* evidence of such purchase.

Drovers not to sell by the quarter.

SEC. 5. Nothing in this chapter contained shall be construed to authorize any person, following the business of a drover for a livelihood, to sell meat by the quarter, unless he shall be licensed under this chapter.

CHAPTER XXXI.

Relative to the Sale of Woodcock, &c.

When woodcock, patridges &c., shall not be sold.

SEC. 1. It shall not be lawful for any person to offer for sale, or sell within the limits of the city of Detroit, or bring into the city for the purpose of selling the same, or for any other purpose, any woodcocks killed between the first day of February and the first day of July in each year, or any quails, partridges or pheasants killed between the first day of March and the first day of October, in each year.

Penalty.

SEC. 2. Any person who shall expose for sale, or sell, or have in his possession for the purpose of selling the same, or for any other purpose, within the limits of said city, any woodcocks, quails, partridges or pheasants killed within the periods specified in the first section of this chapter, shall forfeit and pay the sum of fifty cents for each woodcock, quail, partridge or pheasant, to be recovered in an action of debt before the Mayor's Court of said city, one half of which sum shall be paid upon recovery to the Treasurer of the city of

TITLE V. CHAPTER 32.

Detroit, and one half to the person who shall sue and prosecute therefor.

CHAPTER XXXII.

Relative to the Sale of Hay and Straw.

Weigh master to weigh hay and issue certificate.

SEC. 1. It shall be duty of the Weighmasters, severally, well and truly to weigh any cart, wagon, or sled load of hay, when applied to by any person desiring the same, and make such reduction from the weight of said hay as to him may seem reasonable and just, by reason of said hay being damp, wet or not well cured, and deliver to the person so applying a certificate thereof, for which he may demand and receive of such applicant twenty-five cents.

No hay to be sold unless first weighed

SEC. 2. No person or persons shall sell or offer for sale any hay in said city, by the cart, wagon or sled load, unless the same shall have been first weighed in the manner above prescribed, and as soon as conveniently may be, after unloading said hay, the cart, wagon, sled or other vehicle, bearing the same, with all things and apparatus belonging thereto, at the time of weighing said hay, shall also be weighed; and the seller shall deliver unto the buyer the certificate given by the Weighmaster, at the time of demanding payment for the hay so sold.

Purchaser may have hay weighed.

SEC. 3. The purchaser or purchasers of any hay which shall have been weighed in the manner above directed, may require and cause the same as well as the cart, wagon, sled or other vehicle, bearing the same, to be weighed at his own expense, and the seller of such hay shall not refuse to let the same be so weighed.

How hay carts or other vehicles to stand.

SEC. 4. All carts, wagons, sleds or other vehicles, loaded with hay intended for sale, shall stand at, or adjoining the hay scales, in regular order, one after the other, and in such manner as not to obstruct the centre of any street, and so as to leave access to any house or other building thereon, open and unobstructed.

Provisions of this chapter applied to straw.

SEC. 5. All the foregoing provisions of this chapter shall apply relative to any straw sold or offered for sale in said city, except straw made up into bundles and sold by the bundle.

SEC. 6. Any person offending against the provisions of this chapter, shall be liable to a fine not exceeding fifty dollars and costs of prosecution for each offence. Penalty.

CHAPTER XXXIII.

Relative to Unwholesome Liquors and Provisions.

SEC. 1. No butcher or other person shall sell or offer to sell within the limits of the city of Detroit, the flesh of any animal dying otherwise than by slaughter, nor the flesh of any animal slaughtered when diseased, nor any contagious or unwholesome flesh of any description whotsoever, nor any provisions of any description, except such as are sound, and of pure and wholesome quality; and no baker, brewer, distiller or other person, shall sell, or offer, or expose to sale, any unwholesome bread or other provisions, drink or liquors whatever; and any person offending in the premises shall, on conviction thereof before the Mayor's Court, be fined in a sum not exceeding five hundred dollars, and the costs of prosecution, and be liable to be excluded from the public markets of this city, and from the exercise of his business, notwithstanding such person may have rented a stall or stalls in one or more markets, or paid a license; and it shall at all times be the duty of all the constables and other officers of this city to take notice of, and report all infractions of this chapter. No person shall sell diseased, or unwholesome flesh, bread or drink. Penalty.

SEC. 2. Any person who shall sell or offer for sale, or who shall aid in effecting any sale, or in the manufacture or preparation of sausages or other provisions, composed of bad, impure, decayed or unsound ingredients, shall be liable to the penalties in the foregoing section. Unsound sausages.

CHAPTER XXXIV.

Relative to Sale of Goods at Auction.

SEC. 1. No goods, wares, merchandise or other property, personal or real, shall be sold, or exposed for sale in any street or alley, or

TITLE V. CHAPTER 34.

No goods to be sold in streets save by process of law.

on any side walk, wharf or pier in the city of Detroit, or at the door or window of any store or dwelling in said city, by any auctioneer or other person, except a Marshal, Master in Chancery, Coroner, Sheriff, or Collector, by virtue of an execution or other authority, vested in him by law, except such articles as are permitted to be sold by the second section of this chapter.

What may be sold in the streets.

SEC. 2. It shall and may be lawful for any auctioneer, or other person not prohibited by law, to sell or expose for sale, at auction or vendue, on any wharf, or in any street of said city, all spirituous, vinous and malt liquors, cider and other liquors, in casks which shall contain not less than thirty gallons, ship furniture and tackle, carriages, farming utensils, household furniture, animals of every description, and all other goods, wares or merchandise, in packages or parcels, the size of which shall be equal to the bulk of one barrel, or which shall weigh one hundred pounds: *Provided*, The selling or exposing to sale such articles does not encumber the side walks or obstruct the streets, so that persons, horses or carriages cannot conveniently pass.

Bell men prohibited.

SEC. 3. No bell man, crier, or other means of attracting the attention of passengers, shall be used or employed by any auctioneer or other person, for the purpose of collecting bidders at the sale or auction of any property.

Penalty.

SEC. 4. Any person or persons, who shall violate any of the provisions of this chapter shall, on conviction thereof, before the Mayor's Court of the city of Detroit, be subject to a fine not exceeding fifty dollars and costs of prosecution.

Not lawful to sell cattle in certain parts of city.

SEC. 5. It shall not be lawful for any person to vend or sell at public auction or vendue, any horse or cattle in any of the public streets of the city of Detroit, south of Campus Martius; and any person offending in the premises shall, for every offence, on conviction thereof before the Mayor's Court of said city, pay a fine not exceeding one hundred dollars and costs of prosecution.

Dnty of Marshal.

SEC. 6. It shall be the duty of the Marshal of said city to cause this chapter strictly to be carried into effect.

CHAPTER XXXV.

Relative to the Manufacture and Sale of Bread.

SEC. 1. It shall not be lawful for any person to use or carry on the trade or business of a baker, either in person or by employing any other person to use or carry on the said trade or business, under his or her direction, or for his or her profit or benefit, within said city, without having obtained from the Common Council a permit for that purpose, under a penalty not exceeding fifty dollars. Bakers to obtain permits.

SEC. 2. Every person desirous to use or carry on said trade or business, shall make application in writing to the Common Council, setting forth the street and house in which he or she intends to carry on said trade or business, and shall accompany such application with a recommendation signed by at least twelve respectable householders of said city, certifying that such person is qualified to carry on said business, and that he or she is of good fame and correct and orderly deportment and behavior. How obtained.

SEC. 3. If the Common Council shall grant such application, the Clerk shall deliver such person a permit for the purpose aforesaid, for which he shall be entitled to receive from such person the sum of twenty-five cents; and the said permit shall be in force till the second Tuesday in March then next ensuing. Clerk to deliver permit if granted.

SEC. 4. All bread manufactured by the bakers of this city for sale, shall be made of good and wholesome flour or meal into loaves of one pound and two pounds avoirdupois weight, and every loaf of such bread shall be marked with the numbers indicating the weight of such loaf, and also with the initial letters of the name of the baker thereof; and if any baker or other person shall offer or expose for sale any bread made of unwholesome materials, or any bread not so marked, except as aforesaid, every such baker or other person so offending shall forfeit and pay for each loaf, a sum not exceeding twenty-five dollars. Bread to be made of good flour.

SEC. 5. If any baker shall make for sale, or shall sell or expose for sale, any bread that shall be deficient in weight, according to the requisitions prescribed in the preceding section of this Chapter, he shall Penalty for selling bread under weight

TITLE V. CHAPTER 35.

forfeit and pay for every such offence the sum of ten cents for every ounce that such bread shall be deficient in weight: *Provided, always,* That such deficiency in the weight of such bread shall be ascertained by the inspector of bread, by weighing or causing the same to be weighed in his presence, within eight hours after the same shall have been baked, sold or exposed for sale: *And provided, further,* That whenever any allowance in the weight shall be claimed on account of any bread having been baked, sold or exposed for sale more than eight hours as aforesaid, the burden of proof in respect to the time when the same shall have been baked, sold or exposed for sale, shall devolve upon the defendant or baker of such bread.

Marshal to be bread Inspector.

SEC. 6. The City Marshal shall, ex-officio, be inspector of bread, and it shall be his duty, and he is hereby authorized and required from time to time, and not less than once in each month, at all seasonable hours, to enter into, and inspect and examine every baker's shop, store house or other building where any bread is or shall be baked, stored or deposited, or offered for sale, and to inspect and examine all bread found therein, and also to stop, detain and examine in any part of the said city, any person or persons, wagons or other carriages carrying any loaf of bread, and weigh the same, and determine whether the same are in violation of the true intent and meaning of this Chapter; and if the said inspector shall find any bread not conformable to the directions herein contained, or any part of them, he shall make complaint thereof for the purpose of having such person prosecuted according to law.

Penalty for obstructing Marshal inspecting.

SEC. 7. Any person or persons, who may obstruct, or in any manner impede or wilfully delay any person legally qualified, in the execution of his duties under this act, either by refusing to him or delaying his entrance or admission into any of the places above mentioned, or by refusing or omitting to stop their wagon or carriage as aforesaid, or in any other manner whatsoever, so that the due execution of this act, or any part of it may be impeded or obstructed, every such person shall, for every such offence, on conviction thereof before the Mayor's Court, forfeit and pay a sum not exceeding fifty dollars, and costs of prosecution, and further, his, her or their license as a baker, if any has been granted to such person, shall be forfeited.

CHAPTER XXXVI.

Relative to the Sale of Firewood.

SEC. 1. The Inspectors of Firewood shall have power to appoint one or more deputies, (each of whom shall before exercising the duties of their office, take and subscribe the same oath as their principal hath taken, and file the same in the Clerk's office,) and the said Inspectors and their deputies shall, when required by either the seller or purchaser (but not otherwise) of any firewood brought within the limits of said city, by water craft, wagons or other conveyances, for sale, inspect and measure the same, and give a certificate of the date and amount of such measurement, in words of full length, and they shall receive for every cord or load (if offered for sale by the load) of wood so measured, from the party requiring the same, the sum of six cents, and every cord of wood measured, as aforesaid, under the provisions of this Chapter, shall be computed to contain one hundred and twenty-eight cubic feet, well stowed and packed, due allowance being made for all crooked sticks.

Inspectors of firewood may appoint deputies. They may when required measure wood and give certificate of quantity.

SEC. 2. If any person within the limits of the city, who having obtained such certificate, shall sell or otherwise dispose of such wood contrary to the same, or attempt to impose a false certificate in the sale thereof, he shall for each offence, on conviction before the Mayor's Court, forfeit and pay a fine not exceeding twenty-five dollars and the costs of prosecution.

Persons selling wood contrary to certificate how punished.

SEC. 3. Vendors of Firewood shall not congregate, with their loads, in numbers exceeding three loads, within a space of three hundred feet in length, upon any street, alley, or public ground, within the limits of the city, and when more than three persons shall be found standing, with their loads of wood, within such prescribed distance of three hundred feet aforesaid, each of them shall be liable to a penalty of ten dollars and costs of prosecution, for each offence, upon conviction before the Mayor's Court.

How vendors shall stand in streets.

TITLE VI.
CHAPTER 37.

TITLE SIX.

OF THE PREVENTION OF FIRES.

CHAPTER XXXVII.

Relative to the Fire Department of the City of Detroit.

Relative to the fire department of the city of Detroit.

SEC. 1. The Fire Department of said city shall consist of a Chief Engineer, an Engineer, Assistant Engineer, and as many other Engineers, Fire Wardens, fire engine men, hose men, hook and ladder men, axe men, and bag men, as may from time to time be appointed by the Common Council, and who shall be respectively distinguished by the appellations aforesaid.

Of whom the fire department may consist.

SEC. 2. The Chief and Assistant Engineers, when nominated by the Fire Department, may be appointed in the month of April in each year. The Aldermen of this city shall be ex-officio Fire Wardens for their respective wards: in addition to those who are ex-officio Fire Wardens, there shall be appointed eight Fire Wardens in each ward of said city; such Wardens shall be appointed by the Common Council from among such persons as may be nominated or recommended by the Board of Fire Wardens; and the said Wardens so appointed, together with those who are ex-officio Wardens, shall be and constitute a fire guard: And it shall be the duty of such fire guard to attend at every fire that may occur within the limits of said city, and take charge and possession of all property removed from buildings at fires, and to deliver the same to the City Marshal, or in his absence, to a City Constable, to be delivered to the City Marshal to store, or otherwise protect the same until it is claimed by the owner or owners, and upon such claim to deliver up the same to the owner or owners, upon the payment to the City Marshal of all expenses nesessarily and actually incurred in and about the care and protection of such property, and for which a receipt shall be given by the Chief Warden: And the said fire guard are hereby invested with all necessary authority for the purpose of taking charge and possession of such property, and at every fire every Warden shall report himself to the Chief Warden, and be subject to his directions, and the Chief Warden shall report himself to the Chief Engineer, and be subject to his directions, and to the direction of the the other Engineers of the Fire Department; and it shall be the further duty of said Fire Wardens to prevent the hose from being trodden on, and to keep all idle and suspected persons from the fire and its vicinity, and also to use all proper exertions within their power for the preservation of goods and other property endangered at fires; and all citizens are hereby enjoined and required to comply with the directions of said Fire Wardens: *Provided*, Such directions be not in opposition to the orders of the person having supreme control at said fire.

Duties of Engineers at fires.

SEC. 3. All the said Engineers on an alarm of fire shall immediately repair to the place where the same is, and report themselves to the Chief Engineer or person having command of the Fire Department for the time being, under a penalty for every wilful neglect not exceeding fifty dollars.

Of the Chief Engineer.

SEC. 4. The Chief Engineer shall have full power, control and command over all persons whatever at any fire, except members of Common Council, and in his absence the Engineer shall perform his duties. In the absence of both the Chief Engineer and the Engineer, the Assistant Engineer shall discharge them; and in the absence of all the Engineers, the Mayor, or in his absence the Recorder, shall designate some person to discharge the said duties until the proper officer may arrive.

Duties of Chief Engineer.

SEC. 5. That it shall be the duty of the Chief Engineer to direct at all fires all such measures as he may deem most advisable for the effectual extinguishment of the said fires, and also once in every six months to examine the condition of the fire engines and other apparatus, together with the engine house belonging to the corporation, and report the same to the Common Council, accompanied by the names and number of all the members of the Fire Department, and

TITLE VI. CHAPTER 37.

the respective associations to which they belong, which shall be annually published in the month of December, by the Clerk of said city, in such newspaper of the said city as shall be employed by the Common Council; and whenever any of the said fire engines or other fire apparatus shall require to be repaired, the Chief Engineer shall cause the same to be well and sufficiently done, and he shall report in writing all accidents of fire that may happen in this city, with the causes thereof, as well as can be ascertained, and the number and description of the buildings destroyed or injured, together with the names of the owners or occupants, to the Clerk of the city, who shall keep a faithful register of the same.

Duties of fire companies.

SEC. 6. The fire engine men shall be divided into companies, to consist of as many members as the Common Council shall direct, one of which companies to be assigned to each of the fire engines belonging, or that may hereafter belong to the city, and that each of the said companies shall and may choose out of their own number, a foreman, assistant and clerk, in such manner, and at such times as they may think proper. And it shall be the duty of said fire engine men, as often as any fire shall break out in the said city, to repair immediately upon the alarm thereof, to their respective fire engines, and convey them to or near the place where such fire shall happen, and then in conformity with the directions given them by the Chief Engineer or Engineer, shall work and manage the said fire engines, hose and other implements and instruments thereto belonging, with all their skill and power; and when the fire is extinguished, shall not remove therefrom but by the direction of the Chief Engineer or of the other Engineers; which direction being obtained, they shall return with their respective fire engines, and with the hose and other implements to their several places of deposit, and as soon as may be thereafter, wash and clean the same; and for the more effectually keeping and preserving the fire engines from decay, the said fire engine men, when the season of the year will permit, shall by order of the Chief Engineer, draw out the said fire engines, in order to wash, cleanse, and exercise them; and if any fire engine man shall neglect said duty, he shall forfeit and pay for every default, one dollar; and if he shall neglect to attend to any fire as aforesaid, or leave his fire engine while at any fire, without permission, or not perform his duty on such occasion, without reasonable excuse, he shall for every default forfeit and pay a sum not exceeding five dollars, and also be removed and displaced from his station.

Duties of hosemen.

SEC. 7. The hose, hook, ladder, axe and bag men, shall be divided into companies, to consist of as many members as the Common Council shall direct, and each company shall choose, out of their own number, a foreman, assistant and clerk, in such manner and at such times as they may think proper, and it shall be the duty of such hose, hook, ladder, axe and bag men, to cause their hose, hooks, ladders and other implements to be conveyed to the place where any fire may happen, and to apply and use the same agreeably to such directions as they may receive from the Chief Engineer, or other Engineers; and after such fire shall be extinguished, to return the same, when dismissed by the Chief Engineer, to the places where they are usually deposited, and as soon as may be thereafter wash and cleanse the same; and if any hose, hook, ladder, axe or engine man shall wilfully neglect to perform any of the duties aforesaid, he shall forfeit a sum not exceeding five dollars for every such neglect, and also be removed and displaced from his station.

Certificate of firemen.

SEC. 8. Whenever any fire engine man, hose, hook, ladder, axe and bag man is elected a member of any fire company or to supply any vacancy therein, it shall be his duty to call on the Treasurer of the Fire Department, and procure a certificate within one month from the date of his election, countersigned by the City Clerk, specifying the name and number of the company to which such fire engine man, hose, hook, ladder, axe and bag man shall be elected; and if any fire engine man, hose, hook, ladder, axe and bag man, whose office, from any cause may become vacant, shall be re-elected, he shall take up a new certificate as aforesaid; and it shall be the duty of the Chief Engineer to certify on each certificate whether a vacancy exists in the company to which any fire engine man, hose, hook, ladder, axe and bag man shall be elected as aforesaid. And if such certificate shall not be procured within the time above prescribed, such appointment shall be null and void.

Badges of Mayor &c.

SEC. 9. The Mayor and Aldermen shall severally bear a staff, with a gilded flame at the top, and not be required to bear any other badge of office.

Badge of Chief Engineer.

SEC. 10. The Chief Engineer shall wear a painted leathern cap, with the words "Chief Engineer" painted on the frontispiece thereof,

TITLE VI. CHAPTER 37.

and shall also carry a bright speaking trumpet, with the words "Chief Engineer" painted thereon.

Of Engineers

SEC. 11. The Assistant Engineers shall wear painted leathern caps with the words "Engineer No. 1," and "Engineer No. 2," painted on the frontispiece thereof; they shall also carry a speaking trumpet with the words "Engineer No. 1," and "Engineer No. 2," painted thereon.

Badge of Wardens.

SEC. 12. The Fire Wardens shall severally wear a hat, with the word "Warden" painted on the frontispiece thereof; and shall also carry a staff with the word "Warden" painted thereon.

Badge of Foremen.

SEC. 13. The foreman and assistant foreman of the engine, hose, hook and ladder companies, and the members of said companies shall wear leathern caps of the form heretofore in use, and the said caps shall be distinguished in the manner following, viz: the cap of each foreman shall have the word "Foreman" painted on the frontispiece of the same, together with the number of the engine or company to which he may belong; and each member of an engine, hose or hook and ladder company, shall have the number of the engine or company to which he belongs painted upon the frontispiece of his cap.

Of sections and alarm bell.

SEC. 14. The Sextons of the several churches of this city which now are, or hereafter may be furnished with bells, shall immediately on the alarm of fire, repair to the several churches with which they are connected, and diligently ring said bells during twenty minutes, unless the fire be sooner extinguished, under the penalty of two dollars for every such omission: *Provided*, That when a chimney only shall be on fire either by day or by night said bells shall not be rung.

Duties of watchmen.

SEC. 15. It shall also be the duty of every watchman or patrol, upon the breaking out of any fire, to alarm the citizens by crying out "fire," and mentioning the street where it may be on his going to and coming from the next and nearest watch stations, that the alarm may be rapidly passed from one watch station to another, and the firemen and citizens may thereby be generally directed where to repair.

Penalty and arrest for disobeying orders at fires.

SEC. 16. All persons who at a fire shall refuse to obey any order or direction given by a person duly authorized to order or direct, or who shall resist or impede any officer or other person in the discharge of his duty, shall, in the absence of sufficient excuse, be punished by fine not exceeding fifty dollars, and any member of the Common Council or any Fire Warden may arrest and detain such person in custody until such fire is extinguished; and such person then failing to enter into a sufficient recognizance for his appearance at the next term of the Mayor's Court, may be committed until such term of said Court.

For refusing to work at fires.

SEC. 17. It shall be lawful for the Foreman or Assistant Foreman of any fire engine or other fire company, or for any member of the Common Council, Chief Engineer or Assistant, or any Fire Warden, to require the aid of any citizen or inhabitant in drawing any engine or other apparatus to the fire, or the aid of any bystander at a fire, to work any engine or apparatus at the same, and on neglect or refusal to comply with such requisition, the offender shall pay a penalty not exceeding ten dollars with costs of suit upon conviction thereof, before the Mayor's Court, unless sufficient cause for such refusal or neglect is alleged at the time; and if not deemed to be true or sufficient, is made to appear on the trial. And such person may be arrested and proceeded with, in the same manner as is provided in section 16, and more effectually to carry out the provisions of this section, it shall be the duty of the Chief Warden to nominate to the Common Council one suitable person from each Fire Engine Company, to be appointed by them a Fire Warden, and to be assigned and attached to the company of which he is a member.

Penalty for injuring fire apparatus.

SEC. 18. If any person shall wilfully injure, in any manner, any hose, fire engine or other apparatus, or building containing the same, belonging to this city, the offender shall, for every such offence, forfeit and pay the sum of twenty dollars, besides being liable to an action for the recovery of the damage done.

Duty of Marshal and Constable at fires.

SEC. 19. The Marshal and every Constable shall repair immediately on the alarm of fire, with their staff of office, to the place where the fire may be, and report himself to any member of the Common Council, for the preservation of the public peace, and the removal of all idle and suspected persons, or the preservation of property in the vicinity of the fire; and if the Marshal or any Constable shall neglect to comply with the provisions of this section, he shall pay a fine not exceeding fifty dollars, or be subject to removal from office.

TITLE VI. CHAPTER 37.

Of pulling down build- at fires.

SEC. 20. The hook and ladder and axe men shall, under the direction of the Chief Engineer, and two members of the Common Council present, or in the absence of the Chief Engineer, then under the directions of the Assistant Engineer and two members of the Common Council, or in the absence of all the Engineers, then under the directions of three of the Common Council, if so many be present, cut down and remove any building, erection or fence, for the purpose of checking the progress of the fire.

Fines enure to fire department and duty of Wardens.

SEC. 21. Semi-annually, in the months of March and September, all fines provided by this or the succeeding chapter relative to the prevention of fires, shall enure to the benefit of the Fire Department, when collected, after deducting all costs and expenses incurred in the prosecution thereof; and any specified sum as a fine may be paid by the person liable therefor, to such of the Fire Wardens as shall be designated by the Trustees of the Fire Department, and such Fire Wardens shall note in a book, to be furnished by the said Trustees, all violations of this and the succeeding chapter, and make an annual report thereof to the Treasurer of the Fire Department; and the said Fire Wardens shall also pay all moneys received by them by virtue of this section to such Collector as shall be specially designated by the said Trustees for that purpose.

Unlawful use of fire engines.

SEC. 22. If any person having charge of any engine or other fire apparatus, shall suffer or permit the same to be applied to private uses without the consent of the Mayor, Chief Engineer or Common Council, he shall forfeit the penalty of five dollars, together with the damages occasioned thereto.

Term of office of Wardens.

SEC. 23. Fire Wardens shall hold their office during the pleasure of the Common Council, and upon the requisite number of years' service as such Warden, shall be entitled to the same exemptions as other members of the Fire Department for a like term of service.

Appointment of Wardens.

SEC. 24. The Board of Wardens shall nominate to the Common Council whenever necessary, the names of persons to fill vacancies occurring in their body.

No engine shall be run on sidewalks. Penalty.

SEC. 25. Any member of the Fire Department of the city of Detroit, or other person, who is not a member of said Department, who shall hereafter run, place, or wheel upon any sidewalk, or aid or assist in running, or placing any fire engine, hook and ladder truck, or hose company cart, upon any sidewalk adjoining or laying along side any paved street, or alley, in said city, between the hours of six o'clock A. M., and ten o'clock P. M., or at any time when returning from fires, shall, for every such offence, on conviction thereof before the Mayor's Court of said city, be punished by a fine not exceeding five dollars, with costs of prosecution; and if a member of the Fire Department, by suspension or expulsion, or either, at the discretion of said Court.

False alarms Penalty for.

SEC. 26. It shall not be lawful for any person or persons, without reasonable cause, by outcry, or ringing of the bells, or by proclaiming fire, or by any other means whatsoever, to make or circulate, or cause to be made or circulated in any ward in the city of Detroit, any false alarm of fire, and the person or persons so offending, shall be punished on conviction before the Mayor's Court, or any other proper Court in said city to try the same, by a fine not exceeding one hundred dollars, or by imprisonment in the County Jail not exceeding sixty days: *Provided, however*, That all proceedings under this ordinance shall be had on complaint before the proper Court or Magistrate.

CHAPTER XXXVIII.

Relative to the Prevention of Fires.

Of the board of Fire Wardens.

SEC. 1. The Fire Wardens shall constitute a board, of whom a representation from three or more wards shall be a quorum for the purpose of considering the most efficient and prompt manner of dis-

TITLE VI. CHAPTER 38.

charging the duties imposed on them by the laws and ordinances of the city; they shall choose from their number a Chief and Clerk, at such time and such manner as they may designate. The Fire Wardens of the respective wards shall notice and correct any infractions of the laws and ordinances made for the protection of the city from fires, in their respective wards particularly, and in the city generally, and shall make reports by their foreman, to be by them respectively chosen, of the state and police of their respective wards, as respects danger from exposure to fires, on the first Mondays of June and December in each year to the Chief Warden, who shall make report of the same in reference to the city generally, to the Common Council; and the Board may impose such fines upon the members as, in their judgment, may best secure the performance of the duties of said Fire Wardens, both at fires and in visiting buildings, and in other duties in their several wards, and for non-attendance at regular or special meetings of the Wardens; and any disobedience to such rules shall be reported to the Common Council, and shall subject the Fire Warden so disobeying to fine and removal by the Common Council.

Semi-annual inspection of the city.

SEC. 2. It shall be the duty of the Fire Wardens, or either of them, in their respective wards, twice in each year, viz: in the months of May and November, and as much oftener as may be deemed proper, between sunrise and sunset, to enter into any house or building, lots, yards or premises in said city, and examine the fire places, hearths, chimneys, stoves and pipes thereto, ovens, boilers, or other apparatus likely to cause fire; also, the places where ashes may be deposited, and all places where any gunpowder, hemp, flax, tow, hay, straw, rushes, shavings, or other combustible materials may be lodged; and the said Fire Wardens shall give such directions in regard to the several foregoing matters as they or any of them may think expedient, either as to the removal and alteration, or better care and management thereof; which directions shall be obeyed and complied with by the person or persons directed in that behalf, and at their expense.

Of cleaning chimneys. Penalty if they take fire.

SEC. 3. The said Fire Wardens shall also have authority to cause chimneys to be burned out or otherwise cleaned, whenever they shall deem it necessary, and to require the tenant or tenants, owner or owners of any blacksmith's shop so to alter or construct, (as the case may require,) the chimneys in said shop as to prevent sparks of fire from passing into the open air, and may require the ceiling or sides of any shop or any part thereof to be plastered. Every occupant of premises whose chimneys shall take fire, except when burned out under the direction or by the permission of a Fire Warden, shall be fined one dollar for each infraction of the law; and also to remove or abate, with the consent of the Mayor, Recorder or any Alderman, (and in neglect or refusal of the owner or occupant,) any cause from which immediate danger of fire may be apprehended, at the expense of the person who should have done the same; and to remove or abate, in manner above prescribed, any other cause whatever from which immediate danger of fire may be apprehended, at the expense of the person or persons occasioning the same. The said Fire Wardens are hereby empowered at any regular or special meeting of their Board, to require that chimneys shall be swept or cleaned by owners or occupants, as the case may be, at such periods, and under such regulations as they may prescribe; and for every case of neglect or refusal, the parties offending shall forfeit and pay a penalty of one dollar, and for every subsequent case of neglect or refusal, after being thereto specially required by a Fire Warden, a penalty of one dollar in addition.

Abating cause of danger in chimneys.

SEC. 4. If any person or persons, shall neglect or refuse so to comply with any such directions, as any of said Fire Wardens may give in the premises; or shall obstruct or hinder any Fire Warden or his assistants, in the performance of his duty, the person so offending shall forfeit and pay for every such neglect, non-compliance or hindrance, a sum not exceeding fifty dollars, and for every day which shall elapse after the time alotted for such removal, alteration, better care or management, without compliance with such directions, the said person shall also forfeit and pay a further and additional sum of five dollars; and all expenses caused in carrying into effect the directions of the Fire Wardens, shall in the first instance be paid by the occupant of the premises, and shall be deducted from the rent payable by him, her or them, unless such diections were rendered necessary by the act or default of said occupant, or there be a special agreement to the contrary between the landlord and said occupant; and it shall also be the duty of said Fire Wardens to ascertain whether or not their directions are duly complied with, and in case of non-compliance, or in case of any violation of this chapter, to report the names

Penalty for disobeying Fire Warden.

Owners of premises liable for expenses of executing direction of Wardens.

TITLE VI. CHAPTER 38.

of all the offenders, with the particular circumstances, to the Common Council, who may thereupon cause such offenders to be prosecuted for the recovery of the penalties incurred by them.

Securing stove pipe and burning chimneys.

SEC. 5. No pipe of any stove or franklin shall be put up in any house or building, unless it be conducted into a chimney made of brick or stone; nor shall any person at any time set fire to any chimney for the purpose of cleaning the same, without previous consent of the Fire Warden of the proper ward; any person putting up, or procuring to be put up, the pipe of any stove or franklin, or doing any other act contrary to this section, shall for every offence forfeit five dollars, and the further sum of one dollar for every twenty-four hours the same shall remain so put up, after notice by any Fire Warden to alter the same.

How chimneys shall be constructed.

SEC. 6. Every chimney hereafter to be erected, and all chimneys whatever, shall be plastered with lime and sand on the inside thereof, under a penalty of twenty-five dollars, and a further penalty of ten dollars for every fifteen days neglect to alter or take down the same, after a notice given by any Fire Warden for that purpose. It shall be the duty of the Engineers or Fire Wardens to take notice of all chimneys when the same are being constructed, and ascertain whether they are in conformity with the requirements of this chapter, and if not, make report to the Common Council. Chimneys shall be so constructed or altered as to admit of the flues therein being swept or cleaned from top to bottom, under the same penalties for neglect or refusal as are prescribed in section three.

Of carrying fire through streets.

SEC. 7. No person shall carry fire in or through any street or lot except the same be placed or carried in some close and secure pan or vessel, under a penalty of five dollars for each offence.

Securing ashes.

SEC. 8. No ashes, except at manufactories where ashes are used, shall be kept or deposited in any part of this city, unless the same be in a close and secure metalic or earthen vessel, or brick or stone ash-room, under the penalty of one dollar for every twenty-four hours the same shall remain after notice from a Fire Warden to remove the same.

Of fire works and fire arms

SEC. 9. No person shall fire or set off any squib, cracker, gunpowder or fire works, or fire any gun or pistol in any part of this city, unless by a written permission of the Mayor or two Aldermen, which permission shall limit the time of such firing, and shall be subject to be revoked at any time by the Common Council; and any person or persons violating any of the provisions of this section, shall forfeit the penalty of five dollars for each and every offence.

Of cannon.

SEC. 10. Every person firing a cannon within this city, unless by permission of the Mayor or two Aldermen, shall forfeit the penalty of twenty-five dollars: *Provided*, That nothing in this or the preceding section shall be construed to prohibit any military company from firing any gun or cannon when authorized by their commanding officer or officers.

Of scuttles.

SEC. 11. Every dwelling house or other building more than one story in height within this city, shall have a scuttle through the roof, and a convenient and suitable stair way or ladder leading to the same; and any person constructing such dwelling house or building, without such scuttle, and every owner of any such house or building now erected, (not having other permanent and convenient means of access to the roof,) neglecting to comply with the requisitions of this section for the space of thirty days after notice from a Fire Warden, shall forfeit twenty-five dollars, and the further sum of five dollars for every ten days the non-compliance shall continue to exist.

Of shavings and combustibles.

SEC. 12. It shall not be lawful for any person or persons to have in his or her possession, any shavings, wood or fuel of any description, combustibles, or any materials that may occasion hazard or danger of fire unless the same shall be placed in such situation, and be secured in such manner as shall be directed by the Fire Wardens, or either of them, of the ward in which either of the before enumerated articles shall be deposited; and all carpenters, cabinet-makers, turners, coach makers, wheelrights, coopers, and others, using any trade by which shavings are made, shall respectively, at the close of each day, on leaving off work, cause the place where such shavings are, to be swept, and the shavings to be carefully gathered and placed in boxes, or to be otherwise compactly and securely stowed in some safe place, remote from danger, by means of fire or candle light, and so to be kept until the same shall be taken away from such premises, as aforesaid, under the penalty of five dollars for each omission or offence herein.

SEC. 13. It shall not be lawful to burn any shavings in any street, road or lane, or to kindle any fire or any other combustible matter

TITLE VI. CHAPTER 38.

Fires in the streets.

in any street, road or lane, or on any wharf in this city, under a penalty not exceeding ten dollars for each offence, to be recovered from any person or persons aiding or assisting therein.

keeping of hay and straw.

SEC. 14. No person shall have, put or keep any hay or straw uncovered in stack or pile, within three hundred yards of any building within the limits of this city: *Provided, however*, That nothing herein shall be construed to prevent landing hay or straw on any of the wharves of this city, or to prevent carting the same to or from any part of the said city; nor shall any person have, put or keep, within the said city, any hay or straw, hemp, flax, tow, shavings or rushes, in any stable or other building which is, or shall be, within such distance from any chimney, hearth or fire place, or place for depositing ashes, nor in any dwelling house whatever, as may be deemed unsafe or dangerous by the Fire Warden of the proper ward, under a penalty not exceeding twenty-five dollars for each and every offence, to be recovered with costs of suit, and the further sum of ten dollars for every twenty-four hours the same shall so remain after due notice given in writing to the offender, by the Fire Warden or other officer.

Powder.

SEC. 15. No powder shall be deposited in any magazine, unless the same be approved by the Common Council.

Keeper of magazine.

SEC. 16. The Common Council shall appoint a suitable person to be the keeper of the magazine, and he shall be entitled to demand and have twenty-five cents on each keg of powder received, stored and delivered by him, to be paid by the person for whom it is stored.

Powder to be seized.

SEC. 17. If any fireman, during a fire, and in the vicinity thereof, shall discover in any building, a greater quantity than twenty-eight pounds of powder, it shall be lawful for him to seize, without warrant from any magistrate, and convert the same as forfeited to the use of the Fire Department.

Where and how powder to be kept.

SEC. 18. There shall not be kept within the limits of this city, (except in the magazine of powder of the United States, or of this State,) at any one time, in any one house and its appurtenances, or in any one store and its appurtenances, any greater quantity of gunpowder, than the weight of twenty-eight pounds; which twenty-eight pounds of gunpowder shall be well secured in metal canisters, with metal stoppers or covers, neither of which shall contain more than seven pounds weight. All gunpowder which shall be kept in this city, contrary to the meaning and provisions of this chapter, shall be forfeited by the person or persons so keeping the same; and it shall be lawful for the Mayor, Engineer, or any Fire Warden to seize the same in manner as provided in section 17, and the person or persons so offending shall also forfeit the sum of one hundred dollars for every hundred weight of gunpowder, and in that proportion for a greater or less quantity, so kept contrary to the true intent and meaning of this chapter, to be recovered with costs of suit in the Mayor's Court of this city.

Chief Warden or Marshal to dispose of powder seized, &c.

SEC. 19. It shall be the duty of the Chief Warden or City Marshal to dispose of all gunpowder forfeited and seized as provided in the preceding section, and pay the proceeds arising therefrom to the Treasurer of the Fire Department, for the use of said Department, taking his receipt therefor, and report the same to the President of said Department. And to avoid dangers from gunpowder laden on board of any vessel arriving at this port, *Be it further ordained*, That the commander or owners of every vessel arriving at this port, and having gunpowder on board, shall, within twenty-four hours after her arrival before this city, and before such vessel shall be hauled alongside of any wharf, pier or quay, within the said city, land the said gunpowder by means of a boat or boats, or other small craft, at any place out of the limits, viz: above or below this city, on the Detroit river, and shall cause the same to be stored in some safe place beyond the said limits, until the same shall be conveyed to such magazine as shall be provided by the corporation for the storing of gunpowder, on pain of forfeiting all such gunpowder.

Commanders and owners of vessels having powder on board, how to land the same.

Of conveying powder through the streets.

SEC. 20. For the more safe conveyance of gunpowder through the city, to or from any magazine or powder house, the store keeper shall procure and provide good canvas, tow cloth, or leathern bags, or cases, in order to cover all casks of gunpowder that may be conveyed as aforesaid; and no cartmen or other person shall cart or carry through any avenue, street or lane of this city. by means of any cart, carriage, or by hand or otherwise, any gunpowder, except in tight casks, well headed and hooped, which casks shall be put into such canvas, tow cloth or leathern bags or cases as aforesaid, in such manner as entirely to cover such cask therewith, and the mouths of

TITLE VI. CHAPTER 38.

such bags or cases shall be securely tied, so that no gunpowder may be spilled or scattered in the passage thereof, on pain of forfeiting all such gunpowder as shall be conveyed through any of the avenues, streets or lanes aforesaid, in any other manner than is hereby directed.

Of lading or unlading powder in the city.

SEC. 21. No person, excepting as aforesaid, shall be permitted to lade or unlade any greater quantity of gunpowder than twenty-eight pounds, in or from any vessel at any of the slips or wharves in the city, under the penalty of forfeiting a sum not exceeding one hundred dollars for each offence.

Lights in stables.

SEC. 22. No owner or occupant of any livery or other stable within this city, nor any person in the employment of such owner or occupant, shall use therein any lighted candle or other light, except the same be securely kept within a horn, tin or glass lantern, under a penalty not exceeding ten dollars for each offence, to be recovered with costs of suit.

Liability of parents and masters.

SEC. 23. If any offence shall be committed against this chapter by any child, apprentice or servant, the forfeiture and penalty shall be recovered from and paid by the parent, master, or mistress of the party offending.

CHAPTER XXXIX.

Relative to the erection of certain Buildings within certain limits.

Wooden buildings where prohibited. Penalty.

SEC. 1. No person shall hereafter erect or place any building or any part of a building within the following limits, unless such building or part of a building shall be constructed of stone or brick, with party or fire walls of the same material, rising at least ten inches above the roof, if the same be covered with metal or slate; if with wood, then at least two feet, viz:—Beginning at a point in the Detroit river where the easterly line of St. Antoine street extended will strike said river, thence up said St. Antoine street to a point south of Jefferson avenue, within one hundred feet of the southerly line of Jefferson avenue, thence in a line parallel with said southerly line east to the easterly line of the city, thence northerly alone the easterly line of the city to a point on said line one hundred feet northerly of the north line of Jefferson avenue, thence westerly in a line parallel with said north line, and one hundred feet distant therefrom, till it intersects with St. Antoine street, thence northerly up the centre of said St. Antoine street to the centre of Croghan street; thence along the centre of said Croghan street to the centre of Randolph street; thence along the centre of said Randolph street to Miami avenue; thence along the centre of said Miami avenue to State street; thence along the centre of said State street to the alley between Farmer street and Woodward avenue; thence along the centre of said alley to Grand River street; thence along the centre of said Grand River street to the alley between Griswold street and Woodward avenue; thence along the centre of said alley to State street; thence along the centre of said State street to Cass street; thence along the centre of said Cass street to an alley between Lafayette street and Fort street; thence along the centre of said alley and the continuation thereof to the western line of the city; thence along the said western line of the city to the Detroit river; thence up along the line of said river to the place of beginning. Also, commencing on the north side of Michigan avenue at the corner of Park street and extending up Park street on the east side thereof to Grand River street; thence along Grand River street on the south side thereof to Woodward avenue in said city; thence along the westerly line of Woodward avenue to the northerly line of Michigan avenue; thence along the northerly line of Michigan avenue to the place of beginning: Also, commencing at a point on the east line of Randolph street, one hundred feet southerly of Gratiot street, running thence in a line parallel to the southeasterly line of said Gratiot street and one hundred feet distant therefrom to Russell street; thence northerly along the westerly line of said Russell street to a point one hundred feet northerly of said Gratiot street; thence south-westerly in a line parallel to the north-westerly line of said Gratiot street and one hundred feet distant therefrom to the easterly line of said Randolph street; thence southerly along the easterly line of said Randolph street to the place of beginning of this latter description. Also, commencing on the southerly side of Miami avenue, at the point of its intersection with State street, and extending thence westerly up said avenue to Circus street; thence along the

TITLE VI. CHAPTER 39.

southerly line of Circus street to Woodward avenue; thence along the easterly line of Woodward avenue to State street; thence along the northerly line of State street to the place of beginning, (said description including all that portion of the city which lies between Miami avenue, Circus street, Woodward avenue and State street.) Also, commencing on the westerly side of Cass street, at the point of its intersection with the southerly line of the alley which lies between Howard street and Michigan avenue and Abbott street, thence along the said line of said alley westerly to the westerly line of said city; thence southerly along said westerly line of said city to the centre of the alley between Fort street and Lafayette street; thence easterly along the centre of said alley to the westerly line of Cass street; thence northerly along said line of Cass street to the place of beginning. Also, commencing on the easterly line of Randolph street, at the point of its intersection with the southerly line of Croghan street, thence the said line of said Randolph street to the easterly line of Gratiot street; thence northerly along said Gratiot street to the westerly line of Beaubien street; thence northerly along said line of Beaubien street to the northerly line of Croghan street; thence along said line of Croghan street westerly to the place of beginning. And if any building not made and constructed of stone or brick shall be erected or placed within the aforesaid prescribed limits, contrary to the provisions of this section, the owner or owners, builder or builders thereof shall severally forfeit a penalty of fifty dollars for each and every offence; and also a penalty of fifty dollars for each and every week such building shall so remain within said limits as above prescribed.

Barns and wood houses of certain size permitted.

SEC. 2. Nothing contained in the preceding section shall prohibit the erection within the aforesaid prescribed limits, of any building of wood which shall not be more than eight feet square, nor of any wood house for keeping and storing of fire wood, which shall not exceed twenty feet in length, twelve feet in width, and twelve feet in height, nor of any barn which shall not exceed twenty-four feet in length, sixteen feet in width, and not more than twelve feet in height from the common surface of the earth to the top of the plates, with a roof not to exceed one-quarter pitch, provided such small buildings or wood house or barn shall not be made to front upon any street: *Provided*,

That nothing in this section contained shall be construed to allow more than one such barn or wood-shed on any one lot or premises used as one tenement.

Partition walls.

SEC. 3. The limits prescribed in section one of this chapter, shall be known as the fire limits of the city of Detroit, and the whole of the ground included within said prescribed limits shall be deemed and taken to be within said fire limits; and in all buildings hereafter to be erected of stone or brick, in blocks of two or more buildings, within said limits, there shall be erected partition walls running at right angles with the street upon which such building shall front, or as nearly at right angles with said street as the plan of the city will admit of, constructed of stone or brick, at least one foot in thickness, and extending at least ten inches above the roof, if such roof be covered with metal or slate; but if of wood, then at least two feet above the roof of such building; and every person, whether owner, part owner, or builder who shall erect or cause to be erected a building or part of a building, contrary to the provisions of this section, shall forfeit the penalty of fifty dollars for every month during which such building shall remain so erected.

Certain repairs prohibited. Penalty.

SEC. 4. No person shall raise or elevate from the ground any wooden building now standing within said limits, by constructing thereunder or thereon another story or part of a story, or in any other way increase the height of said building; and if any person shall violate the provisions of this section, then he shall forfeit a penalty of fifty dollars, and also a penalty of fifty dollars for each and every week said building shall remain so raised or erected.

Building not to be removed within the fire limits. Penalty.

SEC. 5. No person shall remove any building of wood from one part, or section, or lot within such fire limits, to any other part, section or lot within the same; and in case any person shall violate the provisions of this section, he shall forfeit the like penalty of fifty dollars; and also a further penalty of fifty dollars for each and every week such building shall be permitted to remain upon the place to which it shall have been removed.

Height of building without fire limits.

SEC. 6. No person shall build, erect or place any building or part of a building, more than twenty-six feet in height, measuring from the established grade, or common surface of the ground of the street or alley upon which such building shall front, to the top of the plate of

TITLE VII. CHAPTER 40.

such building; nor shall the roof thereof exceed a quarter pitch unless such building shall be constructed of stone or brick, as provided in section one of this chapter, in any part of the city whatever. And any owner or owners, builder or builders, for hire, who shall at any time build or place any such building within the limits of the city, contrary to the provisions of this section, shall each and severally, upon conviction thereof before the Mayor's Court, pay a fine for each and every offence not exceeding fifty dollars; and the owners thereof shall, on conviction, be subject to a like penalty of fifty dollars for each and every week he, she, or they shall suffer such building (to be hereafter erected,) to remain within the limits of the city: *Provided*, That nothing in this chapter shall prohibit the erection of steeples or cupola upon any church or any public building, or manufactory establishment.

Lime kilns prohibited.

SEC. 7. No person shall erect or cause to be erected within the limits of the city, any lime kiln or building to be used in the manufacture or burning of lime; and if any person shall violate the provisions of this section, he shall forfeit a penalty of one hundred dollars, and also a penalty of one hundred dollars for each and every weak such lime kiln or building shall be used for the manufacture of burning of lime.

TITLE SEVEN.

OF THE PUBLIC HEALTH.

CHAPTER XL.

Relative to Nuisances.

SEC. 1. How nuisances may be abated; penalty for nuisances.
SEC. 2. Marshal to abate, and property to be assessed for expenses.
SEC. 3. Nuisances to be buried; penalty for not burying.
SEC. 4. Duty of Marshal.

How nuisance may be abated.

SEC. 1. If any person or persons within the boundaries of the said city shall permit or suffer on his, her or their premises, of which he, she or they may be the occupant or occupants, agent or agents having charge thereof, either by exercising any unwholesome or offensive trade or calling, or by permitting any building, sewer or other thing whatsoever, to remain on the premises of which he, she or they shall be the owner or occupant or occupants, agent or agents having charge thereof, until by offensive and ill stenches or otherwise, they, or any of them, shall become offensive, hurtful or dangerous to the neighborhood or travelers, it shall be the duty of the Marshal, or any other officer of said city, appointed or elected, to give notice to such person or persons to remove such nuisances forthwith; and if the owner or owners, occupant or occupants, agent or agents having charge of such premises, on which such nuisance shall be situate, shall neglect or refuse to remove the same for the space of twenty-four hours after such notice shall have been given, he she or they, on conviction thereof shall be liable to pay a fine not exceeding five dollars for each day he, she or they shall have permitted such nuisance to remain after notice as aforesaid.

Penalty for nuisances.

Marshal to abate and property to be assessed for expenses.

SEC. 2. If any person or persons shall, after notice as aforesaid, permit any such nuisance to remain, which shall be manifestly dangerous or improper, it shall be lawful for the Marshal to remove and abate such nuisance, either by removing any putrefactions, or by draining the premises, or by filling them up forthwith, under the direction of the Common Council, and the person or persons permitting the same to remain as aforesaid, shall, on conviction thereof, be liable to pay a fine not exceeding thirty dollars, and the expenses of removing such nuisance, together with the costs of prosecution: *Provided*, The Common Council may, at the time of the abatement of any such nuisance, or at any time within thirty days thereafter, direct an assessment to be made on the lot or lots from which such nuisance shall have been removed, sufficient to pay all the expenses of removing the same, and when such assessment shall have been levied and collected, it shall be a bar to the recovery of the same by any proceedings in the Mayor's Court, but shall not prevent the recovery of any fines or costs under this chapter, to which any person or persons may have become liable for creating such nuisance, or suffering the same to remain after notice: *Provided*, Whenever, in the opinion of any two Aldermen of said city, any nuisance of any kind may be dangerous to the health of said city, they may, without notice, by written instructions, signed by them, direct any officer of said city to abate the same in a manner to be by them directed; and the occupant or occupants, owner or

TITLE VII. CHAPTER 41.

owners, agent or agents having charge or control of the premises on which any nuisance shall be so abated, if they refuse to pay the expense of abating such nuisance, be subject to prosecution in the Mayor's Court, for having suffered the existence of such nuisance, and on conviction shall be liable to a fine not to exceed ten dollars and the expenses of removing the nuisance, together with costs.

Nuisances to be buried and penalty for not burrying.

SEC. 3. No person shall deposit or cause to be left, placed or deposited in any part of said city, any dead animal, or any animal, vegetable or other substance, which is offensive, or which by process of decomposition, may become offensive, unless the same shall be buried at least three feet below the surface of the ground, and any person offending in the premises, shall, on conviction, be liable to pay a fine not exceeding fifty dollars, and the expense of removing such nuisance, together with the costs of prosecution.

Duty of Marshal.

SEC. 4. It shall be the duty of the Marshal to report to the Common Council, the existence of any nuisance whatever in said city, and perform such other acts relative to the same according to the general or special regulations prescribed relative thereto. And the Marshal is hereby required to make complaint to the City Attorney of any violation of this chapter.

CHAPTER XLI.

Relative to Small Pox.

SEC. 1. Taverns and boarding houses where small pox is to close doors.
SEC. 2. Signs to be placed on houses where small pox exists.
SEC. 3. Physicians shall report cases of small pox.
SEC. 4. Diseased persons not to go at large.
SEC. 5. Mayor may confine persons having.

Taverns and boarding houses where small pox is to close doors

SEC. 1. That the keepers of all taverns, hotels and boarding houses within the limits of this city, shall be, and they are hereby required whenever the small pox shall be found to exist therein to close them immediately, and to keep them closed against all customers and lodgers, until the patients are removed, and such tavern, hotel or boarding house shall be thoroughly cleansed and ventilated, under a penalty not exceeding one hundred dollars for each case of the small pox within their premises, to be recovered in the Mayor's Court, with costs.

SEC. 2. That every keeper of a tavern, hotel, boarding house, or house within the limits aforesaid, within whose premises, any person or persons may at any time be sick of small pox shall be, and he or she is hereby required to exhibit openly and publicly at his or her front door or gate, a sign, with the words "small pox," distinctly and legibly written or printed thereon, under such penalty for every wilful omission, not exceeding fifty dollars with costs, as the Mayor's Court may on complaint impose.

Signs to be placed on houses where small pox exists.

SEC. 3. That it is hereby made the duty of every practising physician within the limits of the said city, to report in writing to the Clerk of the city, or to any member of the Common Council, every case of the small pox which he may be called to visit or examine; which report shall contain, as near as may be, a description of the location in the city of each case, and the name of the patient, under a penalty not exceeding one hundred dollars for each day such report shall be withheld.

Physicians to report cases of small pox.

SEC. 4. That it shall not be lawful for any person or persons who may have been, or may be diseased as aforesaid, to go at large within the limits aforesaid, until advised by a physician that said going at large will not endanger the health of others.

Diseased persons not to go at large.

SEC. 5. If any person so diseased shall be found going at large, it shall be competent for the Mayor, Recorder, or either of the Aldermen, to send him forthwith to some suitable place to be provided, and if need be, to confine him there so long as the public safety may require.

Mayor may confine persons having.

CHAPTER XLII.

Relative to filling wharves, and preserving the purity of the Detroit River.

SEC. 1. That no person shall deposit or put into any dock or wharf within the limits of said city, any straw, hay or green boughs, manure, cord wood, or any vegetables or perishable materials whatever, and any person or persons offending against the provisions of this section, shall, on conviction before the Mayor's Court, for every offence, forfeit and pay a sum not exceeding twenty-five dollars, and costs of prosecution.

Perishable materials not to be put into any dock.

TITLE VII. CHAPTER 43.

No carcasses to be deposited within a quarter of a mile of the shore.

SEC. 2. No person or persons shall deposit in the Detroit river, within a quarter of a mile from the shore, in front of this city, or within the distance of half a mile above or below the limits thereof, any dead carcass, or any filthy or offensive matter of any kind whatsoever, or any substance which, by any process, can become putrid or offensive, or which may in any manner render the water of said river within the limits aforesaid, unhealthy or impure, and any person or persons offending herein, shall, on conviction thereof, be fined in a sum not exceeding fifty dollars, with costs of prosecution.

Penalty.

Deposit to be removed.

SEC. 3. It shall be the duty of all the city officers to notice any violation of this chapter, and to require all persons guilty thereof to remove all deposits of the description, and within the limits aforesaid, and on their failing to do so, to cause the same to be removed, at the expense of the corporation, which amount shall be reimbursed by the person or persons guilty of making such deposits, in addition to the penalty imposed by the foregoing section.

No person to expose their naked bodies.

SEC. 4. It shall not be lawful for any person or persons, to expose their naked bodies, by bathing or otherwise, within the limits of said city, or in front thereof, between the hours of four of the clock in the forenoon, and nine of the clock in the afternoon, under a penalty not exceeding ten dollars and costs, for each offence.

Penalty.

CHAPTER XLIII.

Relative to Grave Yards.

Public grave yards.

SEC. 1. That the grave yards lying north of the Fort Gratiot turnpike, are hereby declared to be the only public grave yards within the limits of the city of Detroit, and the plan thereof respecting lots for interment, is hereby continued; and all graves shall be at least five feet deep.

Duty of Sexton.

SEC. 2. It shall be the duty of the Sexton to superintend the grave yards, to take charge of the city hearse, and when required by the friends of any deceased person, or by the Director of the Poor of the said city, he shall, within a reasonable time, cause to be dug a grave of suitable dimensions agreeably to the preceding section, and shall bury the corpse therein; and when it shall be required of the Sexton, he shall deliver the coffin at the house where the corpse may be, furnish a horse for the hearse, and convey the corpse to the grave.

Where corpses to be buried.

SEC. 3. It shall not be lawful for any person or persons to inter or cause to be interred, the corpse of any deceased person in any part of said city, excepting in the public grave yards aforesaid.

The Sexton may demand and receive fees.

SEC. 4. The Sexton may demand and receive for his services the following fees, to wit: for digging a grave and burying the corpse, one dollar and fifty cents; for delivering the coffin at the house where the corpse may be, twenty-five cents; for furnishing a horse and carrying the corpse to the grave, one dollar and seventy-five cents. *Provided*, That whenever the corpse is to be buried less than one mile beyond the limits of said city, the Sexton shall be entitled to demand and receive for digging a grave and burying the corpse, two dollars, and for furnishing a horse and carrying the corpse to the grave, one dollar and seventy-five cents.

Lots and half lots how purchased.

SEC. 5. Any person who may be desirous of purchasing a lot in the new cemetery, may make application to the City Clerk, and if the same be granted, the applicant shall pay the sum of ten dollars to the City Treasurer, and take his certificate therefor. Nothing in this section shall prohibit the sale of half lots, if any there should be, at the price of five dollars, and no lot shall be divided for this purpose so long as any half lot remains unsold.

Clerk to convey lots &c.

SEC. 6. The purchaser or his assigns shall deposit said duplicate with the City Clerk, who shall thereupon execute and deliver a deed for the lot described therein to the person entitled thereto, and charge the Treasurer for the price paid.

No one to be buried without permission.

SEC. 7. No person shall inter or cause to be interred the corpse of any deceased person, in either of said gave yards, without the permission of the person or persons, or corporation owning the lot.

Penalties.

SEC. 8. Any person or persons who shall violate any of the provisions of this chapter, shall forfeit and pay a sum not exceeding twenty-five dollars with costs of suit; and if any Sexton shall neglect or refuse to perform the duties herein required, or demand for his services a sum greater than is provided by the fourth section of this chapter, he shall, on conviction thereof before the Mayor's Court, be fined in a sum not exceeding twenty-five dollars with costs of suit.

Clerk to register lots sold

SEC. 9. The Clerk shall keep a register of all lots heretofore or hereafter to be sold in the new cemetery—by which it shall appear the name of the person or persons owning the lot, the description of the same, the price paid therefor, and the time when the deed was executed and delivered.

Allyes in grave yards not to be obstructed.

SEC. 10. It shall not be lawful for any person to obstruct or cause to be obstructed, nor permit or suffer any obstruction occasioned by him or those under whom he claims, to be or remain in, any of the alleys of the public grave yards of said city. And it shall be the duty of the Sexton to remove all such obstructions at the expense of the persons occasioning or permitting the same as aforesaid, which upon conviction, shall be included in the fine adjudged against him.

Lots for burying strangers.

SEC. 11. The Common Council shall, whenever necessary, designate suitable lots in the new cemetery for the interment of the corpse of any deceased poor person or stranger; and it shall be the duty of the Sexton to inter any such corpse in any lot so designated, when he shall be of opinion that such corpse cannot be lawfully interred in any other place in the public grave yards.

A Register to be kept of interments and report to be made to the Common Council.

SEC. 12. It shall be the duty of the Sexton to keep a register of all interments made in the public grave yards, in which shall be stated the name of the deceased person, the time of his decease, his late residence, the place of his birth, his occupation, and the disease or complaint of which he died, and to report the same on Mondays of each week to the City Clerk; such report to include the particulars of all interments for the full week ending on Saturdays previous to the date of such report; the Sexton shall also at the expiration of his term of office, deliver said register to his successor in office; and no person or persons other than the Sexton or his employees shall dig or open any grave in the said grave yards, on pain of fine not to exceed fifty dollars for each offence, on conviction therefor.

CHAPTER XLIV.

Relative to Sluices and Low Grounds.

Assessment for low grounds, sluices, &c.

SEC. 1. Whenever it may be deemed necessary or expedient to make and open any sluice, and make any wharf or embankment on the margin of the Detroit river, or fill up any low grounds or lots covered or partially covered with water, adjacent to said river, or when it shall be necessary for the abatement of any nuisance to fill up or level any lots or low grounds not adjacent to said river, but within the limits of said city, the Common Council shall, by a written resolution to be entered on their journal, authorize some competent person to make an assessment for making such sluice, wharf, embankment, or filling up such low grounds or abating such nuisances; and upon approving and filing such assessment the Common Council shall order that the owner, occupant or proprietor of such wharf, low grounds or lots, (describing them,) shall make such sluice, wharf, or embankment, or fill up such low grounds or lots, or abate such nuisance within a certain time, and in such manner as may be in such order specified.

Marshal to give notice of order to fill low grounds.

SEC. 2. It shall be the duty of the Marshal to give notice in writing to such owner, occupant or proprietor personally, or by leaving the same at his place of residence in said city, requiring him to comply with such order, a copy of which shall be annexed to such notice, and also that within ten days after the service of such notice, he shall enter into a bond to the Mayor, Recorder, Aldermen and Freemen of the city of Detroit, with approved security, conditioned for the performance and execution of such order, and the Marshal shall make due return or report to the Common Council of his doings in the premises: *Provided*, That if any such person cannot be found, or has no place of residence in said city, the Marshal shall cause such notice to be published four weeks in some paper in said city, unless the Common Council shall otherwise order, and an affidavit thereof shall be filed with the Clerk.

When Council may order a lot to be filled.

SEC. 3. Whenever it shall appear to the Common Council that the notice required by the preceding section has been given, and that such bond has not been executed, within the time limited therefor,

TITLE VIII. CHAPTER 45.

then the Common Council may cause such sluice, wharf or embankment to be finished and completed, or such low ground or lots to be filled up, or such nuisance abated in such manner as they may deem expedient and necessary; and the expense thereof shall be deemed a valid assessment, from the time of filing the same as aforesaid.

Clerk to deliver the assessment to collector to be collected.

SEC. 4. The Clerk shall record in the assessment register all assessments made by virtue of this chapter, and the date of the same; and immediately after said work mentioned in said order shall have been finished and completed, the Clerk shall make out and deliver to the Collector a copy of such assesment, to be collected as other special sssessments.

TITLE EIGHT.

OF THE PUBLIC PEACE.

CHAPTER XLV.

Relative to Breaches of the Peace and Disorderly Conduct.

Persons concealed for the purpose of crime.

SEC. 1. Any person who may hereafter be found lurking, lying in wait, or concealed in any house or other building, or in any yard or premises within the limits of said city, with intent to do any mischief, or to pilfer, or commit any crime or misdemeanor whatever, shall, for every such offence, on conviction thereof before the Mayor's Court of said city, be punished by a fine not exceeding two hundred dollars, and imprisonment for a period not exceeding three months, or either, at the discretion of the Court, and may moreover be held to bail for good behavior.

Riot, disturbance, insulting language, conduct, &c.

SEC. 2. Any person who shall make, aid, countenance or assist, in making any noise, riot, disturbance, or improper diversion, who shall be guilty of *any indecent, immoral or insulting conduct, language or behavior*, in the streets or elsewhere in said city, and all persons who shall collect in bodies or crowds in said city for unlawful purposes, to the annoyance or disturbance of the citizens or travelers, shall for each offence, on conviction before the said Mayor's Court, be liable to the punishment mentioned in the foregoing section.

SEC. 3. The Marshal or any Constable of this city may arrest all such offenders as are before mentioned, and bring them forthwith before any member of the Common Council, who may either discharge the same, or on the oath of one credible witness commit such offenders to the county jail, unless they shall enter into a recognizance with one or more sufficient sureties, in a sum not exceeding five hundred dollars, conditioned that such offender or offenders shall be and appear before the Mayor's Court at the next ensuing term thereof, to do and receive what shall be then and there required by said Court, and shall be of good behavior and keep the peace in the meantime; and if from any reason, no member of the Common Council can be found immediately after such arrest as aforesaid, such offender or offenders shall be committed for safe keeping, until some one member of the Common Council be enabled to attend to the case.

Duty of Marshal and Constable.

CHAPTER XLVI.

Relative to Houses of Ill Fame.

SEC. 1. Any person or persons who shall, within the limits of the city of Detroit, keep a disorderly or ill-governed house or place, or a house for the resort of persons of evil name or fame, or of dishonest conversation, or who shall procure or suffer to come together, at such house or place, persons of evil name or fame, or who shall commit or suffer to be committed therein, any immoral, improper or indecent conduct or behavior, or any tippling, revelling, rioting or disturbance, every person or persons so offending, or who shall aid or assist in any manner, in offending in the premises, shall, on conviction thereof before the Mayor's Court of said city, be punished by fine not exceeding five hundred dollars, together with costs of prosecution, and imprisonment in the common jail of the county of Wayne, or both, and may, moreover, be held to enter into recognizance with sufficient surety in a suitable penal sum to keep the peace for a period not exceeding one year.

Penalty for keeping houses ill fame, &c.

SEC. 2. When any such house or building, so occupied, or kept as aforesaid, shall be deemed by the Common Council to be a nuisance,

When such houses to be abated.

it shall be the duty of the Common Council to abate such nuisance by any legal means they may deem proper.

Punishment for letting house to be kept for lascivious and disorderly purposes.

SEC. 3. It shall not be lawful for any persons to demise, let or hire, any house or other building, or premises, within the limits of the said city of Detroit, to any person or persons for any of the purposes in the first section of this ordinance mentioned; or to any person or persons who are of evil name or fame, or of dishonest conversation or who have or has the reputation of keeping a common, ill-governed or disorderly house or brothel; neither shall it be lawful for the owner or occupant of any such house, building or other premises, to permit or suffer any such person or persons to occupy any such house or premises, or otherwise harbor such person or persons; and if any person shall knowingly offend against any of the provisions of this section, he or she shall be liable on conviction thereof before the Mayor's Court, to be punished by a fine not exceeding one hundred dollars and costs of prosecution, or imprisonment in the common jail of the county of Wayne, or both.

Punishment for suffering rioting, quarreling, &c., in houses.

SEC. 4. No person or persons shall, within the limits of the city of Detroit, commit, or suffer to be committed, in any house or other building or premises by him, her or them occupied, any rioting, quarreling, fighting, reveling, drunkenness, noise, or any other disorderly conduct, calculated to disturb the neighborhood, or any travelers or others. . Any person violating the provisions of this section shall, upon conviction before the Mayor's Court, for each offence, be liable to a fine of not exceeding five hundred dollars and costs of prosecution, and moreover may, at the discretion of said Court, be imprisoned in the jail of the County of Wayne, for a period of not exceeding three months, and required to enter into recognizance with sufficient surety in a suitable penal sum to keep the peace, for a period not exceeding one year.

Duty of officers.

SEC. 5. It shall be the duty of the Marshal and Constables of the said city of Detroit, to take notice of, and report all infractions of this chapter, that every person offending may be dealt with according to law; and it shall be competent for said Marshal or any of said Constables, to arrest any person or persons who may have violated the provisions of the first and fourth sections of this chapter, and to bring such person or persons before the Mayor, Recorder, or any of the Aldermen of said city, who are hereby authorized to hold any such person or persons to bail, for his or their appearance at the ensuing term of the Mayor's Court, to answer to any alleged offence in any such case, and for want thereof to commit such person or persons to jail.

CHAPTER XLVII.

Relative to Injuries to Public Property.

SEC. 1. If any person shall destroy, deface, impair, injure, or wantonly force open any gate or door, or in any way whatsoever destroy, injure or deface any part of the State capitol building, or the appurtenances, fences, trees or fixtures thereunto belonging or appertaining, the city magazine, hospital, city hall, market houses, water works, water pipes, water screws, hydrants, or any fixtures appertaining to the hydraulic works, weigh scales, street lamps and posts, public wharves, fire engine houses, fire apparatus, public grave yards or trees growing therein, or any grave, tomb or fence around either of them, sidewalks or crosswalks in any street, or any shade or ornamental trees in any street, or any other property whatever, of the State of Michigan, the county of Wayne, or the corporation of the city of Detroit, within the limits of said city, he, she or they so offending, shall forfeit and pay for every such offence a fine not exceeding one hundred dollars and costs of prosecution, together with the expense of repairing the property so injured: *Provided*, That when the injury is accidental, no further fine shall be imposed than the amount of the costs of prosecution and the expense of making such repair. Punishment for injury to public property.

SEC. 2. If any of said property should be owned by individuals, it shall nevertheless be deemed, for the purposes of this chapter, the property of the corporation of said city. Private property.

SEC. 3. Any person or persons who shall hereafter be guilty of using for any private purposes whatever, any of the fixtures, apparatus, ladders, or other property attached or belonging to any of the fire engines, hose, or hook and ladder companies of the city of Detroit, without due permission for that purpose first had and obtained of the Punishment for using property of the fire department.

TITLE VIII. CHAPTER 48.

Chief Engineer, or some one in charge of said property, shall, on conviction thereof in the Mayor's Court, be fined in a sum not exceeding fifty dollars and costs of prosecution, together with the expense of repairing said property, if the same shall in any manner be injured by such unlawful use.

Punishment for injuries to gas and gas lights.

SEC. 4. Any person who shall, without lawful authority, light or extinguish any of the public gas lamps of said city, or who shall in any way change, alter, or turn the stop cock, or any fixture belonging thereto; or who shall break, injure or tarnish any of said lamps, or the posts on which they are erected, shall for each and every offence pay a penalty not exceeding fifty dollars and the costs of prosecution, together with the expense of repairing the property so injured: *Provided*, That when such breaking or injury is accidental, no further fine shall be imposed than the amount of the costs of prosecution and the expense of making such repair.

Penalty.

Duty of officers.

SEC. 5. It shall be the special duty of the Marshal and all the Constables of said city, to make complaint of all violations of this chapter.

CHAPTER XLVIII.

Relative to Injuries to Reservoirs.

SEC. 1. Punishment for injuries to public Reservoirs.

Punishment for injuring public reservoirs.

SEC. 1. Any person who shall injure any public reservoir, or who shall break or enter the same, and draw off, or cause to be removed, any of the water therefrom, except in case of fire, or unless duly authorized by the Common Council of said city, or by the Chief Engineer of the Fire Department, (except in case of inspection of fire engines,) shall forfeit and pay a sum not to exceed one hundred dollars, on complaint and conviction in the Mayor's Court of the said offence.

CHAPTER XLIX.

Relative to a Night Watch.

SEC. 1. Mayor may organize a Watch.
SEC. 2. Duties of Watch.
SEC. 3. Powers of Watchmen.
SEC. 4. All persons to assist Watchmen, when.
SEC. 5. Duty of Marshal.
SEC. 6. Watchmen may be removed.
SEC. 7. What to be done with persons arrested.

Mayor may organize a watch.

SEC. 1. The Mayor of the city is hereby vested with full power and authority to establish and organize a Night Watch, in and for said city; and for that purpose, he may appoint as many discreet and suitable persons as, in his opinion, the public safety may require. The persons appointed as aforesaid, shall, before entering on the performance of their duties, take an oath or affirmation, that they will faithfully and honestly discharge the duties of their office, to the best of their ability.

Duties of watch.

SEC. 2. The members of said watch, and each of them, are hereby authorized, and it shall be their duty, between the hours of nine o'clock at night, and the dawn of the succeeding morning, to apprehend any and every person who shall be reasonably suspected of having committed any crime or misdemeanor, or who shall be detected by either of the members of said watch in the violation of any of the ordinances of said city, or of an intent to commit any crime or misdemeanor, and to detain such person until morning; and thereafter, it shall be the duty of such watch to report all persons so apprehended to the Marshal of said city, who shall thereupon have the custody of all such persons, until discharged by due course of law.

Powers of watchmen.

SEC. 3. That the said watch and every member thereof, shall have power and authority, on reasonable ground of suspicion, during the hours or period of watch aforesaid, to enter in a peaceable manner, or if resisted, (after demand made,) with force into any house, store, shop, grocery or other building whatever in said city, in which any person or persons may be suspected to be for unlawful purposes, and if any person or persons shall be found therein guilty of any crime or misdemeanor, or who may be reasonably suspected thereof, the said watch to apprehend and keep in custody any such person or persons, in manner as hereinbefore prescribed.

All persons to assist watchmen, when.

SEC. 4. It shall be the duty of all persons in said city when called upon by any member of said watch, promptly to aid and assist him in the execution of his duties, and if any person shall neglect or refuse to give such aid and assistance, he shall, on conviction, forfeit a sum not exceeding one hundred dollars and costs of prosecution.

Duty of Marshal.

SEC. 5. It shall be the duty of the Marshal of said city, to bring such persons apprehended by said watch before the proper authority, for examination, within a reasonable time; and all persons who shall resist, or in any manner interfere with the members of said watch in the discharge of their duties, shall, on conviction, forfeit a sum not exceeding one hundred dollars and costs of prosecution.

TITLE VIII. CHAPTER 50.

Watchmen may be removed.

SEC. 6. The Mayor shall have power to remove from office any member of the watch, when, in his opinion, there shall be just cause therefor.

What to be done with persons arrested.

SEC. 7. All persons apprehended by said night watch, in the performance of their aforesaid duties, shall be confined in a room in the City Hall, provided for that purpose, during the night in which said person or persons shall be apprehended, subject to the custody and control of said Marshal: whose duty it shall be to take such person or persons, for the purpose of examination, during the morning succeeding their arrest, before the Mayor or Recorder, or in their absence, one of the Aldermen of said city, who shall, as conservator of the peace of said city, attend at the City Council room, at nine o'clock A. M., of each and every day except Sunday, during the continuance of said watch, for the purpose of hearing such examination: *Provided*, That persons so apprehended during any Saturday night, shall, on the following morning, be committed to the county jail, to be examined as aforesaid, on the Monday following.

CHAPTER L.

Relative to process and proceedings in the Mayor's Court, and to the recovery of Fines.

SEC. 1. When process may be issued from the Mayor's Court.
SEC. 2. When security for costs may be required.
SEC. 3. Who to execute process.
SEC. 4. Bond upon arrests.
SEC. 5. Execution to issue against body, goods and real estate.
SEC. 6. When complainant to pay costs.
SEC. 7. Constable and Marshal's returns.
SEC. 8. Clerk to report quarterly to Council.
SEC. 9. Penalty for obstructing officers.
SEC. 10. Duty of officers when it is not convenient to bring prisoner before the Recorder, Aldermen, &c.
SEC. 11. Duty of Jailor.

When process may be issued from the Mayor's Court.

SEC. 1. That upon complaint on oath or affirmation being made to any member of the Common Council, or the Clerk of the Mayor's Court, that any person has violated any of the laws or ordinances of said city, the Clerk shall issue a *capias ad respondendum*, unless a summons be specially prescribed for the arrest of such person, and shall be returnable any day in the present or ensuing term of said Court.

SEC. 2. Before issuing such process, the Clerk may, if he shall deem it necessary, require the complainant to enter into a bond, with sufficient surety, to the Mayor, Recorder, Aldermen and Freemen of the city of Detroit, conditioned for the appearance of the complainant at the term of the Mayor's Court at which such process shall be made returnable, to give evidence against the person or persons complained of by him; and if upon trial the defendant shall be discharged, that the complainant shall pay the costs of prosecution, if so ordered by the said Court.

When security for costs may be required.

SEC. 3. It shall be the duty of the Marshal or Constable to whom the writ shall be directed to arrest the defendant therein named if he be found, who may give bail for his appearance at the time such writ shall be returnable, and in default thereof the officer shall take him before any member of the Common Council, who may commit, let to bail, or discharge the defendant according to his discretion.

Who to execute process.

SEC. 4. The bail required in the preceding section, shall be by bond payable to the Mayor, Recorder, Aldermen and Freemen of the city of Detroit, with at least one sufficient surety, in a sum not less than fifty dollars, and not more than double the amount of the penalty provided in the by-law or ordinance which may be violated, and shall be conditioned for the due appearance of the defendant before the Mayor's Court at the time such writ shall be returnable, and that the defendant shall comply with the judgment of the Mayor's Court, and not depart without leave, and in the mean time, keep the peace towards all the good people of said city: *Provided*, That if such bail should be insufficient or irresponsible, the officer taking the same shall be liable in an action of debt for the amount thereof, to be recovered in the name of the corporation.

Bond upon arrest.

SEC. 5. Executions returnable at the next term, may issue upon any judgment of the said Court, against the body, goods and chattels of the defendant, or party prosecuted, (unless such party be in actual custody for the offence on which judgment was rendered,) for the amount of such fine and the costs of prosecution, which execution may be levied upon the goods and chattels or body of such party, and all goods and chattels so levied upon, shall be sold in the same manner in all respects, that personal property is directed by the laws of this State to be sold, except that six days' previous notice of sale shall be sufficient, and the officer levying the same shall return the execution at the next term of the Mayor's Court, with his doings thereon. And if such execution be returned unsatisfied in whole or in part, an execution may be issued

Execution to issue against body, goods and real estate.

TITLE VIII. CHAPTER 50. against the real estate of such defendant, which shall be executed according to the laws of this State.

When complainant to pay costs. SEC. 6. If in any trial it shall appear to the Court that the complaint was wilful or malicious, or without probable cause, or if the complaint does not appear and testify in the cause, the Court may order and adjudge the complainant, (and if he has entered into a bond as required by this ordinance, then against him and his surety,) to pay the costs of such prosecution, and thereupon an execution as in other cases, shall issue for the same.

Constable and Marshal's returns. SEC. 7. The Marshal and Constables, once in each month, and whenever it can be done, at least three days prior to the term of the Mayor's Court, shall return to the City Clerk all process issued out of said Court, with their doings in each case endorsed thereon, and shall also at such times pay over to the said Clerk all moneys collected by them in pursuance of such process, except in civil cases; and all moneys collected in civil cases shall be paid to the City Attorney. And if any such officer shall neglect or refuse to comply with the provisions of this section, or shall knowingly do any other act inconsistent with the just and faithful discharge of his duties, he shall, on conviction, be liable to pay a penalty not exceeding one hundred dollars, and costs of prosecution.

Clerk to report quarterly to Council. SEC. 8. The Clerk shall once in three months make a report to the Common Council of all the particulars and business of the Mayor's Court—the number of persons tried, and the amount of fines and costs of each term, and the amount collected and paid into his hands: and he shall once in every three months pay over to the City Treasurer all moneys by him received belonging to the corporation, together with all witness' or jurors' fees then on hand, and shall at the time of making his reports exhibit the receipts of said Treasurer for such moneys.

Penalty for obstructing officers. SEC. 9. If any person or persons knowingly or wilfully obstruct, resist, or oppose the Marshal or any of the Constables of said city, or other person or persons duly authorized in serving or attempting to serve any writ or process, rule or order issued out of said Mayor's Court, or while executing or carrying into effect any order, rule, or determination of the Common Council of said city, or shall resist or impede any person duly authorized, or any member of the Common

Council of said city, in the performance of any of their duties or powers, or if any person shall aid or assist any person legally in custody, to escape, or conceal him after the escape, every person offending in the premises, shall, on conviction before said Mayor's Court, be punished by fine not exceeding one hundred dollars and costs.

Duty of officers when it is not convenient to bring prisoner before Recorder, Aldermen, &c.

SEC. 10. If any officer shall arrest any person, at a time that may be inconvenient to bring him before any proper officer for an examination, the officer making the arrest may place such person in the custody of the Jailer of the County of Wayne, and within fifteen hours thereafter, he shall bring him before some member of the Common Council for examination, and if such officer shall neglect to comply with the requirements of this section, he shall be liable to pay all the expenses of keeping such prisoner in jail: *Provided*, That if the said period of fifteen hours shall terminate on the Sabbath day, said examination shall be had during the forenoon of the next ensuing Monday.

Duty of Jailor.

SEC. 11. The keeper of the jail of the county of Wayne shall not permit or suffer any person committed by virtue of a process of the Mayor's Court, or other authority of said city, to leave or depart said jail without the permission of some member of the Common Council, or the City Attorney, under the penalty of a sum not exceeding one hundred dollars, and costs of prosecution.

CHAPTER LI.

Relative to Fees in Mayor's Court.

SEC. 1. Fees of Officers, &c.
SEC. 2. Fees not herein provided for.
SEC. 3. Fees not chargeable to city, when.
SEC. 4. All fines and proceeds of Mayor's Court to be a fund for payment of the officers thereof.

Fees of officers, &c.

SEC. 1. That the several officers and persons in attendance, in the Mayor's Court shall, in civil and criminal cases, to which the same respectively apply, be entitled to demand and receive the fees and compensation following, that is to say:

Court Fees.

For the officer holding the court, in each cause or prosecution, $1 00

Clerk's Fees.

For each cause or prosecution, tried without jury, and without continuance, - - - - - - - - - - $1 00

For continuance,	6
For certified copies of rules, the same as for entering such rules,	12
For every report upon an assessment of damages, or other matter referred to him,	12
For calling and swearing a jury,	19
For swearing a constable to take charge of a jury,	12
Reading and filing a certiorari,	12
Entering special bail,	6
Entering exoneration or surrender,	6
Issuing commission to take depositions,	25
Administering oath or affirmation,	6
Taking bond or recognizance,	25
Search of the records or files, if a copy is not required, for each year, except for officers of the court,	10
Copies and exemplifications of records and pleadings to be returned on certiorari or appeal, copies and exemplifications of all records, pleadings, and proceedings furnished on request, where no special provision is otherwise made, for each folio,	8

Marshal's and Constable's Fees.

For serving every writ, (subpœna excepted,) and return thereof, for one defendant,	25
For each additional defendant,	12
For making arrest without process,	25
For every commitment to prison,	25
Serving every subpœna on each witness,	6
Summoning a jury,	38
Traveling fees upon writs or precepts served without the city, and within the county of Wayne, to be computed from the place of service to the place of return, for each mile,	6
Serving an execution against the property,	50
Collecting moneys and paying over the same, five per cent. upon the sums collected, exclusive of costs.	
Serving citation by order of the court,	25
Attending upon jury,	25
For each bond or recognizance taken by him,	12

Juror's Fees.

TITLE VIII.
CHAPTER 38.

To each juror empannelled in a cause where a verdict is rendered, - - - - - - - - - - - 25

Witness' Fees.

Each witness, for every day's attendance, in any cause or prosecution, - - - - - - - - - . - 25

Attorney's Fees.

For each criminal case, where defendant is tried and found guilty, - - - - - - - - - - - - 1 00

For each civil case, where judgment is rendered for the city, 3 00

Fees not herein provided for.

SEC. 2. When any service shall be performed by any officer of the Mayor's Court, for which no compensation is provided by this chapter, the officer or person performing the same shall be entitled to the same fees as are prescribed for such services in the Circuit Court for the county of Wayne.

Fees not chargeable to city, when.

SEC. 3. The Marshal of said city shall not be allowed a per diem for attending the Mayor's Court; nor shall any juror or witness, or the City Marshal in any cause or prosecution be entitled to demand or receive any of said fees, as against the corporation of said city; but when any such fees shall be collected and paid to the Clerk, it shall be his duty, on demand, to pay the same to the officers or persons entitled thereto.

All fines and proceeds of Mayor's Court to be a fund for payment of the officers therof.

SEC. 4. Hereafter all fines and other proceeds of the Mayor's Court of said city, shall be kept as and constitute a separate and distinct fund, to be used for the payment of the officers of said Court, and other expenses thereof, and for no other purpose whatever—and no charge or account, whether the same be for the fee of any officer or other expense of said Court, shall be paid, save out of said fund: *Provided*, That whenever said fund has accumulated beyond what the Council may deem sufficient for the payment of said fees and expenses, the Common Council may direct the surplus to be appropriated to any other purpose they may deem proper.

TITLE NINE.

OF STRAY ANIMALS.

CHAPTER LII.

Concerning Pounds and certain Animals Impounded.

SEC. 1. When pounds shall be established and how kept.
SEC. 2. Certain animals not to run within certain limits; penalty.
SEC. 3. Minors not to impound.
SEC. 4 Duties of Pound keepers.
SEC. 5. Pound Keepers to pay moneys to City Treasurer.
SEC. 6. Fees of Pound Keepers.
SEC. 7. Injuries to pounds; penalty.
SEC. 8. Punishment for obstructing persons driving animals to Pound.
SEC. 9. Punishment of Pound Keepers for neglecting to distrain and detain animals.
SEC. 10. Punishment for permitting animals to run at large.

When pounds shall be established and how kept.

SEC. 1. That the Street Commissioner, when directed by the Common Council, shall construct one or more good and suitable pounds, at such place or places in said city as shall be designated for such purpose by said Common Council, to be placed under the care and direction of a Pound Keeper for each pound in said city, to be appointed by the Common Council, who shall act as such Pound keeper during the pleasure of said Common Council.

Certain animals not to run within certain limits

SEC. 2. Hereafter no swine, sheep, horses, mares, asses, mules, neat cattle, goats, or geese, shall be permitted to run at large within the following limits of said city, to wit: Beginning at the Detroit river, on the channel bank thereof, at the eastern line of the said city, and running thence north along said line to the point of intersection of said eastern line and the Fort Gratiot road; thence along said road to Riopelle street; thence north along said Riopelle street to Cemetery street; thence along said Cemetery street west to Russell street; thence south along said Russell street to the Fort Gratiot road; thence along said Fort Gratiot road to Rivard street; thence north along Rivard street to Winder street; thence west along Winder street to Woodward avenue; thence north along said Woodward avenue to Sproat street; thence west along Sproat street to the eastern line of the Cass farm; thence south along the eastern line of said farm to the Grand River road; thence west to the western line of said city; thence south along said western line to the channel bank of the Detroit river; thence east along said channel bank to the place of beginning. And if found running at large within the limits aforesaid, each and every of such animals may be impounded in the common pounds of said city, from whence they shall not be released until the owner or owners, or some other person, shall pay to the Pound Keeper the sum of fifty cents per head for all horses, mules, asses, and neat cattle, and ten cents per head for all sheep, goats, swine, and geese so distrained by him; and the Pound Keeper shall be entitled to four cents per head for all the said animals so impounded, and the owner of any such animal, upon conviction of permitting any such animal to run at large, shall be subject to pay a fine not to exceed five dollars, in the discretion of the Court, and costs of prosecution, for every such offence.

Penalty.

SEC. 3. It shall not be lawful for any minor, unless arthorized by a written certificate directed to some Pound Keeper of said city, signed by the parent or guardian of such minor, to take up, distrain or impound any such animals as aforesaid, within said pound limits, and no Pound Keeper shall impound any such animal or animals mentioned aforesaid, taken up or distrained by any minor, except the same be accompanied by a certificate signed by the parent or guardian of said minor, and directed to said Pound Keeper, authorizing said minor to deliver up such animal or animals to said Pound Keeper, to be impounded in the common pounds of said city.

Minors not to impound.

SEC. 4. It shall be the duty of each Pound Keeper to provide necessary sustenance for all animals so impounded; and the reasonable cost for providing such sustenance for each animal, shall be paid to the Pound Keeper before such animal shall be released from the pound; and it shall be lawful for Pound Keepers to sell at public vendue any animal or animals impounded as aforesaid, at any time after the expiration of three days from the time they shall be so impounded, the Pound Keeper giving at least forty-eight hours' previous public notice of the time and place of sale, by four advertisements, one of which shall be put up at the City Hall in some conspicuous place, another at the Post Office, another in the division of the city in which such animals were found so running at large, and the other in the most public place in the division of the city where said animals may be impounded; but if said animals or any of them are redeemed, or an offer is made to redeem by paying the Pound Keeper's fees, and the fine prescribed in the preceding section, together with the

Duties of Pound Keepers.

TITLE IX. CHAPTER 52.

expenses of sustenance as aforesaid, at any time before they are actually sold, the same shall not then be sold, but shall be released by the Pound Keeper. The Pound Keeper shall render to the Common Council quarterly a true statement of all fees and all moneys received by him, either for fines, or for animals sold by him, together with the names of persons paying him the same and owning such animals; and if he shall fail to render such account he shall be snbject to removal from office. No Pound Keeper shall purchase, or be interested, directly or indirectly, in any manner in the purchase of any animal sold by him as Pound Keeper, under a fine of twenty dollars and forfeiture of his office.

Pound Keepers to pay moneys to City Treasurer.

SEC. 5. All moneys received by the Pound Keepers, by virtue of this ordinance, for animals sold by him or them, after deducting therefrom the fees and charges for sustenance, shall be promptly paid by him or them to the City Treasurer; but the city shall not in any case be liable to the Pound Keeper for or on account of any fees or expenses due to him on account of any animal which may be impounded.

Fees of Pound Keepers.

SEC. 6. Pound Keepers shall exact and receive for his or their fees in receiving and discharging, or selling every horse, the sum of fifty cents and no more; for each ass, fifty cents; for each head of neat cattle, fifty cents; for each swine, sheep, goat, or goose, ten cents; and for suitable and proper sustenance for each horse, twenty-five cents; for each mule, twenty-five cents; for each ass, twenty-five cents; for each head of neat cattle, twenty-five cents; for each swine, sheep or goose, twelve cents for every twenty-four hours the same shall be kept.

Injuries to pounds.

SEC. 7. If any person or persons shall break open or in any manner, directly or indirectly, aid or assist in breaking open any city pound, said person or persons shall severally, on conviction thereof before the Mayor's Court of said city, be punished by a fine not exceeding five dollars and the costs of prosecution, and imprisonment for the period of five days, or either, in the discretion of said Court.

Penalty.

Punishment for obstructing persons driving animals to pound.

SEC. 8. Each and every person who shall hinder, delay or obstruct any person or persons in driving to the pounds any animal or animals, beast or beasts, liable to be impounded in the city pounds, shall, for each and every hindrance, delay or obstruction, and for each and every person delayed, pay a fine of not less than ten dollars, nor more than twenty dollars.

Punishment of Pound Keepers for neglecting to distrain and detain animals.

SEC. 9. If any Pound Keeper appointed as aforesaid shall refuse or neglect to take up, detain or impound any horses, neat cattle, swine or other animal, liable to be impounded, known by him to be running at large contrary to the ordinances of the city, he shall be subject to pay a fine, on conviction of any such offence in the Mayor's Court of said city, of fifty dollars and costs of prosecution for any such neglect.

Punishment for permitting animals to run at large.

SEC. 10. Any owner of any horse, neat cattle, or other animal liable to be impounded, who shall permit the same to run at large within the aforesaid limits of said city, shall for each offence pay a fine of five dollars and costs of prosecution, upon conviction thereof in the Mayor's Court of said city, for each animal so permitted to run at large.

CHAPTER LIII.

Relative to Pound Keepers, Fence Viewers, &c.

Duties of pound keepers.

SEC. 1. Pound Keepers shall have and exercise the same power, duties and privileges, and be subject to the same restrictions, so far as the said power, duties, privileges and restrictions are consistent with chapter fifty-two of these ordinances, and the laws of the State prescribe relative to the keeper of a public pound.

Fence viewers.

SEC. 2. The Street Supervisors of said city shall have and exercise the same powers, duties and privileges, and be subject to the same restrictions and penalties, as the laws of this State prescribe relative to Fence Viewers.

Laws of this state applicable to pounds may be enforced in Mayor's Court.

SEC. 3. Every provision of the law of this State relative to Pound keepers thereof, Fence Viewers, stray cattle or beasts in the pound, are hereby adopted, and all violations of the same shall be prosecuted in the Mayor's Court of said city.

TITLE IX.
CHAPTER 54.

CHAPTER LIV.

Relative to Dogs.

Dogs may be taxed.

SEC. 1. Every person residing in this city, owning or having in his possession, or suffering to be kept on his or her premises any dog, shall be liable to be assessed and pay for the same, the following taxes: for one dog the sum of fifty cents per annum, (commencing on the first Monday in April,) for every additional dog two dollars, to be assessed and collected in the same manner as taxes upon personal property in said city.

Owners of dogs to report to assessors.

SEC. 2. Every person residing in this city, owning or having in his or her possession, or suffering to be kept on his or her premises any dog, shall, on or before the third Monday in March, in each year, report to the Assessor of his proper ward, the name and description of every dog so owned or possessed by him, and shall put upon the neck of every dog a metal strap or collar, on which shall be engraved in legible letters the name of the owner. Any person neglecting any of the provisions of this section, shall forfeit the penalty of five dollars for every neglect.

Dogs may be killed.

SEC. 3. It shall be lawful for any person to shoot, or otherwise kill or destroy, any dog found running at large in this city, contrary to the requirements of the preceding section.

Assessor to keep register of dogs, &c.

SEC. 4. It shall be the duty of the Assessors to keep a record of the name and description of all dogs reported to them as aforesaid, together with the name and description of any other dog which they shall ascertain at the time of making their annual assessment, and return the same to the City Clerk, who shall deliver the same to the Collector.

All sluts and bitches shall be killed.

SEC. 5. No slut or bitch shall be kept, or allowed to be kept or remain within the limits of the city, and such as may be found or shall be seen going at large within the limits aforesaid, shall be liable to be killed by the Marshal or any other person.

SEC. 6. No person shall be allowed to keep or suffer to run at large, any dog or slut of vicious or ferocious character or disposition, under penalty for each offence, not exceeding ten dollars, and the City Marshal or any other person is hereby required to kill, or cause any such dog or bitch to be killed, if found running at large, or that an injury has been wantonly caused by any such dog or slut to any person. Vicious dogs may be killed

SEC. 7. It shall not be lawful for any dog, slut or bitch, to run at large within the limits of the city of Detroit, unless muzzled, as hereinafter provided for. Dogs to be muzzled.

SEC. 8. No dog, slut or bitch shall be allowed to run at large within the limits of said city unless muzzled with a good and sufficient muzzle rendering it impossible for such dog, slut or bitch to do any mischief by biting any person or animal. Dogs running at large to be muzzled.

SEC. 9. It shall be the duty of the Marshal to kill every dog, slut or bitch found running at large within the limits of said city, contrary to the provisions of the preceding sections. Marshal to kill dogs when.

SEC. 10. It shall be lawful for the Marshal, when the safety of the citizens shall require the vigorous enforcement of this chapter, to employ such number of discreet persons to kill all dogs, sluts and bitches as shall be found running at large *unmuzzled*, or with defective muzzles: *Provided*, The expense shall not exceed twenty-five cents for every dog, slut or bitch so killed. May employ assistant dog killers.

SEC. 11. The operation of the four preceding sections may be suspended at any time when the public safety shall, in the opinion of the Common Council, authorize such suspension. Suspension of four preceding sections when.

TITLE TEN.

OF FERRIES, HACKS, AND DRAYS.

CHAPTER LV.

Relative to Ferries.

SEC. 1. Ferries to be licensed; penalty.
SEC. 2. License how obtained, and recognizance.
SEC. 3. Number of ferries allowed; illegal fees; penalty.
SEC. 4. Time of attendance on ferry; no persons to be detained; penalty.
SEC. 5. Ferry place not to be changed; gaming, &c., prohibited; penalty.
SEC. 6. Rates of fare.
SEC. 7. Keeper to post a list of rates.

SEC. 1. That no person shall use or keep any ferry or boat for

TITLE X. CHAPTER 55.

Ferries to be licensed.

transporting for hire across the river Detroit, any persons, cattle, carriages, or other matter whatever, from within the limits of the city of Detroit, without having previously obtained a license from the Common Council of the said city, under a penalty not exceeding twenty-five dollars for each offence, to be recovered for the use of the said city with costs.

Penalty.

License how obtained and recognizance

SEC. 2. Each license shall be for the term of one year, and shall issue only on the petition or recommendation in writing, of at least twelve respectable freeholders of the said city, stating that a ferry is needed at the place therein designated, and that the applicant is a person suitable to keep the same, and if the prayer of such petition be granted, such applicant shall, before receiving such license, pay to the Treasurer of said city, such sum as the Common Council shall deem reasonable for such license, and shall also enter into a recognizance to the Mayor, Recorder, Aldermen and Freemen of the city of Detroit, by himself in the sum of one hundred dollars, and two sufficient sureties in the sum of fifty dollars each, conditioned that he shall faithfully keep in complete repair one or more sufficient and safe boats and scows as may be necessary for the safe conveyance of persons, wagons, carriages, cattle, horses, and all other articles necessary to be transported, and shall, at all times, when the said river is passable, give due attendance with a sufficient number of hands, to work and manage said boats and scows at the said ferry, during such hours in each day and night, and at such prices or rates for ferriage as shall be, from time to time, prescribed by the said Common Council, which recognizance shall be taken and remain in the Clerk's office of said city; and upon the perfection thereof and payment of the aforesaid sum, a license for such right of ferriage shall be issued to the said applicant.

Number of ferries allowed.

SEC. 3. The granting of any license for the aforesaid purpose shall not be deemed to deprive the Common Council of the power to grant as many more as they may think proper, and no greater fee or payment shall be demanded for ferriage at any time other than as fixed by law, under a penalty of not more than fifty dollars for each offence, with costs of suit, and such penalty shall be independent of and in addition to any remedy on the aforesaid recognizance.

Illegal fees. Penalty.

SEC. 4. Each ferry keeper shall attend his ferry from sunrise in the morning until sundown in the evening, and shall be liable to be deprived of his license by the Common Council in case of failure or omission to comply with the directions of this chapter, or the conditions of his recognizance. And such ferry keeper during the period aforesaid, when such river is passable, shall not detain any person, or any person with his goods, cattle or other property, necessary and proper to be transported, more than fifteen minutes from the time application is made by such person to be ferried over said river with his goods and other property aforesaid; and for every such offence he shall forfeit a sum not exceeding twenty-five dollars and costs of prosecution.

Time of attendance on ferry. No person to be detained.

Penalty.

SEC. 5. No ferry keeper shall remove his ferry to any other place in said city, than that designated in his said application for license, without the permission of the Common Council; nor shall any ferry keeper at any time, permit any gaming for money or other value, or suffer any drunkenness, quarreling, fighting, blasphemy, or any rude disorderly, or immoral conduct, on any boat or scow engaged or used by him in ferrying said river. And any person offending in the premises, on conviction, shall forfeit a sum not exceeding fifty dollars for each offence, and be liable to have his license suppressed and declared void.

Ferry place not to be changed. Gaming, &c., prohibited.

Penalty.

SEC. 6. The rates of ferriage shall be as follows, to wit: from the first day of April to the first day of November in each year, for each person twelve and a half cents; for each horse twenty-five cents; for one horse and carriage and persons thereto belonging, not exceeding two, fifty cents; for a carriage and two horses, and persons as last aforesaid, seventy-five cents; for every additional horse, eighteen and three-fourth cents; for each head of horned cattle, twenty-five cents, and for each sheep or hog, six cents. And from the first day of November to the first day of April following, for each person, twelve and a half cents; for each horse, thirty-seven and a half cents; for each horse and carriage and persons thereto belonging, not exceeding two, seventy-five cents; for each carriage and two horses, and persons as last aforesaid, one dollar and twenty-five cents; for each additional horse, twenty-five cents; for each head of horned cattle, thirty-seven and a half cents; and for each sheep or hog, six and a quarter cents.

Rates of fare.

SCE. 7. It shall be the duty of every person authorized to keep a ferry within the limits of said city, to cause to be affixed, and at all

Keeper to print a list of rates.

TITLE X. CHAPTER 56.

times to keep, in some conspicuous place near the ferry landing, and in each boat or scow used for the purpose of ferriage, a list of the rates of ferriage; which shall be painted on a board in plain and legible characters, so that it may be seen by the public, and shall be headed thus: "Legal charges for ferriage across the river Detroit, as established by law." And if any person shall neglect or refuse to comply with the provision of this section, he shall, on conviction, forfeit the sum of five dollars and costs of prosecution, for every day's omission.

CHAPTER LVI.

Relative to Cabs, Hackney Coaches, Omnibusses, and Carriages, &c.

Cabs, &c to be licensed.

SEC. 1. The City Clerk may issue a license, under the corporate seal of the city, to any trustworthy person or persons, of the ages of twenty-one years, or upwards, who shall be resident of said city, authorizing such person or persons to keep cabs, hackney coaches, carriages, omnibusses, or other vehicles, for hire, upon such person or persons complying with the provisions of this ordinance, and giving proper security, and upon paying five dollars to the City Treasurer for every cab, hackney coach, carriage, omnibus or other vehicle, authorized to be kept by such license. Such license shall state the number of each cab, coach, carriage, omnibus, or other vehicle, allowed to be kept under said license, with the name of the person to whom it is granted, and shall, in all cases, continue in force for the period of one year next ensuing the date thereof. And no person shall keep, or use any hackney coach, cab, carriage, omnibus, or other vehicle, for hire, in said city of Detroit, without being licensed as aforesaid; and, in case any person shall keep or use any such hackney coach, carriage, cab, omnibus, or other vehicle, for hire, without having taken out license for that purpose, as aforesaid, he shall, upon conviction of the offence, in the Mayor's Court, pay a fine of ten dollars and costs of prosecution. Penalty.

SEC. 2. Every person to whom a license shall be granted, as provided for in the foregoing section, shall execute a bond, to the Mayor, Recorder, Aldermen, and Freemen of the city of Detroit, in the sum of two hundred dollars, with sufficient sureties, to be approved by the City Auditor; conditioned, that such person will pay all fines, costs, penalties or damages, for which he may become liable, on account of the use of any cab, hackney coaches, carriages, omnibusses, or other vehicles, kept or used by such person, under his license as aforesaid; and no license shall be of any validity until such bond has been duly executed and filed with the City Clerk. Bond given on license issued.

SEC. 3. The prices which may be charged by the owners, or drivers, of hackney coaches, cabs, carriages, omnibusses, or other vehicles, shall not exceed as follows, viz: For conveying one person, for each drive, less than an hour, twenty-five cents; for conveying two or more persons, for each drive, less than one hour, twenty-five cents for each person; for the use of a cab, carriage, hackney coach, or other vehicle, (except an omnibus,) by the hour, to carry not more than four persons inside, at the rate of one dollar per hour: *Provided*, That children between two and twelve years of age, shall be conveyed at one-half the foregoing rates; and infants under two years of age shall be carried free if in charge of any other person. Prices.

SEC. 4. When a cab, carriage, hackney coach, or other vehicle, shall be used for a longer time than one hour, the owner, or driver thereof, shall be entitled to charge and receive from the person or persons using the same, the sum of one dollar for each full hour the same shall have been used; and for fractional parts of an hour he shall only charge and receive at the rate of one dollar per hour, as aforesaid. Price when cab used more than an hour.

SEC. 5. For each trunk carried on any cab, carriage, hackney coach, omnibus, or other vehicle, the owner, or driver thereof, may charge and receive the sum of twelve and one-half cents, and no more: *Provided*, That each person hiring or using any such carriage, cab, omnibus, or other vehicle, shall be allowed to carry thereon Price for baggage.

TITLE X. CHAPTER 56.

any ordinary traveling bag, valise, or bundle, weighing less than forty-five pounds, free of all charge.

Rates of fare at night.

SEC. 6. When a cab, carriage, omnibus, hackney coach, or other vehicle, shall be hired or used between the hours of eleven o'clock in the evening, and five o'clock in the morning, the owner or driver thereof, shall be entitled to charge and receive one-half more than the rates prescribed in the foregoing section, and no more.

Charge not to exceed amount allowed for an hour, when

SEC. 7. In no case shall any person, or any number of persons, less than five, be charged for the use of a cab, carriage, hackney coach, or other vehicle, more than the sum allowed for the use thereof for one hour, unless the same shall be used more than one hour, although the person or persons using the same may have stopped at several places during the time, he, she, or they may have been using such cab, carriage, hackney coach, or other vehicle.

Punishment of cabmen, &c., for what.

SEC. 8. A fine of not less than twenty-five dollars, nor more than one hundred dollars and costs of prosecution, shall be imposed by the Mayor's Court upon the owner or driver of any hackney coach, cab, carriage, omnibus, or other vehicle, who shall demand or receive higher or greater prices or rates, for the use of his cab, carriage, hackney coach, omnibus, or other vehicle, than those named and fixed by the foregoing sections of this ordinance; and a fine of ten dollars and costs of prosecution shall be imposed by the Mayor's Court upon the owner or driver of the foregoing named vehicles, or any other vehicles used for hire in said city, who shall unreasonably refuse or neglect to convey any person or persons within the bounds of said city, when applied to for that purpose, and being at the time unemployed; and the like fine shall be imposed by said Court, upon the owner or driver of either of the foregoing named vehicles, or any other vehicles used for hire in said city, who shall neglect to place upon such vehicle, in a conspicuous place inside, a card, on which shall be legibly printed the number of the license under which such vehicle is used, the name of the owner thereof, and the prices or rates fixed by this ordinance for the use of cabs, hackney coaches, carriages, omnibusses, and other vehicles.

SEC. 9. All keepers of livery stables within said city shall pay the sum of five dollars to the City Treasurer for every carriage, cab, or other vehicle which they may at any time place on a public stand, or run as a public conveyance within said city; and all carriages or other vehicles placed by any livery stable keeper on a public stand, shall be regularly numbered, and subject to all the provisions hereinbefore contained relative to rates or prices of conveyance; and in case any livery stable keeper shall place a carriage or other vehicle on a public stand without paying the said sum of five dollars to the City Treasurer, and placing a number on his carriage, or other vehicle, he shall, upon conviction of the offence in the Mayor's Court, be fined ten dollars and costs of prosecution.

Livery stables to pay five dollars to Treasurer for each vehicle; and suject to provisions of this ordinance.

SEC. 10. No hotel keeper who may keep an omnibus, carriage, or other vehicle, for the purpose of carrying passengers to and from steamboats and railroad depots, or other places in said city, shall be permitted to use the same for carrying any person or persons for hire in and through said city, except on taking out a license according to the provisions of section one of this ordinance, and paying the regular fee therefor; and for every violation of the provisions of this section, the person or persons offending, on conviction in the Mayor's Court, shall be fined ten dollars and costs of prosecution.

Hotel keepers to obtain licences.

SEC. 11. The Mayor's Court, in its discretion, may order any person or persons found guilty of a violation of any of the provisions of this ordinance, to be imprisoned in the common jail of Wayne county for a term not exceeding ninety days, besides the fines and costs hereinbefore authorized; and the Mayor or Recorder, or any three Aldermen of the city, may at any time revoke the license of any person who shall be found guilty of having violated any of the provisions of this ordinance.

Mayor's Court may order persons violating this ordinance imprisoned, and Mayor or Recorder or any three Aldermen may revoke license.

SEC. 12. In all cases where complaints shall be made by a stranger or non-resident of said city for a violation of any of the provisions of this ordinance, and the person or persons complained of shall be found guilty, upon trial in the Mayor's Court, or shall plead guilty, the complainant shall be entitled to receive one-half of the fine imposed upon the person or persons complained of, after the same has been collected and paid to the City Treasurer; and it shall be the duty of the City Treasurer, on receiving such fine, to pay one-half thereof to such complainant, on demand, and take a receipt therefor.

When one half of fine to go to non-resident complainants.

SEC. 13. All sleighs, cutters, or other conveyances used by persons for hire, within said city, during the season of sleighing, shall be

TITLE X. CHAPTER 57.

Sleighs and cutters subject to provisions of this ordinance.

subject to all the provisions of this ordinance in regard to rates or prices of hire for cabs, carriages, hackney coaches, omnibusses, or other vehicles.

Clerk to keep register of persons licensed and of numbers of vehicle.

SEC. 14. The City Clerk shall keep a register of the names of all persons licensed according to the provisions of this ordinance, in which shall be stated the number and date of the license granted to each person, and the number of cabs, carriages, coaches, omnibusses, or other vehicles, allowed to be kept or used under each license; and at the time of granting each license, the Clerk shall give to the person or persons taking the same, a number for each of the vehicles allowed to be kept by such person or persons, and also enter such number on his register; and every person taking out a license as aforesaid, shall forthwith place, or cause to be placed, in conspicuous figures, on the outside of the door or doors of each vehicle kept or used under such license, the number given him by the City Clerk, as aforesaid; and in case there are no doors to such vehicle, the number shall be placed on both sides of the box of such vehicle, in a conspicuous place. Any person or persons failing to comply with the provisions of this section, on conviction thereof, in the Mayor's Court, shall be fined ten dollars and costs of prosecution. The Mayor or Recorder, may, at any time, in their discretion, revoke such license granted as provided in the preceding sections of this ordinance.

CHAPTER LVII.

Relative to Stands of Public Carriages, &c.

SEC. 1. Place where cabs, &c. to stand.	SEC. 4. Vehicles to occupy centre of street.
SEC. 2. Stands for drays, &c.	SEC. 5. Penalty.
SEC. 3. Driver to remain on his vehicle.	

Places where cabs, &c., to stand.

SEC. 1. That hereafter all hackney coaches, carriages, cabs and other vehicles used for carrying passengers, plying for hire within the limits of the city, shall, while waiting for employment, occupy the following stands, and no others, that is to say: The centre of Jefferson avenue, from a point fifteen feet easterly of the east line of Woodward avenue, to a point fifteen feet westerly of the west line of Bates street; the centre of Jefferson avenue from a point fifteen feet westerly of the west line of Woodward avenue, to a point fifteen feet easterly of the east line of Griswold street; the centre of Woodward avenue, from a point fifteen feet northely of the north line of

Jefferson avenue, to a point fifteen feet southerly of the south line, of Larned street; the centre of Woodward avenue, from a point fifteen feet southerly of the south line of Jefferson avenue, to a point fifteen feet northerly of the north line of Woodbridge street.

Stands for drays, &c.

SEC. 2. All drays, carts, wagons and other vehicles used for the transportation of goods, merchandise, and other wares, plying for hire within the limits of the city, shall, while waiting for employment, occupy the following stands, and no others, that is to say: The centre of Jefferson avenue, between Griswold street and Third street; the centre of Jefferson avenue, between Bates street and Brush street; the centre of Woodward avenue, between Larned street and the Campius Martius; the centre of Woodward avenue, between Woodbridge street and the river: *Provided*, That none of the said vehicles shall stand within fifteen feet of any cross street.

Driver to remain on his vehicle.

SEC. 3. The driver of any carriage, cart or other vehicle mentioned in this ordinance, shall, while waiting for employment as aforesoid, remain upon his said vehicle.

Vehicles to occupy centre of streets.

SEC. 4. The said vehicles, while occupying the stands aforesaid, shall stand in the centre of said streets, and in a line parallel with the course of said streets.

Penalty.

SEC. 5. Any person violating any of the provisions of this ordinance, shall, for each offence, upon conviction before the Mayor's Court, forfeit and pay a fine of not more than fifty dollars and costs of prosecution.

CHAPTER LVIII.

Relative to Drays, Carts, &c.

Drays &c., to be licensed.

SEC. 1. No person shall ply any cart, dray or wagon within the limits of said city, for hire, without a license, under the penalty of five dollars for each and every offence.

Who may be licensed and how.

SEC. 2. That any resident of the city of Detroit, and who has been such resident for three months and more, may have a license as cartman, drayman, or wagoner, by applying to the City Clerk thereof and paying the Clerk one dollar for the same: *Provided*, That any non-resident, or any person who has been here less than three months,

TITLE XI. CHAPTER 59.

may have a license on payment in addition to what is required above, of the sum of five dollars to the City Treasury, said license to run one year from the first of August in each year.

No license to be assigned.

SEC. 3. No person licensed as above shall asssign his license or permit any other person to drive his wagon, cart or dray, without permission of the Mayor or one of the Aldermen of said city endorsed on the back of his license, and having such transfer entered on the registry kept by the City Clerk, under a penalty of five dollars for each and every offence.

Drays, &c., to be numbered

SEC. 4. Each person having a cart, dray or wagon licensed as aforesaid, shall cause the number of his license to be painted upon each side of his cart, wagon or dray, with black paint on a white ground, so as to be easily seen on the square of the after part of the shaft, and to continue the same under a penalty of one dollar for every day he shall drive his cart, dray or wagon without having the same so numbered.

Penalty.

Rates.

SEC. 5. The price to be demanded and received by persons as above licensed, shall not exceed eighteen and three-quarter cents for each load.

Penalty for violation.

SEC. 6. If any person or persons acting with authority for any person licensed under this chapter, shall ask, demand or receive any greater charge than is herein established, or shall be guilty of any embezzlement or deceit in the execution of his duty, or of cruelty to his horse, he shall forfeit and pay the penalty of five dollars for each and every offence.

Clerk to keep a registry of licensed drays, &c.

SEC. 7. The City Clerk shall keep a registry of all persons licensed under this chapter, and of the date of their licenses.

TITLE ELEVEN.

OF PLACES OF REFRESHMENT AND RECREATION.

CHAPTER LIX.

Relative to Ordinaries and Groceries.

SEC. 1. No person or persons who may keep an ordinary, victualin house or grocery, within the limits of the city of Detroit, nor any person employed by, or acting for him or her, shall at any time, knowingly permit any gaming for money, or for other value, within his, her, or their premises, or suffer any drunkenness, reveling, quarreling, fighting, blasphemy, or any other disorderly or immoral conduct, or keep his, her or their establishment open during any part of the Sabbath, or sell any liquors or beverages prohibited by the laws of this State, or keep open any house at any time after half-past ten o'clock at night; any person or persons offending in the premises, on conviction thereof before the Mayor's Court of the city of Detroit, shall forfeit and pay for every such offence, for the use of said city, a sum not exceeding one hundred dollars, with the costs of prosecution, and be liable to have his, her or their license suppressed and declared void.

Of the internal order of groceries and ordinaries.

SEC. 2. It shall be the duty of the Marshal and Constables to notice and enquire into all offences under this chapter, and to notify the City Attorney of the same, who, upon such notification, shall cause proceedings against the guilty party or parties to be instituted in the Mayor's Court.

Duty of Marshal and Constables.

CHAPTER LX.

Relative to ball alleys, billiard and other tables.

SEC. 1. No person or persons shall keep, or permit to be kept, in his, her or their premises, within the limits of said city, any ball alley, or any billiard table, or other tables for the purpose of playing at any game whatsoever, or to allow any person or persons to play at such alley, or such table or tables, unless the person keeping the same, has been previously licensed to do so, by the authority of the Common Council of said city.

Keepers of ball alleys, &c to be licensed

SEC. 2. It shall be the duty of any person or persons who may be desirous of keeping any ball alley, billiard table or other table, to make application to the Common Council of said city for license; and such license may be granted on paying the sum, and on filing the bond hereinafter required: but no such license shall be granted for a shorter period than three months.

License, how obtained.

TITLE XI. CHAPTER 61.

Amount of license, recognizance, &c.

SEC. 3. No person shall receive such license until he shall have paid to the Treasurer of said city, such sum as the Common Council may determine for one year, for each and every ball alley, billiard table or other table; the person applying for any such license shall also enter into recognizance to the Mayor, Recorder, Aldermen and Freemen of the City of Detroit, himself in the sum of hundred dollars with two sufficient sureties, in the sum fifty dollars, to be taken and acknowledged before the City Clerk, conditioned that such applicant shall well and truly observe and keep all the requirements of this chapter, and shall neither do nor permit to be done anything contrary thereto.

Premises closed when, no gambling, &c.

SEC. 4. No person licensed as aforesaid, shall at any time permit, or suffer any gaming for money or other value, within any ball alley or billiard table, or other such establishment kept by him; nor shall any person be guilty of betting or gaming for money or other value therein; nor shall any person so licensed, suffer therein or thereabouts, any drunkenness, quarreling, fighting, or any other disorderly conduct, nor keep any such establishment open during any part of the Sabbath or first day of the week, or after the hour of ten o'clock in the evening, or before the hour of eight o'clock in the forenoon of any day, nor permit to play thereon or thereat, any minor, apprentice, or servant, after the parent, guardian, master or mistress of such person, shall have notified such keeper not to permit such minor, apprentice or servant, to play.

Penalty.

SEC. 5. Any person or persons who shall offend against any of the provisions of this chapter, shall, on conviction thereof, be liable to a fine not exceeding one hundred dollars and costs of prosecution, for each offence, and on conviction a second time, the person so licensed, shall be liable to have his license suppressed and annulled.

CHAPTER LXI.

Relative to Shows, Theatrical Entertainments, &c.

SEC. 1. Persons keeping shows, &c., to be licensed; penalty. | SEC. 2. Common Council to license.

Persons keeping shows, &c to be licensed

SEC. 1. It shall not be lawful for any person or persons to make or exhibit any show or shows, or to perform any plays, games, theatrical or any other performances or exhibitions whatever, or to exhibit any natural or other curiosities for which pay or compensation of any kind shall be required, demanded or received, without having previously been licensed so to do, by the authority of the Common Council of the city of Detroit; or the Mayor or two Aldermen may give any such person permission to make such exhibitions if deemed proper; any person or persons offending against the provisions of this chapter, shall be liable to pay a fine not exceeding one hundred dollars for every offence; and the Marshal of the city of Detroit is hereby authorized in any case wherein the provisions of this chapter shall be violated, or not complied with, to arrest the person or persons offending against the same, and bring him or them before the Mayor, Recorder, or any of the Aldermen of said city, who are hereby authorized to hold such persons to bail for their appearance at the ensuing term of the Mayor's Court, to answer to any alleged offence, in any such case: *Provided*, Any such person may be discharged by the Mayor or any two Aldermen upon paying such sum as they may direct, and costs. Penalty.

SEC. 2. It shall be the duty of all or every such person or persons, who may be desirous of exhibiting any natural or other curiosities or shows, or to perform any games or theatrical exhibitions, or any other games, shows or exhibitions whatever, for which money, or pay, or any compensation whatever shall be required or received, to make application to the Mayor, Recorder and Aldermen of the city of Detroit for a license; and the said license may be granted by the Common Council, whenever payment to the Treasurer of the city of Detroit has been made of such sum as may be prescribed by the Common Council, for the use of the said city. Common Council to license.

CHAPTER LXII.

Relative to Taverns and Inns.

SEC. 1. No person to keep a tavern without license; penalty.	SEC. 4. License to be allowed by Council; recognizance.
SEC. 2. Form and manner of applying for license.	SEC. 5. When license annulled.
SEC. 3. Amount to be paid for license.	SEC. 6. Internal order of house.
	SEC. 7. To keep signs over doors.

SEC. 1. No person, unless licensed agreeably to the provisions of this chapter, shall keep a tavern, inn or hotel, within the limits of the said city, and if any person shall offend against the provisions of this section, such person shall, upon conviction thereof, before the Mayor's Court of the said city, be fined in a sum not exceeding twenty-five dollars for every such offence. No person to keep a tavern without license. Penalty.

TITLE XI. CHAPTER 62.

Form and manner of applying for license.

SEC. 2. Every person desiring to keep a tavern, inn or hotel, within the limits of the said city, shall make application in writing to the Common Council, setting forth the street and house in which he or she intends to keep the same, and shall accompany such application with the names of his or her securities, and also a recommendation signed by at least twelve respectable freeholders of the said city, stating his or her means and qualifications to keep a tavern, inn or hotel, and certifying that he or she is of good fame and moral character, and correct and orderly deportment and behavior; and the Common Council shall take such application under consideration, and grant or refuse the same, as in their opinion the interests and well being of the city may require. And no license shall be granted unless the applicant is possessed of stabling sufficient for ten horses, and accommodation for at least eight guests.

Amount to be paid for license.

SEC. 3. Every person to whom the Common Council shall grant license to keep a tavern, inn or hotel, shall, before the same be issued, pay into the Treasury for the use of the Mayor, Recorder, Aldermen and Freemen of the city of Detroit, such sum as may be required by the Common Council, having a proper regard in each case, to the apparent advantages of each petitioner's situation for the business and profit of a tavern, hotel or inn.

License to be allowed by Council.

SEC. 4. Whenever the Common Council shall decide in favor of any petitioner, and grant him or her a license for keeping a tavern, hotel or inn, the Clerk of the said city shall give such petitioner a certificate of the granting of such license, and of the price fixed for the same; on the said applicant producing a receipt from the Treasurer of the said city for the payment of the sum so fixed, he or she shall be entitled to receive a license under the hand of the Mayor, and the seal of the said city, and attested by the said Clerk, authorizing him or her to keep a tavern, hotel or inn, for the term of one year, and no longer, in the house designated, and in no other house: *Provided*, That every person to whom license shall be granted as aforesaid, shall, before he or she be entitled to receive such license, or to act by virtue thereof, enter into recognizance to the Mayor, Recorder, Aldermen and Freemen of the city of Detroit, him or herself in the sum of one hundred dollars, with two or more sufficient sureties in the sum of fifty dollars each, conditioned that he or she

Recognizance.

shall keep and maintain an orderly and well regulated house, during the continuance of such license, and shall at all times provide and keep good sufficient meat, drink, bedding and stabling, for the convenience and accommodation of travelers and other guests, who may apply for and require the same, for a reasonable compensation, and shall keep, observe and obey the provisions and regulations which are or may be prescribed and ordained from time to time, regulating taverns, hotels and inns within the city of Detroit; which recognizance shall be taken and be acknowledged before the City Clerk.

When license annulled.

SEC. 5. In case any person is declared and adjudged to have forfeited his or her recognizance, it shall be in the power and discretion of the Mayor, Recorder and Aldermen in Common Council convened, to vacate and annul the license granted to such person as aforesaid, and thereupon such person shall be disqualified, or to order a new recognizance to be entered into, within a limited time; and in case the said order is not complied with, the said license shall from that time be null and void.

Internal order of house.

SEC. 6. It shall not be lawful for the keeper of any tavern, inn or hotel, within the said city, to suffer in or about his or her house or premises, upon the Sabbath day, any person or persons drinking, tippling, rioting, and making a disturbance, or at any time to sell any liquors prohibited by the laws of this State, nor shall it be lawful for the keeper of any such house as aforesaid, to permit or suffer any cards or other games of chance to be played for money or other article of value, in his or her house, out house or enclosurs, or to suffer or permit any gambling or betting of money or other property whatever, within his or her said house, out house or enclosures, which are or may be prohibited by the laws of this State: and if any person shall offend against the provisions of this section, he or she shall be considered as having broken his or her recognizance, and shall be further liable to be fined upon conviction thereof before the Mayor's Court, in a sum not exceeding twenty-five dollars for every such offence: *Provided, always*, That the prosecution for offending against this chapter shall be commenced within one year after the commission of such offence, and at no time thereafter.

To keep signs over doors.

SEC. 7. Every person to whom a license under this chapter shall be granted, shall fasten and keep over the front door of the tavern, inn or hotel kept by him, a sign having painted thereon in large and legible letters, the word "tavern," "inn," or "hotel," as the case may be, together with the name of the person keeping the same; and every person neglecting or refusing to comply with this section, shall be liable to pay a fine not exceeding five dollars for every day he or she shall so neglect or refuse.

CHAPTER LXIII.

Relative to the Collection of License Moneys.

License moneys to be paid before delivery of license.

SEC. 1. It shall be the duty of the Clerk of the city of Detroit to make out all grocery, tavern and other licenses, which shall from time to time be granted by the Common Council, but no such license shall hereafter be issued or delivered until the sum required for the same has been fully paid to the Treasurer of the city of Detroit.

TITLE TWELVE.

OF PORTERS, RUNNERS, AND THE ARRIVAL AND DEPARTURE OF BOATS AND CARS.

CHAPTER LXIV.

Relative to Licensing Porters and Runners.

Porters, and runners to be licensed.

SEC. 1. The Mayor of the city of Detroit for the time being shall have power from time to time to issue licenses under his hand and seal to so many and to such persons as he shall think proper to carry on the business of public porters or runners for hotels, and all omnibus agents, omnibus drivers, and drivers of baggage, and all other persons when acting as porters or runners for hotels; and the Mayor or Recorder, or any three Aldermen of the city, shall have power to revoke all or any of such licenses.

SEC. 2. All such licenses shall expire on the seventh day of April next after the date thereof, and may be renewed on application of the holders thereof. When license to expire.

SEC. 3. For every such license shall be paid by the person applying for the same, the sum of one dollar, and for every renewal the same sum. Fees for license.

SEC. 4. No person shall act or engage in the business of a public porter or runner for any hotel, or as an omnibus agent, omnibus driver, or driver of baggage, acting as porters or runners for hotels, without being duly licensed as such by the Mayor, under a penalty not exceeding five dollars, in the discretion of the court, and costs of prosecution, for every such offence. Persons not to act without license.

SEC. 5. Every public porter or runner, omnibus agent, omnibus driver and baggage driver, and all other persons acting as runners for hotels, shall wear a badge on his hat, and in a conspicuous place on his body, on which shall be legibly and plainly engraved or printed, his name and the number of his license, under a penalty not to exceed five dollars, in the discretion of the court, and the costs of prosecution, for each neglect of the provisions of this section. Porters and runners, &c., to wear a badge.

SEC. 6. Every public porter or runner, omnibus agent, omnibus driver or baggage driver, and all other persons acting as porters or runners for hotels, shall have on a card or a plate, printed or engraved, his name and the number of his license, and also the prices or rates of fare allowed by law for omnibuses, hackney coaches, &c., in legible characters, which shall be nailed on a conspicuous part of his carriage, omnibus, wagon, sleigh, wheel-barrow or hand cart, under a penalty not to exceed five dollars, in the discretion of the court, and the costs of prosecution, for every violation of the provisions of this section. Porters, runners, &c., to have a card containing his name, &c. in carriage.

SEC. 7. Every person to whom such licenses shall be granted, shall first execute to the Mayor, Recorder, Aldermen and Freemen of the city of Detroit, a bond with one or more sufficient sureties, to be approved by the Mayor, in the penalty of five hundred dollars, conditioned that he will conduct himself in a decent and orderly manner while acting as such porter, runner, omnibus agent, omnibus driver, or driver of baggage, when acting as porters or runners for hotels, and in all respects comply with the provisions of this ordinance: *Provided, however*, That it shall be lawful for such sureties or either of Porters and runners to execute bond them to vacate such bond by giving ten days' notice in writing to the Mayor or Recorder, and in such case the said license shall be annulled and made void, unless other sureties are furnished as above provided.

Not to approach within twenty feet of boats and cars, when.

SEC. 8. No porter, runner, omnibus agent, omnibus driver, driver of baggage or other persons acting as porters or runners for hotels, so licensed as aforesaid, shall, on the arrival of any steamboat or railroad cars in the city of Detroit, for a period of fifteen minutes thereafter, go upon or approach within twenty feet of the wharf or depot where such steamboat or railroad cars have made fast or stopped running, or are about to make fast or stop running; unless such porter, runner, omnibus agent, omnibus driver, or driver of baggage be requested by a passenger to remove some trunk or other baggage from said wharf or depot, in which case it shall be lawful to go near, in or upon such steamboat or depot for such purpose, under a penalty not to exceed five dollars, in the discretion of the court, and costs of prosecution, for every such offence.

Punishment for acting without license.

SEC. 9. No person shall act as porter or runner, or omnibus agent, omnibus driver or baggage driver when acting as runner or porter for any public house or hotel in the city of Detroit, without being duly licensed according to the provisions of this ordinance, under a penalty not to exceed twenty-five dollars, in the discretion of the court, for every such offence.

When license forfeited.

SEC. 10. On conviction of any porter, runner, omnibus agent, omnibus driver, or baggage driver, or other person acting as porter or runner for any hotel or public house, licensed as aforesaid, before the Mayor's Court, of any violation of the provisions of this ordinance, the Mayor or Recorder shall, in his discretion, be authorized, in addition to the fines hereinbefore provided, to vacate and annul any such license that may then be held by any such porter, runner, omnibus agent, omnibus driver or driver of baggage, and to declare the bond of such person forfeited.

When City Attorney to put bond in suit.

SEC. 11. On the forfeiture of the bond of any such porter, runner, omnibus agent, omnibus driver, driver of baggage or other person, as provided in the preceding section, it shall be the duty of the City Attorney to prosecute the principal and sureties named in such bond for the benefit of the city.

CHAPTER LXV.

Relative to the Departure and Arrival of Boats and Cars.

SEC. 1. That no person shall, on the arrival of any railroad cars in said city, nor for the period of thirty minutes previously to the departure of any railroad cars from said city, have or keep any carriage, wagon, cart or other vehicle within twenty feet of the place where such railroad cars shall have ceased running, or are about to depart from said city.

Carriages not to be kept within twenty feet of depot on arrival of cars.

SEC. 2. No person shall, on the arrival of any steamboat or vessel, at any wharf in said city, nor for the period of thirty minutes thereafter, nor for the period of thirty minutes previously to the departure of such steamboats or vessels, have or keep any carriage, wagon, cart or other vehicle, within sixty feet of the place where such steamboat or vessel has or is about to be made fast, or depart from said city. Any person violating this or the preceding section, shall, for every violation, on conviction before the Mayor's Court, forfeit a sum not exceeding one hundred dollars and costs of prosecution.

Where carriages to stand on arrival and departure of steamboats.

SEC. 3. All carriages, wagons, carts and other vehicles, the keepers whereof are waiting for employment, from any railroad cars, steamboats or vessels, shall stand on either side of the street or alley, so as to leave the centre thereof, and access to each house thereon, open and unobstructed, for the free passage of carriages, wagons, carts and other vehicles, and foot passengers. Any person violating this section, shall, for every violation, on conviction before the Mayor's Court, forfeit a sum not exceeding fifty dollars and costs of prosecution.

Further regulations.

SEC. 4. If any person shall, on the arrival or departure of any railroad cars, steamboats or vessels, at or from said city, or for the period of thirty minutes after the arrival or before the departure of such railroad cars, steamboats or vessels, and within sixty feet of the wharf or depot where such railroad cars, steamboats or vessels, have or are about to stop running or being made fast, or depart from said city, make, aid, countenance or assist in making, any loud or boisterous noise, disturbance or improper diversion, or shall be guilty of any

Disorderly conduct at boats and cars prohibited.

32

TITLE XIII. CHAPTER 66.

indecent, immoral or insulting conduct, language or behavior, such person shall, for every such offence, on conviction before said Mayor's Court, forfeit a sum not exceeding one hundred dollars and costs of prosecution.

False representation to strangers—punishment.

SEC. 5. If any person shall, by any false or decitful representations to any stranger or traveler in said city, induce or prevail on such stranger or traveler, to go to, and put up at any hotel, tavern, grocery or other house of entertainment in said city, such person shall, for every such offence, on conviction before the Mayor's Court, forfeit a sum not exceeding one hundred dollars and costs of prosecution.

Duty of officers.

SEC. 6. It shall be the special duty of the Marshal and all the Constables of said city, to make complaint of all violations of this chapter.

Teamsters may haul freight.

SEC. 7. Nothing contained in the first and second sections of this chapter shall be construed to prevent any teamster from hauling freight to any steamboat or vessel about to depart from said city.

Propellors to be provided with spark catchers—penalty.

SEC. 8. No propeller shall be permitted to approach within fifty feet of any wharf in this city, or lie at any wharf in this city, while fired up, unless her smoke-pipe shall be covered with a good and sufficient spark-catcher, or other covering to prevent the emission of sparks or coals from her said pipe; and in case the captain or officers of any propeller shall permit the same to approach or lie at any wharf, contrary to the provisions of this section, he or they shall be liable to a fine not exceeding one hundred dollars, to be recovered with costs by prosecution in the Mayor's Court.

TITLE THIRTEEN.

OF PAUPERS.

CHAPTER LXVI.

Relative to Paupers and their Support.

SEC. 1. Vessels not to land paupers in city.	SEC. 3. Penalty.
SEC. 1. Persons bringing paupers to city to support same.	SEC. 4. Director of Poor—their duties and powers.

Vessels not to land paupers.

SEC. 1. If any owner, captain or master of a vessel, or other person, shall, by land or water, bring and leave within the limits of this city, any person or persons, poor and unable to maintain themselves, they shall forthwith, or as soon as may be thereafter, transport the same back to the place whence they were taken; and shall provide all the necessary means of comfort and subsistence for such paupers, if requested by them or by any citizen, until so transported.

Persons bringing paupers to support them.

SEC. 2. In case of refusal or neglect to provide for such paupers the necessary means of comfort and subsistence according to the foregoing section, and any member of the Common Council, or Director of the Poor, shall make such provision, the same may be recovered back, and may form part of the judgment in a prosecution for a violation of this chapter.

Penalty.

SEC. 3. Any violation of the two preceding sections of this chapter, may be punished with a fine not exceeding fifty dollars and costs of prosecution.

Director of poor, his duties.

SEC. 4. The Director of the Poor for said city, shall have and exercise the same powers and duties, and be subject to the same liabilities and restrictions as the laws of this State prescribe relative to Directors of the Poor in any township of this State; and the laws of this State relative to township and county paupers shall be observed with respect to such paupers in said city; and all suits and prosecutions for violations of such laws, may be brought in the Mayor's Court of said city.

TITLE FOURTEEN.

MISCELLANEOUS.

CHAPTER LXVII.

Relative to Cancelling the orders, warrants, and due bills of the City of Detroit.

Treasurer to cancel warrants, &c.

SEC. 1. That the City Treasurer shall, without delay, procure a proper cancelling hammer, such as is ordinarily used by banking institutions, with which he shall immediately cut, mark and cancel every order, due bill, warrant or other evidence of debt, issued by the Mayor, Recorder, Aldermen and Freemen of the city of Detroit, or by the Common Council of said city, or under their direction, which now are in the City Treasury; and hereafter, the said Treasurer shall, as

TITLE XIV. CHAPTER 67.

soon as any order, due bill, or warrant or other evidence of debt heretofore issued, or which hereafter shall or may at any time or times be issued by said Mayor, Recorder, Aldermen and Freemen, or by said Common Council, or by or under their direction or authority, shall come or be paid into the Treasury of said city, cut, mark and cancel the same with said cancelling hammer.

To keep cancelled warrants.

SEC. 2. After the City Treasurer shall have so cut, marked and cancelled said orders, warrants, due bills, or other evidences of debt, as aforesaid, he shall carefully and safely file and keep the same until the further order or action of said Common Council.

To record the same.

SEC. 3. It shall be the duty of the City Treasurer, from and after the passage of this chapter, to keep a book or record, in which he shall enter as soon as he receives the same, the number, date and amount of each and every warrant, order, due bill, and evidence of debt, as aforesaid, received into the City Treasury; and whenever the City Treasurer shall report to said Common Council any amount of warrants, orders, due bills or other evidences of debt, as hereinafter provided for, he shall accompany his report with a schedule or list of said warrants, orders, due bills or other evidences of debt so reported, with the number, date and amount of each.

Warrants, &c to be returned to Council and destroyed.

SEC. 4. Whenever the City Treasurer shall have in his possession one thousand dollars of cut, marked and cancelled warrants, orders, due bills or other evidences of debt, issued or hereafter to be issued, as aforesaid, he shall report the fact to the said Common Council, whilst in session, and thereupon, at the same session of said Council, or at the next regular meeting, said Council shall cause said orders, due bills, warrants or other evidences of debt aforesaid, to be carefully examined and checked on the warrant book, in presence of the Council, by a committee of three, to be appointed from time to time by the Mayor, of whom the Clerk shall be one, and the same having been so counted, examined and checked, shall be forthwith burned, or otherwise destroyed, in the presence of the Council, and the amount so destroyed, with the number or other suitable designation of each, shall be entered on the journal of the Council.

AN ORDINANCE to give effect to the Revised Ordinances of eighteen hundred and fifty-five.

Be it ordained by the Mayor, Recorder and Aldermen of the city of Detroit, in Common Council convened:

SEC. 1. That the edition of the ordinances of the city of Detroit collated and published by, and under the direction of the Special Committee of this Council, appointed for that purpose, on the thirteenth day of February, A. D., eighteen hundred and fifty-five, shall be called "The Revised Ordinances of the City of Detroit, for eighteen hundred and fifty-five," and the same, together with this ordinance, shall take effect and go into operation from and after the fifteenth day of August, A. D., eighteen hundred and fifty-five.

SEC. 2. It shall be the duty of the Special Committee who have arranged the same, to record, or cause to be recorded, in the book of ordinances kept by the City Clerk, a full, fair and correct copy of all the ordinances collated by the said committee, and published under their direction as aforesaid; and the said copy, so recorded, shall be carefully preserved in the office of the City Clerk.

SEC. 3. All by-laws and ordinances, or parts of by-laws and ordinances, repugnant to, or in any manner inconsistent with, the edition of ordinances so arranged and published by the said Special Committee as aforesaid, shall be repealed from and after the taking effect of the said revised ordinances arranged and published by said Special Committee.

SEC. 4. The repeal provided for in the preceding section, shall not affect any act done, or any right accruing or accrued or established, or any suit had or commenced for any purpose whatever before the time when such repeal shall take effect; nor shall any offence committed, or penalty or forfeiture incurred, under any of the ordinances or by-laws repealed by the preceding section, and before the time when such repeal shall take effect, be affected by such repeal.

SEC. 5. No suit or prosecution, pending at the time of the said repeal, for any offence committed, or for the recovery of any penalty or forfeiture incurred, under any of the ordinances or by-laws repealed as provided for in section three, shall be affected by such repeal, except that the proceedings in such suit or prosecution shall be conformed, when necessary, to the provisions of said revised ordinances.

SEC. 6. All persons who at the time when the said repeal shall take effect, shall hold any office under any of the ordinances or by-laws so as aforesaid repealed, shall continue to hold the same according to the tenure thereof.

SEC. 7. No ordinance or by-law, which has heretofore been repealed, shall be revived by the repeal provided for in section three.

SEC. 8. Whenever an ordinance or by-law, or any part thereof, shall be repealed by a subsequent ordinance or by-law, such ordinance or by-law or any part thereof, so repealed, shall not be revived by the repeal of such subsequent repealing ordinance or by-law.

SEC. 9. All ordinances and by-laws hereafter to be passed by the Common Council shall be promulgated by being printed in such manner as the Common Council shall direct; and every ordinance or by-law which does not expressly provide the time when it shall go into operation, shall take effect on the tenth day after the same has been passed.

SEC. 10. This ordinance shall take effect and be in force from and after the fifteenth day of August, A. D. 1855.

Ordained and dated in Common Council the fifteenth day of August, A. D., 1855. HENRY LEDYARD, *Mayor.*

Attest: RICHARD STARKEY, *City Clerk.*

At a session of the Common Council of the city of Detroit, held on the thirteenth day of February, A. D., 1855, the following resolution was unanimously adopted:

Resolved, That the Recorder, City Attorney, and City Auditor be a special committee whose duty it shall be to proceed and collate the charter of the city of Detroit, and all the present existing amendments thereto, all the ordinances of said city now in force or existing, omitting all amendments or ordinances repealed or not now in force, together with the standing rules of this Council, and have the same published at the expense of the city, and furnished to each member and officer of the Common Council, with all convenient speed.

HENRY LEDYARD, *Mayor.*

Attest: RICHARD STARKEY, *City Clerk.*

STANDING RULES

OF THE

COMMON COUNCIL OF DETROIT.

RULE I.

The Common Council shall hold regular sessions upon Tuesday of every week, at 7 o'clock P. M., unless the Council shall otherwise order. When sessions of Council to be held.

RULE II.

The Mayor (and in his absence the Recorder) shall take the Chair, at the hour appointed for the Council to meet, whether in special or regular session, and call the members to order. On the appearance of a quorum, he shall cause the minutes of the preceding session to be read, at which time, mistakes, if any, shall be corrected. He shall preserve order and decorum, and shall decide questions of order, subject to an appeal to the Council. He shall appoint all committees, subject, at the announcement thereof, to concurrence therein by the Council; and an appointment being disagreed to, that committee shall be elected by ballot. He shall vote upon a division, or a call of ayes and noes. Mayor—his duties at sessions of Council.

RULE III.

The Chair or any two members may have a call of the Council, and the names of absentees shall be noted by the Clerk. Every such absentee not offering a reasonable excuse for his absence, when called upon or when summoned for that purpose, shall be fined for each default, such sum, not exceeding two dollars and fifty cents, as the Council may deem proper. Members may be fined for absence.

RULE IV.

When a question is put by the Chair, every member present shall vote, unless the Council, for special reasons, shall excuse him; but if interested, he shall not vote. In doubtful cases, the Chair may direct, or any member call for a division. The yeas and nays shall be called upon the requisition of the Chair, or of any member. Who to vote.

RULE V.

Motions to be in writing.

Every motion (except to adjourn, postpone or commit) shall be reduced to writing, if the Chair or any member requires it. When made and seconded it shall be stated by the Chairman; or being written, shall be read by the Clerk; and may be withdrawn before decision or amendment, or any disposition thereof has been made, or a vote had thereon.

RULE VI.

Motions to adjourn.

A motion to adjourn shall always be in order, and shall be decided without debate.

RULE VII.

Members to rise when speaking.

When a member is about to speak, he shall rise, and address himself to the Chair; nor shall he speak more than twice on any question without leave of the Council, nor more than five minutes any time.

RULE VIII.

Who to have precedence in speaking.

When two or more members rise at once, the Chairman shall designate which is to speak first.

RULE IX.

Member called to order, to take his seat &c.

A member called to order shall resume his seat, unless permitted to explain, and the Council, if appealed to, shall decide on the case—on any appeal, no member shall speak but once without leave of the Council.

RULE X.

Mayor to leave chair in committee of the whole.

On forming a committee of the whole Council, the Mayor or Recorder shall leave the Chair, and shall call some member to preside.

RULE XI.

Order in which questions shall be put.

All questions, whether in committee or in the Council, shall be put in the order they were named—except in cases of privileged questions; and in filling blanks, the longest time and the largest sum shall be first put.

RULE XII.

Rules of Council to be observed in committee.

The rules of the Council shall be observed in committee of the whole as far as they may be applicable, except the rule limiting the time of speaking; and the previous question shall not be put in a committee of the whole.

RULE XIII.

A motion that the committee rise, shall always be in order, and shall be decided without debate. Motion in committee.

RULE XIV.

The Clerk shall not enter upon the journal the proceedings of a committee of the whole, except as the same may be reported to the Council. Proceedings of committee of the whole not to be recorded.

RULE XV.

When a question is under debate, no motion shall be received, unless to postpone, amend, to take the previous question, to commit, or to adjourn. What motions in order during debate.

RULE XVI.

The previous question shall be put in these words, "Shall the main question now be put?" It shall be admitted on demand of any two members, and until decided shall preclude all amendments under debate of the main question. Previous questions, how put.

RULE XVII.

Any member may call for a division of the question, when the same will admit thereof. Division, &c.

RULE XVIII.

Every ordinance shall be introduced by a committee, to whom the subject matter thereof may have been referred, by resolution or otherwise; or, by a member, upon leave asked and granted. Any notice of intention to move for such leave, shall be given at a previous regular session. Ordinances, how introduced.

RULE XIX.

Every ordinance shall recive two several readings, previous to its passage, but shall not be read at any other than regular sessions; nor twice read at the same session without special order of the Council. Reading of ordinances.

RULE XX.

The second reading of an ordinance, shall be first by sections, at which time amendments are to be offered; but the reading of a succeeding section, shall not preclude the offering of an amendment to a preceding one. If no amendment is made, the question shall be, "Shall this ordinance pass?" If amendments are made, the chair shall so report, and the ordinance shall be so read as amended, before the question on its passage is taken. Amendm'ts to ordinances how made.

RULE XXI.

Reconsideration of questions.

When a question has been taken, it shall be in order for any member to move a reconsideration thereof, at the same or the succeeding meeting; but no question shall be a second time reconsidered without the consent of two-thirds of the Council.

RULE XXII.

Petitions &c., how presented.

Petitions and other papers addressed to the Council, shall be presented by any member in his place; who shall make a brief statement of the contents thereof, when introducing the same.

RULE XXIII.

Ord'nances, how kept.

After an ordinance shall have passed, a fair copy thereof shall be made by the Clerk, and after having been compared by the Mayor, or in his absence by the Recorder, with the original, shall be signed and deposited with the Clerk, to be filed and recorded.

XXIV.

Clerk, his duties, &c.

It shall be the duty of the Clerk to keep a correct journal of the proceedings of the Council; to cause committees, members of the Council, and its officers to be informed of such duties as they may be charged with by the Council from time to time; and to perform such other duties as appertain to him as Clerk. He shall suffer no journal, accounts or papers to be taken from the table, or out of his custody, other than by the regular mode of business of the Council; and if any paper in his charge should be missing, he shall make a report to the chair, that it may be enquired into.

RULE XXV.

Who may sit within bar of Council.

No person, other than the members of the Council, shall be admitted to a seat within the bar of the Council, but the Clerk, City Attorney and Marshal, unless invited by a member of the Council.

RULE XXVI.

Standing committees.

The following standing committees shall be appointed, viz:

A Committee on Claims and Accounts, to consist of two members, who shall examine and report upon all matters of account or claim, in favor of or against the city, which may be referred to it.

A Committee on Ways and Means, to consist of two members, whose duty it shall be to examine and report upon all such matters relative to the revenue of the city as may be referred to them; to inquire into the state of the city debt, the revenue, and the expenditures; and whether any, and what retrenchment can be made with advantage; and to report from time to time, such provisions and arrangements, as may be promotive of economy, order and accountability, in the conduct of the fiscal concerns of the city, and all such claims as are not properly referable to the Committee on Claims and Accounts, shall be referred to the Committee on Ways and Means.

A Committee on Streets, to consist of two members, one for each street district, who shall examine and report upon all such matters relating to streets and sidewalks, within the city, as may be referred to them, and to report from time to time, upon such matters generally, as properly fall within the sphere of their duties in the premises.

A Committee on Health, to consist of two members, one for each street district, who shall examine and report upon all such matters, relating to, or in any way affecting the public health as may be referred to them, or which shall properly fall within the scope of their appointment.

A Committee on the Fire Department, to consist of two members, one for each district, whose duties shall be such, relative to the fire Department of the city, as are devolved by the rules upon the other committees, relative to their duties.

A Committee on Hydraulic Works, who shall examine and report upon all matters referred to them, in any way relating to the Hydraulic works of the city.

A Committee on Markets.

A Committee on Taxes.

A Committee on Printing.

A Committee on Gas Lights.

A Committee on Sewers.

A Committee on Public Buildings.

A Committee on Parks.

A Committee on Licenses, who shall respectively examine and report upon all matters referred to them, properly falling within the scope of their appointment.

RULE XXVII.

Every member about to leave the city for the space of twenty days, shall notify the Mayor, or in his absence the Recorder, thereof, that his place in committees may be temporarily filled.

Members to notify Mayor when about to leave the city.

RULE XXVIII.

Order of business at sessions of Council.

In the ordinary transaction of business, the following order shall govern: 1st. Petitions and applications to the Council. 2d. Reports from officers of the Council. 3d. Reports from Committees. 4th. Unfinished business remaining from preceding sessions in the order in which it was introduced. 5th. Resolutions and other matters offered for the consideration of the Council.

RULE XXIX.

How rules may be altered.

These rules not to be altered, amended or rescinded, but by the vote of two-thirds of the members present.

A true copy. RICHARD STARKEY, *City Clerk.*

APPENDIX TO CITY ORDINANCES.

AN ORDINANCE relative to the width of sidewalks on Fort street.

Be it ordained by the Mayor, Recorder, and Aldermen of the City of Detroit, in Common Council convened:

SEC 1. That the width of wagon way on Fort street, from the west line of Griswold street to the western line of the city, shall be forty-four feet, from curb to curb, and that the width of walk on each side thereof, shall be twenty-eight feet.

SEC. 2. That all ordinances, or parts of ordinances, conflicting with this ordinance, are hereby repealed.

Ordained and dated at Detroit, this twenty-fourth day af July, A. D. 1855.

HENRY A. MORROW,
Recorder and Acting Mayor.

Attest: RICHARD STARKEY, *City Clerk.*

MEMBERS OF COMMON COUNCIL AND CITY OFFICERS, 1855-56.

Mayor—HENRY LEDYARD.

Recorder—HENRY A. MORROW.

Aldermen:

First Ward—Wm. C. Duncan, Albert Marsh.

Second Ward—Edward A. Lansing, Wm. Craig.

Third Ward--Isaac W. Ingersoll, Anthony Dudgeon.

Fourth Ward—Isaac Finehart, Bradley H. Thompson.

Fifth Ward—Henry H. Leroy, Robert W. King.

Sixth Ward—Alanson Sheeley, Wilson W. Wilcox.

Seventh Ward—Edward Doyle, Robert Reaume.

Eighth Ward—Francis Mayhew, Stephen Martin.

Regular session of Common Council Tuesday evening of each week.

Regular sessions of Mayor's Court second Monday of each month.

OFFICERS OF THE CORPORATION FOR 1855-6.

City Attorney—J. Knox Gavin.
" *Clerk*—Richard Starkey.
" *Treasurer*—John Campbell.
" *Comptroller*—Charles Peltier.
" *Marshal*—Eli Laderoot.
" *Assistant Marshal*—Patrick McGinnis.
Chief Engineer Fire Department—William Duncan.
City Physician—John B. Scovel.
" *Surveyor*—Thomas Campau.
Director of the Poor—Luther B. Willard.
City Sexton—Frederick Deneke.
Street Commissioner—John King.
Clerk of City Hall Market—John Robson.
Weigh Master Upper Hay Scales—Enos Lebot.
" " *Lower Hay Scales*—Chas. H. Damn.
Wood Inspectors—Francis Lesperance, Henry Decker, A. Wing.
City Printer—Wilbur F. Storey.

Assessors.

First District—James Hanmer.
Second District—John Reno.
Third District—A. H. Stowell.

A LIST OF THE MAYORS OF THE CITY OF DETROIT, SINCE 1824.

John R. Williams, - - - - - - -	Elected 1824
John R. Williams, - - - - - -	" 1825
Henry I. Hunt, - - - - - - -	" 1826
Jonathan Kearsley, - - - - - -	" 1826
John Biddle, - - - - - - - - -	" 1827
John Biddle, - - - - - - -	" 1828
Jonathan Kearsley, - - - - - -	" 1829
John R. Williams, - - - - - -	" 1830
Marshal Chapin, - - - - - - -	" 1831

Levi Cook,	Elected	1832
Marshal Chapin,	"	1833
Charles C. Trowbridge,	"	1834
Andrew Mack,	"	1834
Levi Cook,	"	1835
Levi Cook,	"	1836
Henry Howard,	"	1837
Augustus S. Porter,	"	1838
DeGarmo Jones,	"	1839
Zina Pitcher,	"	1840
Zina Pitcher,	"	1841
Douglass Houghton,	"	1842
Zina Pitcher,	"	1843
John R. Williams,	"	1844
John R. Williams,	"	1845
John R. Williams,	"	1846
James A. Van Dyke,	"	1847
Frederick Buhl,	"	1848
Chas. Howard,	"	1849
John Ladue,	"	1850
Zachariah Chandler,	"	1851
John H. Harmon,	"	1852
John H. Harmon,	"	1853
Oliver M. Hyde,	"	1854
Henry Ledyard,	"	1855

RECORDERS SINCE 1826.

Jonathan Kearsly,	Appointed	1826.
E. P. Hastings,	"	1827
B. F. H. Witherell,	"	1828
Joseph Torrey,	"	1829
Augustus S. Porter,	"	1830
Henry S. Cole,	"	1831
Edmund A. Brush,	"	1832
Edmund A. Brush,	"	1833
Augustus S. Porter,	"	1834

Henry Chipman, - - - -	Appointed 1835
Alex. D. Frazer, - - - - -	" 1836
Ross Wilkins, - - - - - -	" 1837
Edmund A. Brush, - - - -	" 1838
Alex. D. Fraser, - - - - -	" 1839
B. F. H. Witherell, - - - -	" 1840
B. F. H Witherell, - - - -	" 1841
B. F. H. Witherell,- - - - -	" 1842
E. Smith Lee, - - - - -	" 1843
Alpheus S. Williams, - - - -	" 1844
Edmund A. Brush, - - - -	" 1845
Edmund A. Brush, - - - -	" 1846
Edmund A. Brush, - - - -	" 1847
James F. Joy, - - - - -	" 1848
Marshal J. Bacon, - - -	Elected 1849
David E. Harbaugh, - - - -	" 1850
Joseph H. Bagg, - - - - -	" 1851
Joseph H. Bagg, - - - -	" 1852
Geo. V. N. Lothrop, - - - -	" 1853
Wm. A. Cook, - - - - -	" 1854
Henry A. Morrow, - - - -	" 1855

Estimate of the population of the city of Detroit, August 1, 1855, 50,000.

INDEX

TO

CITY CHARTER

AND ACTS RELATIVE TO

CITY OF DETROIT.

INDEX TO CITY ORDINANCES.

ERRATA.

Chapter 15, for "City Surveyor," whenever the same occurs, read "Street Commissioner."

Chapter I5, page 139, insert "the" between words "to" and "Avenue," in the 6th line of section 16.

Chapter 15, page 139, insert "to" between the words "the" and "notice," in the 4th line of section 18.

Chapter 15, page 140, for "Street Commissioner" read "City Collector," in the 8th line of section 23.

Chapter 39, page 203, for "alone," in the 11th line of section 1, read "along."

Chapter 39, page 206, for "of," in 6th line of section 7, read "or."

Chapter 50, page 223, for "complaint," in the 3d line of section 6, read "complainant."

Chapter 56, page 235, for "City Auditor," in the 5th line of section 2, read "City Comptroller."

www.ingramcontent.com/pod-product-compliance
Lightning Source LLC
LaVergne TN
LVHW020227110826
845151LV00003B/843

* 9 7 8 1 4 2 5 5 3 1 5 3 9 *